# Possibilities
# of Poetry

## Also by Richard Kostelanetz

THE THEATRE OF MIXED MEANS
MASTER MINDS
VISUAL LANGUAGE
METAMORPHOSIS IN THE ARTS
(*As Author*)

THE NEW AMERICAN ARTS
(*As Co-Author and Editor*)

ON CONTEMPORARY LITERATURE
TWELVE FROM THE SIXTIES
THE YOUNG AMERICAN WRITERS
BEYOND LEFT AND RIGHT
IMAGED WORDS & WORDED IMAGES
SOCIAL SPECULATIONS
MOHOLY-NAGY
JOHN CAGE
(*As Editor*)

# Possibilities
# of Poetry

## AN ANTHOLOGY OF AMERICAN CONTEMPORARIES

Selected and introduced by

## RICHARD KOSTELANETZ

A DELTA BOOK

Grateful acknowledgment is made to the following for permission to reprint copyrighted material:

"Gunner," "The Death of the Ball Turret Gunner," "Losses," "The State," "Mail Call," "A Lullaby," "The Orient Express," "A Girl in a Library," "The Difficult Resolution," "Hope," and "Variations," by Randall Jarrell: Reprinted from *Selected Poems* and *Little Friend, Little Friend* by permission of Mrs. Randall Jarrell.

"The Heavy Bear Who Goes With Me," "In the Naked Bed, in Plato's Cave," and "The Ballad of the Children of the Czar," by Delmore Schwartz: Reprinted from *Selected Poems*, by Delmore Schwartz. Copyright 1938, 1950 by New Directions. Reprinted by permission of New Directions Publishing Corporation.

"The City of Satisfactions," by Daniel Hoffman: From *The City of Satisfactions*, by Daniel Hoffman. Copyright © 1963 by Daniel Hoffman. Reprinted by permission of Oxford University Press.

"Exploration," by Daniel Hoffman: From *A Little Geste*, by Daniel Hoffman. Copyright © 1960 by Daniel Hoffman. Reprinted by permission of Oxford University Press.

"Words for Dr. Williams," by Daniel Hoffman: From *Striking the Stones*, by Daniel Hoffman. Copyright © 1968 by Daniel Hoffman. Reprinted by permission of Oxford University Press.

"Cycle for Mother Cabrini," by John Logan: From *Cycle for Mother Cabrini*, Grove Press, 1955. © by John Logan. Used by permission of the author.

"To My Wife," "To the Reader," and "Doctor Drink," by J. V. Cunningham: From *The Exclusions of a Rhyme*, by J. V. Cunningham, Swallow Press, Chicago, Illinois. Copyright 1960. Used by permission.

"Mr. Edwards and the Spider" and "The Quaker Graveyard in Nantucket," by Robert Lowell: From *Lord Weary's Castle*, copyright 1944, 1946 by Robert Lowell. Reprinted by permission of Harcourt, Brace & World, Inc.

"Skunk Hour" and "To Delmore Schwartz," by Robert Lowell: From *Life Studies*, by Robert Lowell. Copyright © 1958 by Robert Lowell. Reprinted with the permission of Farrar, Straus & Giroux, Inc.

IN APPRECIATION

*Jonathan Cott*

*Harvey Shapiro*

*Suzanne and Philip Gossett*

*Rachel and Harvey Nachman*

# EPIGRAPHS

It has been perceptible for several years that not one but three English literatures exist—that written by Irishmen, that written by Americans, and that composed by the English themselves. —T. S. ELIOT, "The Three Provincialities," *The Tyro* (1922).

The only Americans I can possibly imagine as British are minor poets with a turn for light verse like [James Russell] Lowell and Holmes; and the only British poets who could have conceivably been American are eccentrics like Blake and Hopkins.

The first thing that strikes a reader about the best American poets is how utterly unlike each other they are. . . . The danger for the American poet is not of writing like everybody else but of crankiness and a parody of his own manner. —W. H. AUDEN, "American Poetry" (1956).

Taken as a whole, literature in democratic ages can never present, as it does in the periods of aristocracy, an aspect of order, regularity, science and art; its form will, on the contrary, ordinarily be slighted, sometimes despised. Style will frequently be fantastic, incorrect, overburdened, and loose—almost always vehement and bold. Authors will aim at rapidity of execution, more than at perfection of detail. Small productions will be more common than bulky books; there will be more wit than erudition, more imagination than profundity; and literary performances will bear marks of an untutored and rude vigor of thought—frequently of great variety and singular fecundity. —ALEXIS DE TOCQUEVILLE, *Democracy in America* (1834).

I take SPACE to be the central fact to man born in America, from Folsom cave to now. I spell it large because it comes large here. Large, and without mercy. —CHARLES OLSON, *Call Me Ishmael* (1947).

To maintain that poetry has but little influence in our day is to be blind to the obvious fact that . . . the poet has often performed the function of the lookout aboard ship. It is true that this poetry has few readers, and that it sometimes discourages readers; nevertheless, it registers the slightest change in the atmosphere, it makes the gesture that others will imitate and develop (in writings that will be read and rewarded) and it is first to utter the long-awaited word. —MARCEL RAYMOND, *From Baudelaire to Surrealism* (1933).

Poets are not simply men devoted to the beautiful. They are also and especially devoted to truth, in so far as the unknown can be penetrated, so much that the unexpected, the surprising, is one of the principal sources of poetry today. And who would dare say that for those who are worthy of joy, what is new is not beautiful? —GUILLAUME APOLLINAIRE, "The New Spirit and the Poets" (1917).

The stupid or provincial judgment of art bases itself on the belief that great art must be like the art that it has been reared to respect. —EZRA POUND, "The Serious Artist" (1913).

Poetry, as nearly as I can understand it, is a statement in words about a human experience, whether the experience be real or hypothetical, major or minor; but it is a statement of a particular kind. Words are symbols for concepts, and the philosopher or scientist endeavors as far as may be to use them with reference to nothing save their conceptual content. Most words, however, connote feelings and perceptions, and the poet, like the writer of imaginative prose, endeavors to use them with reference not only to their denotations but to their connotations as well. —YVOR WINTERS, *The Function of Criticism* (1957).

The poetry of Dante . . . is a test (a positive test, I do not assert that it is always valid negatively) that genuine poetry can communicate before it is understood. —T. S. ELIOT, *Dante* (1929).

He works by piling up many distant suggestions at once, and half the time is not "saying anything" in the ordinary meaning of the term. You are not expected to take in the whole of this poem on a first reading as the eye goes down the page, which is what good prose ought to allow you to do; the thing is meant to grow in the mind, or at least echo about there. On the other hand, I think there is no reason to feel that "modern" poetry is some obscure new trick. Poets have always worked by piling up suggestions. —WILLIAM EMPSON, "How To Read a Modern Poem" (1947).

The poem is not an "idea" or an "experience" rendered into metrical language; still less is it an attitude toward an experience. A poem is a symbol in which idea, experience, and attitude are transmuted into feelings; these feelings move in significant arrangements: rhythmically. It is prosody and its structures which articulate the movement of feeling in a poem, and render to our understanding meanings which are not paraphrasable. —HARVEY GROSS, *Sound and Form in Modern Poetry* (1963).

I believe that . . . the poet, in order to be true to what is most universal in himself, should not rely on allusion; should not comment or employ many judgment words; should not meditate (or maunder). He must scorn being "mysterious" or loosely oracular, but be willing to face up to genuine mystery. His language must be compelling and immediate; he must create an actuality. . . . He works intuitively, and the final form of his poem must be imaginatively right. If intensity has compressed the language so it seems, on early reading, obscure, this obscurity should break open suddenly for the serious reader who can hear the language; the "meaning" itself should come as a dramatic revelation, an excitement. —THEODORE ROETHKE, "Open Letter" (1950).

In contemporary poetry, if not in astronomy too, the Ptolemaic system—where the poet stands for the earth—is more suitable to creation of important poetry than the Copernican system—where types and myths stand for the sun. . . . The two great long American poems of the century—Pound's *Cantos* and William Carlos Williams' *Paterson*—are, for all their disguises, personal in the extreme. Pound does nothing less than incorporate in himself the personae of Master Kung, Odysseus, Malatesta, John Adams, et al., while Williams discovers man himself to be a city, "beginning, seeking, achieving and concluding his life in ways which the various aspects of a city may embody." —JONATHAN COTT, "Poetry," *The New American Arts* (1965).

For it seems unlikely that the number of potential poets born varies as much from age to age as literary history might lead one to suppose. What varies is the use made of talent. And the use each age makes of its crop of talent is determined largely by the preconceptions of "the poetical" that are current, and the corresponding habits, conventions, and techniques. —F. R. LEAVIS, *New Bearings in English Poetry* (1932).

# PREFACE

Anthologies are perhaps the most important harbingers of lasting-ness that a writer's work may know during his lifetime; thus, they have come to seem a kind of trial immortality for all good poems. —JAMES DICKEY, "In the Presence of Anthologies" (1958).

The anthology can have another use which . . . lies in the interest of comparison, of being able to get, in a short space, a conspectus of the progress of poetry; and if there is much that we can only learn by reading one poet entire, there is much to learn by passing from one poet to another. —T. S. ELIOT, "What Is Minor Poetry?" (1944).

The most important thing that criticism can do for a contempo-rary poet is to establish that atmosphere of interested respect which gets his poems a reasonably careful reading. —RANDALL JARRELL, "Poetry and the Age" (1953).

It is easier in America to be discovered as a poet than to endure as one. —NORMAN HOLMES PEARSON, "Decade" (1969).

One would, quite frankly, be mad to attempt yet another anthology of contemporary American poetry unless he felt that each of the collections already in print was deficient in a crucial respect—either so biased that the variousness of re-cent achievement is hardly represented, so parochial that the selections become interminably repetitious, so diffuse that no patterns emerge from the whole, or so swamped by second-rate work that the book is simply unreadable. "It is hard to know," Randall Jarrell once jabbed at an anthologist, "whether he is printing a poem because he likes it, because his acquaintances tell him he ought to, or because he went to high school with the poet." The task of the anthologist must inevitably demand critical responsibility, for a book collecting the choice work of an historical period is, in effect, the result of a discriminating scrutiny in which several score unabridged quotations are offered in support of the critic's measure, as well as the historian's definition, of a discrete body of artistic work. In this case the subject is post-World War II North American poetry, and the exposition of the critical introduction approximately parallels the order in which the subsequent selections appear, while each large roman numeral in the text demarks a distinct jump from one rough stylistic tendency to another. For these reasons, just as a critic would be foolish to do yet another study of Anton Chekhov if he regarded the existing critical literature as satisfactory, so *Possibilities of Poetry*, as an extended historical-critical essay, is intended at minimum to remedy some earlier confusions, deficiencies, and evasions.

What primarily distinguishes post-World War II American poetry from pre-War poetry is the stylistic diversity of excellences; for whereas the greatest works of the previous generation came from authors united more or less in a common cause—for modernism in its various forms, in reaction to decaying Victorianism—the best poems of the past twenty-five years blossom from a greater variety of positions, persuasions, and preoccupations. Moreover, if the achievements of 1920–1940 focused upon two giants, Ezra Pound and T. S. Eliot, excellences in recent poetry are more diffused, distributed among several first-rate, yet stylistically different, figures. This diversity in part explains why the American poetry scene as a whole seems more cluttered and confused in 1969—marked by opposing claims and scores of publicized reputations, as well as several establishments of chiefs and Indians—than, say, American fiction or theater today, where a particular hierarchy of approximate reputations commands all but general assent. There has not yet been, indicatively, an acknowledgedly definitive critical book on the corpus of recent verse, whose achievements have been, and can be, interpreted in many ways; another sign, as well as reason, is the fact that there are more publishing poets in the U.S. today than in any time past, or perhaps in the entire rest of the world. Indeed, American poetry a decade or two ago had a comparatively clearer definition in the minds of those who care than the scene today; and as I suggest in the Introduction, this comparative diffuseness is largely the result of a succession of willed reactions to the post-Eliot ambience that appeared to be so pervasively established during the years immediately following World War II.

Indicatively again, today's persistent readers of poetry tend to be more catholic in their taste than comparably avid readers of, say, twenty years ago; for they seem to acknowledge that the kinds of values and pleasures exemplified by Allen Ginsberg are different, though not contrary, to those in Robert Lowell's poems. As a survey of first-rate recent work, *Possibilities of Poetry* is designed not only to present the best individual poems of the past quarter century, allowing readers to judge each poet by his most outstanding works, but also to capture the variousness of recent poetic activity in America; inevitably, the selection aims to cull the best poems from all the competing schools and positions—to swim in the warring seas and yet retrieve the best fish to dry land. By its title, this book is more open than closed in its esthetic outlook, including pieces which were not necessarily conceived (or even published) as "poetry," such as John Cage's "Diary," or written by authors who are not members in the Church of Poets, as well as visual arrangements of *words* that conservative critics might dismiss as "not poetry," whatever or wherever that may be.

Recent American poetry is, to all commentators, distinctly different from pre-War verse; but the task of drawing the chronological lines between one period of an art's history and another invariably poses knotty problems. In general practice, the historical record of significant intellectual activity has less to do with when something was written than, first, when it was published and, second, when it had its decisive impact. For instance, those who speak of American music between 1900 and 1920 mention Horatio Parker, Henry F. G. Gilbert, Edward Burlingame Hill, and other all-but-forgotten names. Generally omitted from such discussions is Charles Ives, who, though he wrote all his major works in that period, went unpublished and unperformed until after 1920; and not until the 1930s, long after he stopped composing, did Ives have his greatest "contemporary" influence. In literature, an analogous example is Emily Dickinson, whose poetry, written in the middle of the nineteenth century, was not published until 1890, well after her death, and was not widely appreciated until 1910–1920.

*Possibilities of Poetry* focuses upon the poetry of the post-World War II period, upon poets who made their primary mark after 1945, even though some were born as early as 1893 and some of the poems included here, such as those by Stanley Kunitz, Louis Zukofsky, Delmore Schwartz, and Theodore Roethke, were in fact written and first published some years before that crucial date. On the other hand, these criteria necessitate the exclusion of recent poems by Robert Penn Warren, Ezra Pound, Langston Hughes, Louise Bogan, Allen Tate, and Yvor Winters, all of whom belong to an earlier period of poetry (and even the fine early poems of James Agee, who as a poet existed in the earlier period; as a novelist, in the later one). On the more recent side, the cut-off date is the last possible moment the publisher allowed me for additions. In general, an individual's poems appear roughly in the order in which they were first published.

Beyond that, all the poems here are by Americans, which is to say poets who contribute to American culture, even if their birthplace or current residence is abroad; excluded are British poets, who inhabit a poetic world of different current concerns and traditions (if not language), even if they should presently live in the U.S. Also excluded from this selection are verse translations, even though some of the finest recent poems in English were derived from other languages. In principle, I would have preferred including more pieces by poets under thirty; in practice, several pieces I tentatively selected did not in the end stand strongly to the rest of the book. By intention, I wanted more poetry about public issues; in practice, aside from those included, nearly all the political poems I read were, for one reason or another, less than persuasive. (As a general rule, political comment in poetry, to have minimal literary validity, must offer perceptions, images, or criticisms considerably different from those commonly available in prose, particularly newspapers and periodicals.) Also, as many major recent poems run longer than a few pages, some are reprinted in their entirety, while others appear here in excerpt. There are no "double standards" here, neither for young poets nor black poets nor friends, and there is also no tokenism—the attempt to include just one and only one poem of every race, reputation, allegiance, or position.

As for my criteria in selecting individual pieces, the less specific the exposition the better, except that I react negatively to both needless incoherence and excessive obscurity, as well as to both patent piety and inauthentic language. Anyone who has read more than two hundred books of contemporary poetry, as I recently have, can only agree with James Dickey's description of "a number of totally unconvincing postures [that induce] a kind of disbelief in the reader completely different from that cited by Coleridge." On the other hand, this selection favors poems that treat perceptively experiences familiar to us, that create a convincing realm, that possess an understanding to which another human being can assent, that reveal a genuine adventurousness in both conception and execution, that contain language which moves and evokes without resorting to the crutches of cliché, that achieve a form appropriate to their theme and perception, that use the materials of poetry in an intense and imaginative way; and the number of pages devoted to a poet's work inevitably represents a rough measure of his overall importance and achievement. Beyond these points, let me offer the general observation that great poems, even those in avant-garde styles, create the persuasion, perhaps the illusion, of inevitability—the sense that from the point of inception all of the poem's dimensions, of form as well as content, have to fall together as they do. Finally, perhaps there is some significance in the fact that this is the first anthology of recent work selected not by a participant in the wars of contemporary poetry but a distant, disaffiliated yet appreciative observer who also authors an eccentric kind of poetry.

*Possibilities of Poetry* is regrettably far too short for its purposes; and were the book larger, I would include several more works by the poets already represented here, as well as pieces by many other poets I admire. Furthermore, although the budget for reprint permissions was more than generous, the fees that certain publishers quoted were so far in excess of my capacity to pay that I feel obliged to extend genuine condolences to a dozen poets whom I intended to include but could not, as well as another dozen whose following selections are less than I originally wished and their achievement deserves.

Without the encouragement of Richard Huett at Dell Books, there would be no anthology; thanks go first to him and his associates, Ross Claiborne, Joanne Dolinar, Irene Yuss, and Donna Jo Brewer. This collection, in turn, draws from my selections for *Piccola antologia della nuova poesia americana* (1968), which Franco Floreanini asked me to compile for his fine Italian journal *Nuova Presenza;* and the following Introduction originally appeared in *Chelsea Review.* For critical advice I am particularly indebted to Jonathan Cott, whose scandalously unnoticed essay on poetry in *The New American Arts* continues to inform my taste; and it was Stanley Kunitz who concluded an intense discussion of the current anthologies by dramatically (and persuasively) suggesting that I should compile a better book—may the selection that follows fulfill his faith. To the people to whom *Possibilities of Poetry* is dedicated, I am indebted for various favors and encouragements over the years; each of them, in his own way, made this and other books possible. A fellowship in intellectual history from the John Simon Guggenheim Memorial Foundation supported much of the research informing the Introduction; to them I am also grateful. Finally, let me thank publishers and librarians who supplied me with countless books of poetry; and since I made every possible effort to secure permission from scores of copyright holders, I would appreciate hearing of any mistakes or omissions, which will be rectified in future editions.

Richard Kostelanetz
New York, New York
14 May, 1969

# Contents

I

# INTRODUCTION

## Reactions and Alternatives: Post-WW II American Poetry

Free verse gave wings to lyricism; but it was only one stage of the explorations that can be made in the domain of form. —GUILLAUME APOLLINAIRE, "The New Spirit and the Poets" (1917).

The history of the American arts from 1900 on is often a record of successful flank attacks made by "outsiders" upon an entrenchment of taste and technique against which straightforward frontal attack would have failed. —LOUISE BOGAN, *Achievement in American Poetry* (1951).

The history of literature—the record of the relatively few works that ultimately count—generally assumes the form of a succession of chronological periods, each of a distinct character, in each of which certain styles of writing became more predominant or influential than others; and the beginnings and ends of literary eras usually coincide with important public events, such as major wars or economic booms and busts. With this in mind, we can see, even in close retrospect, that for literature as well as life the years after World War II were considerably different from the twenty years that went before. For verse written in English, the period between 1920 and 1940 represents the establishment of literary modernism, as defined by the achievements and impact of two great American poets, T. S. Eliot and Ezra Pound, in addition to two complementary English figures, the young W. H. Auden and the rejuvenated William Butler Yeats. These were the poets who made the decisive and persuasive breaks with entrenched nineteenth-century practice, as well as wrote the innovative masterpieces admired by the succeeding generations. "I do not know for certain," wrote William Empson of Eliot, eighteen years his senior, "how much of my own mind he invented, let alone how much of it is a reaction against him or indeed a consequence of misreading him." However, even though Eliot, Pound, and Auden lived into the post-WW II period, continuing to publish new work, as did several secondary American masters of that earlier period —Marianne Moore and E. E. Cummings, Conrad Aiken and John Crowe Ransom, Robert Frost and Wallace Stevens— the definition of recent American poetry has been shaped by younger hands. In distinct contrast to the promising post-WW II English poets who repudiated Eliot and Pound for pre-1920 styles, the young American successors went beyond the elder greats in various ways. For one thing, this period after 1945 has been decidedly more plural than its prede-cessor, as many apparently valid directions were intensively explored and no particular conception of poetic art or indi-vidual poet became pervasively influential—how different in coherence and tone and point of view are such indubitably major poets as Robert Lowell and Allen Ginsberg, Theodore Roethke and Kenneth Koch, David Ignatow and Gary Snyder, John Berryman and Galway Kinnell. Nonetheless, what per-haps unifies the variety of the period is the sense that most of the important work represents alternatives to Eliot's and Pound's (and, to lesser extents, Auden's and Yeats's) ways of making poems.

Indeed, the impact of these masters of modernism was so powerful and pervasive that it was hard for a maturing poet, coming of age between 1922 and 1945, not at least to sound like them; even some contemporary Africans writing in Eng-lish still echo Eliot. This ubiquitous influence is perhaps the primary reason why the more powerful "flank attacks" oc-curred not at the end of the War but about a decade later, largely from poets who came of intellectual age after 1945 —not from the second generation of modern poetry, whose birthdates fall between 1900 and 1922, but from the third, poets born after 1923. (Indeed, the one older poet who be-came so influential his work was all but contemporary, William Carlos Williams, was a college friend of Pound, perhaps the first of his many literary pupils; for not only did Williams develop before Eliot's influence but Eliot reportedly

4

kept Williams unpublished in England during his lifetime.)

Roughly and generally, the established style of poetry in 1945 was intricate in meter, approximately regular in length of line, ironic and elegant and sometimes aphoristic, controlled in texture and restricting in form, complex in thought and solemn in tone. It was rich in allusions to the history of literature and culture, distinctly formal in diction (the taste in language reflected in the choice of specific words), impersonal in ambience (as formulated by Eliot's "objective correlative"), observational in perspective, cosmic in concern, associational in poetic syntax, reverent toward both the tradition and the work of poetry, and implicit in ultimate subject, which the reader generally has to deduce. To Donald Hall, this is "a poetry of symmetry, intellect, irony and wit." These were poems, in Howard Nemerov's phrases, "which want to be read hard and which respond to closest attention." To Louise Bogan, "It was a style which tended to veer, it is true, toward verbalism on the one hand, and extreme condensation of meaning and idea, on the other. At its worst, a core of overcompressed thought was surrounded by an envelope of overinflated words." Perhaps because most of the great poems of the period between the Wars exemplified this brace of approaches to the problems of poetry and the materials of human experience, the "promising" young poets in the late forties tended to appropriate most, if not all, of these strategies, perpetuating the established styles of 1920–1940 well into the fifties. Nonetheless, the significant developments in recent verse, as well as the remarks that follow, focus upon diverse snappings of the stylistic threads woven by Eliot, his contemporaries, and his immediate artistic heirs. The history of art, it is true, sometimes portrays a certain style as a string on the stage of history running through the heads of many individual artists; yet not only is this image an analytic convenience for regarding continuities amid idiosyncracies, but it is also a reasonably accurate metaphor for how literary ideas and artistic structures actually pass from one articulate mind to another. One reason is that the influence of immediate predecessors and particular contemporaries is generally more apparent in an artist's work than his debts to specific figures in the common tradition.

The new poets who commanded the most attention during and immediately after the War tended to echo these predominant stylistic traits of their elders, as well as their archetypal and mythological concerns. Among these prematurely mature poets were Robert Lowell, whose characteristic subjects then included Jonathan Edwards and other aspects of historical New England and whose metrical language was audibly indebted to Gerard Manley Hopkins; John Berryman, who wrote in retrospect, "I wanted something that would be both very neat, contained and at the same time thoroughly mysterious"; and Delmore Schwartz, who favored philosophic poems inspired by Plato and Socrates, in addition to weaving elaborate Freudian symbols for psychic dramas:

> The heavy bear who goes with me,
> A manifold honey to smear his face,
> Clumsy and lumbering here and there,
> The central tone of every place,
> The hungry beating brutish one
> In love with candy, anger, and sleep.

So powerful was the post-Eliot establishment at the time that other ways of making poems went all but unnoticed.

Certain poets, such as Randall Jarrell and Karl Shapiro, who first adopted the dominant style and received critical acclaim, recognized after their war experiences that strictly structured forms do not allow for certain expressions of immediate concerns and they therefore explored alternative styles. Jarrell discreetly revealed his personal history in poems published just before his death in 1965, while Shapiro even excised from his work poems reflecting Eliot's influence and resorted, in *The Bourgeois Poet* (1964), to prose paragraphs that repudiated rhyme, versification, the line breaks, and much other nineteenth-century baggage. Indeed, the old style so dominated the blossoming poetic imaginations that no recent native poet captured the post-WW II disappointment as effectively as *The Waste Land* did for a comparable earlier post-War period, or as Paul Celan's "Todesfuge" (1952) did for German-speaking readers. The truth is that persuasive art about unprecedented history invariably demands radically new forms.

Reactions to Eliot, even among the epigones, were perhaps inevitable, although less extreme. In 1949, Delmore Schwartz, who only four years before lauded Eliot as "The International Hero," publicly questioned the benefits of his "literary dictatorship"; and within a few years, more sensitive critics could easily mock the stylistic, experiential, allusive, and tonal uniformity of the younger poets included in the expanded post-WW II editions of the major classroom anthologies of "Modern Poetry." By the sixties, poetry based upon these familiar strategies became known as "academic" verse, whose representatives and advocates included such professor-poets as Anthony Hecht, Paris Leary, Robert Pack, Donald Finkel, Donald Hall, Louis Coxe, and Daryl Hine, in addition to such Anglican immigrants as W. H. Auden, Stephen Spender, and Thom Gunn. True, not all academics wrote "academic" verse, but nearly all such poetry came from full-time professors; but too often in this work, as James Dickey judged, "Painfully contrived arguments in rhyme substitute for genuine insight." By the late sixties, many of these writers offered statements and manifestos so defensive in stance that they seemed to know as well as the avant-gardists that the time for neoclassicism had passed.

Even though a particular style in art may command primary attention, as well as inform the masterpieces of a certain moment, its widespread impact can never prevent the simultaneous development of other techniques. In America, all through the thirties, a number of talented poets, most of them scarcely recognized, if not barely published, were working in alternative ways. The critic Yvor Winters, himself a skilled poet, fathered a school of unashamedly "reactionary" poets—the best is J. V. Cunningham—who offered declarative statements in rhyme; another tendency, represented by such otherwise different figures as Robert Penn Warren, Muriel Rukeyser, and Winfield Townley Scott, favored dramatic narratives. A third alternative direction that, unlike the other two, subsequently earned more interest and acclaim, grew from the example of the late Theodore Roethke, author of many of the greatest individual poems of the recent period, and his closest compatriot in poetry at the time, Stanley Kunitz, whose work is similar but usually more difficult, more considered, and more intellectual. As early as 1934, Roethke wrote to a friend, "I'm tired of all this Eliot-Pound worship"; and he dissented, as did Kunitz, from the canon primarily in using personal materials, particularly the stuff of dreams, in rather restricted, traditional rhythmic structures patently more indebted to Yeats than to Pound or Eliot:

> My secrets cry aloud.
> I have no need for tongue.
> My heart keeps open house,
> My doors are widely swung.
> An epic of the eyes
> My love, with no disguise.

The result was an American kind of surrealism, different from the more European hysterical surrealism of San Francisco-born Philip Lamantia, as Roethke and Kunitz dealt largely in restrained monologues, occasionally in outright songs, whose landscapes are invariably interior and whose symbols are personally revealing. Twenty years ago, unlike now, such work represented a considerable departure. Both men continued more or less in this lyrical mode, tending toward longer lines and more open structures. Roethke's last poems include titles like "Journey to the Interior," the "interior" being of course his own psyche, and Kunitz in 1963 wrote:

> What's best in me lives underground:
> Rooting, and digging, itching for wings.

By the late fifties, John Berryman staked his position on personal materials, creating elegant yet ragged, evocative yet obscure, symbolic fantasies he called "Dream Songs." At first many of these pieces seem impenetrable; but once their source is identified as psychic processes and their theme as, in Berryman's words, "the turbulence of the modern world, and memory, and wants," then the previously puzzling metaphors and symbols often all but explain themselves.

One of the earlier alternatives to Eliot was already defined by Ezra Pound, whose role in the stylistic history of modern poetry is rather dichotomous. On one hand, he supported both Frost and Eliot, even editing the latter's *The Waste Land* and receiving its dedication as *"il miglior fabbro."* On the other hand, through his later *Cantos*, as well as his post-WW II correspondence, Pound directly influenced the spatially open, idiomatic, metrically irregular, academically irreverent word-collages of William Carlos Williams, Louis Zukofsky, Charles Olson, and younger poets vehemently opposed to Eliot's ways. Williams rejected verbal ornamentation and English metric in addition to "the ash-heaps of the past," instead rooting his poetry in concrete understanding, realistic portrayal, visceral perception, immediate detail, concentrated statements, American idiom, and formal freedom ("Finally I let the form take care of itself"). The major work of his post-WW II career, *Paterson* (1946–1958), extended these principles through a long poem, as well as evoked a universe of life out of the microcosm of a New Jersey city. (Behind nearly every major contemporary long poem in Americanese, as Leslie Fiedler notes, stands the example of Ezra Pound.) Olson, a generation younger than Williams, drew from both him and Pound to evolve, in the late forties, a theory of "projective verse." In an essay of that title, somewhat obscured by a bombastic and convoluted style, Olson's major points include preferences for American language and experience, the formal idea of the poem as an open (more precisely, unclosed) field of energy, cognizance of the expressive possibilities intrinsic in the typewriter, freedom from constraint in the shape and syntax of poetry—how words may be laid out on the page or grammatically connected to each other. (Thus, he logically opposed both the sentence's period and the closed parenthesis as encouraging the completion of expression.) Olson's theory notwithstanding, his own poetry is incorrigibly erratic, both in wholes and in parts, as words and phrases spread asymmetrically across the page, all informed by nonmetrical prosody, generally mundane language that is sometimes incantatory and often slips into outright prose, anthropological resonances, associational coherence, and esoteric allusions (that conclusively repudiates certain claims made for its antiacademicism—in sum, a kind of abstract poetic shorthand for discontinuously organizing a great range of concrete and universal material. Thanks in part to his personal charisma, his commandingly grandiose physical presence and several vociferous disciples, Olson became the father of the "Black Mountain" school of American poetry, named after the late, lamented North Carolina experimental college where all its members taught or studied—Robert Creeley, Robert Duncan, John Wieners, Jonathan Williams, Edward Dorn, among others; and nearly all these writers also emulate Olson's unusual prose style. Yet, perhaps because none of them is imaginatively as extreme and unconstrained as Olson, or intellectually as rich (except for Duncan), their work seems considerably less interesting than the master's—at worst, merely exercises in line-breaking. Instead, some of the more adventurous extensions of Olson's suggestions have come from writers outside his immediate camp. The composer John Cage, a sometime colleague at Black Mountain, has developed in several word-pieces entitled "Diary" a stylistically inventive shorthand for miscellaneous remarks, and the architect-dymaxicrat Buckminster Fuller, another Black Mountain compatriot, evolved a concretely speculative, if not visionary, poetry, while two younger writers, John Giorno and Ronald Gross, have both ingeniously made expressive poetry entirely out of sentences lifted verbatim from newspapers, advertisements, and other popular sources; and an even younger poet, Dan Graham, roots his work in immediate, unedited factual detail. In short, all these imperfect, exploratory, structurally open poetries seem inevitable responses to an open, exploratory, imperfect age.

One inevitable reaction to Auden's and Eliot's poetic impersonality was the direct exposure of personal experience, not with the symbolic shields of Roethke and Kunitz, but in declarative statements made in the first-person voice of the poet. The most compelling poems in this mode deal with the most intimate of aggravations—the state of the poet's marriage or current affair, the tensions of close relationships, major operations, sojourns in mental institutions, social and spiritual insufficiencies. To the critic Jonathan Cott, this poetry represents the "projection of exacerbated sensibilities"; to other critics, this is "confessional" poetry, written partially to purge the poet's mind of haunting preoccupations. However, in the best pieces, the lines evoke not an individual's problem but a more general experience, as W. D. Snodgrass, who reportedly influenced his teacher Lowell to risk also more intimate subjects, writes in "April Inventory":

> I taught myself to name my name,
> To bark back, loosen love and crying;
> To ease my woman so she came,
> To ease an old man who was dying.

Another Lowell pupil, Sylvia Plath, declares in "Elm," written just before her suicide:

> I am terrified by the dark thing
> that sleeps in me.

A related process informs the recent work of Brother Antoninus (né William Everson), who descends stylistically not from Eliot, Williams, and Lowell but from Robinson Jeffers, to arrive at an approximately similar poetic position. His best poem, "In Savage Wastes," includes such stanzas as:

> I too, O God, as You very well know,
> Am guilty.
> For I sought and found not,
> I searched, but was not successful.
> When I failed, You drew back the veil,
> And I am in terror.

However, in contrast to Antoninus's work, most "confessional" poetry uses more formal, less mundane diction, stricter prosody (if not occasional rhymes) and forms more transparent than blatant; for these characteristics in particular distinguish it from the kind of first-person poetry developed by and from Allen Ginsberg.

The writers called "beats" are important in the history of recent poetry less for the publicity their activities accrued—publicity, like other forms of journalism being inherently ahistorical—than their all-but-comprehensive attack upon the post-Eliot establishment; and their claims to greater vitality inevitably capitalized on both the smug dreariness of a declining style and the diminished energies of its former masters. It was not only that Ginsberg, Lawrence Ferlinghetti, Gregory Corso, and poets trailing in their wake created rather persuasive literature but that they challenged nearly everything previously pious in poetry. For reverent solemnity, they substituted irreverent blasphemy; for impersonality, they put anarchistic egotism; instead of ironic personas and other symbolic artifices, they used man-to-man address and explicit statements. They phased out elegant diction and consistent texture for jagged surfaces and lines of wildly irregular length and mundane words, which were sometimes so profane that Ginsberg's *Howl*, for one, became the subject of an "obscenity" case. Rather than a second-hand world drawn from the history of literature and culture, the beat poets treated their own immediate experience, in specific places and at specific times, often in response to current social malaise; and instead of elliptical associative coherence, they resorted to less obscuring, more accessible kinds of poetic syntax. Moreover, they identified not with the great tradition of English verse but with countertraditions of rebellious, if not mad, poets, from Rimbaud to Artaud, from Whitman to the Ezra Pound of the late *Cantos*. In addition, they eschewed not only classical and mythological allusions but also contrived complexity and obscurity in favor of a public, if not popular, poetry of comparatively simple statements and clear-cut attitudes, all of which was appropriately conducive to public declamation.

Precisely because these poets rejected the established modes so completely, they became an issue over which the activists in poetry chose up sides. Several older figures of a similarly anti-Eliot bent gravitated to the beats' support—among them Kenneth Rexroth, who became their most articulate literary publicist; Charles Olson, whose poetic theory was regarded as relevant; William Carlos Williams, who gave *Howl* a combative introduction that concluded, "Ladies, we're going through hell"; and eventually Karl Shapiro, whose reaction to Eliot-Auden propelled him to one polar extreme. Of *Howl*, Rexroth, long an anarchist, wrote in *New Directions*, #16 (1957), "This is the real thing, bona fide revolutionary poetry. Mike Gold [the Communist polemicist] would give his left nut to have written ten lines of it." By the late fifties, the American poetry scene became split, by observers as well as poets, into two warring camps known, variously, as square and beat, cooked and uncooked, academic and antiacademic, each of which had its magazines, its critics, its publishers, its students and, inevitably, its anthologists; and in this apocalyptic war, every poet of note was either in one camp or the other. By the middle sixties, however, as even a professor-poet like William Jay Smith emulated Ginsberg's freely formed long poetic line, this dichotomy had less to do with genuine stylistic differences than irrelevant social habits—less what or how a poet wrote than whom he knew and hung around with.

Since Eliot and Pound dealt with large abstractions, spectacularly cosmic concerns and distant places, another reaction was toward a poetry that focused upon immediate perceptions, pedestrian experiences, and natural landscapes. This persuasion not only had its own veteran advocates in William Stafford, Gary Snyder, Richard Eberhart, and Kenneth Rexroth but it also won several talented poets previously in the Eliot-Auden ambience—among them James Wright, David Wagoner, and James Dickey. Nearly all of them produced comparatively short poems, emphasizing image over symbol and subjectivity over objectivity, in lines varying from metered to free, generally in an authentic first-person voice whose tone occasionally echoes Robert Frost. The subject of these poems is usually an experience or quality distinctly of the premachine age. Perhaps because

the narrator's intelligence regards things observed as more
persuasive than myth and nature as a basically beneficent
force, past literature is sometimes seen as threatening his
perceptual innocence. Gary Snyder remarks in passing,
in "Mid-August at Sourdough Mountain Lookout":

> I cannot remember things
> I once read.

While looking at a newborn child in "Mary Bly," James
Wright says:

> I feel the seasons changing beneath me,
> Under the floor.

Between this position and the older one stands a poet
like A. R. Ammons, whose most famous work, "Corsons
Inlet," perceives a metaphysical dimension in a familiar rural
scene. While such modest, mundane approaches to experience are not usually the processes behind inarguably great
poetry, this poetic stance, as a reaction in part to earlier
excesses, has for this moment an immensely persuasive
impact.

A parallel stylistic preoccupation in recent verse deals
unsentimentally with experience in urban environments;
and this too is not a poetry of symbols but a literature in
which the immediate perception or the scene described sym-
bolizes something larger than itself. This position, generally
indebted to William Carlos Williams, informs the best
poetry of David Ignatow, Denise Levertov, Harvey Shapiro,
Alan Dugan, as well as occasional pieces by Galway Kinnell,
Paul Goodman, and Weldon Kees. Their works are usually
short in length, informal in language, anecdotal in manner,
and swift in development, functioning at minimum to define
order or significance in the chaos of the city; and a particular perception, if not a developed theme, usually provides
more of the poem's cohering gravity than image or rhythm.
In "Get the Gasworks," David Ignatow writes:

> Get the gasworks into a poem,
> and you've got the smoke and smokestacks,
> and mottled red and yellow tenements,
> and grimy kids who curse with the pungency
> of the odor of gas. You've got America, boy.

In one of the late Weldon Kees's poems, the visiting narrator notes of his host's anonymous metropolitan apartment:

> All day the phone rings. It could be Robinson
> Calling. It never rings when he is here.

At times this kind of poetry seems on the verge of what James Dickey calls "metaphysical reportage," investing immense importance in a familiar urban circumstance, usually in New York, such as a Lower East Side street in Galway Kinnell's "The Avenue Bearing the Initial of Christ into the New World" (perhaps echoing the span to Brooklyn in Hart Crane's *The Bridge* [1932]), or the imposing Brooklyn warehouse, near Harvey Shapiro's home, emblazoned "National Cold Storage Company," which becomes a symbolic ashcan of American history.

> I myself have dropped into it in seven years
> Midnight tossings, plans for escape, the shakes.
> Add this to the National total—
> Grant's tomb, the Civil War, Arlington,
> The young President dead.

A curious fact is that until Eliot the best American poetry conspicuously avoided the urban scene that so preoccupied, say, Charles Baudelaire; but now that America has become a predominantly urban society and its social and spiritual problems assume an urban focus, it seems appropriate that by the middle sixties an unprecedentedly high percentage of the best poets of all persuasions have gravitated to New York City. This observation in turn suggests that perhaps urban American verse is establishing an historical beachhead for English poetry in an urbanizing world.

One circle of poets mistakenly placed among the anti-academics, primarily because they were abundantly included in Donald Allen's beat anthology *The New American Poets* (1960), collected around John Ashbery, Kenneth Koch, and Frank O'Hara; and to Jonathan Cott, in his 1965 survey of recent efforts, they represented "the most original school of poetry today." Here the professor-proletarian dichotomy simply did not relate to their individual natures; for not only did each of the three have a Harvard B.A., as well as a further degree, but Koch himself, heaven forbid, earned a doctorate and then took a regular teaching position squarely in the enemy's camp, Columbia University. The first mature work of these writers, dating from the middle fifties, followed certain tendencies in modern French literature (where free verse and prose paragraphs typify the major poets) by questioning established concepts of poetic structure through various explorations of *acoherence*—an effort analogous to atonality in music, and this preoccupation continues to inform their work, as well as that of younger poets working in their wake, such as Ted Berrigan and David Shapiro, and perhaps Allen Ginsberg in his "Wichita Vortex Sutra." Koch's *When the Sun Tries To Go On* (1953) is an interminable nonsense poem in a regularly irregular meter, evenly measured lines and consistent diction that, to Cott, "defies explication or even persistent reading," while his incredible *Ko, or a Season on Earth* (1959) is an absurd narrative in heroic meter. In "Europe" (1960) Ashbery broke through the rectangular format of poetry, using a variety of meters and printed lines, dictions and syntaxes, so that the page became an open field full of fragments—images and remarks, phrases and even single words—whose relation to each other would be tenuous, ambiguous, and perhaps multiple; to Cott, who regards Ashbery as more concerned with connotation than denotation, "Europe" represents the "difficult but adroit construction of a disconnected journey." The fifty-second stanza in its entirety runs as follows:

                    The rose
                              dirt
                    dirt you

                    pay
                    The  buildings
                    is tree

          Undecided protest This Planet.

In this radical restructuring of poetry's words, the
problem, for writer and reader alike, becomes making poetic
sense without depending upon the familiar clues provided
by either a distinct subject or an expository format; yet
what makes such works coherent are the familiar devices of
poetry, such as associative imagery, spatial disposition, con-
notative relation, consistent diction, and sometimes cohe-
sive meter. Precisely because it defies conventional analysis
and definite paraphrase, this spatial poetry is extremely
obscure by conventional standards, if not inexplicable and
perhaps too precious; yet like all radical writing, these lines
ask critical readers to revise not only their standards of
coherence in literature but also their strategies for attentive
reading; like so much that is truly adventurous in contemporary art, this kind of poetry asks the most experienced
perceptor to discern structure in what at first seems chaos.
   A series of "flank attacks" upon an established style invariably produces a spate of alternative artistic conceptions
—witness the diversity of reactions to romanticism in nineteenth-century music. If only to avoid the smug restrictive-
ness that plagued more parochial eras (and seems
embarrassing in retrospect), the more sophisticated readers
and critics of poetry today are justifiably reluctant to dismiss
one or another stylistic alternative as "not poetry," or simply
out of bounds. Such tolerance toward adventurous art and
thought is, to my mind, all to the good, if only because in
this era of pluralism and upheaval, the currently accepted

definitions of reality and potentiality shift, like the seasons, right under our feet.

Some of the more radical possibilities for poetry today deal with its structural essentials—the discrete word, the printed line, and the overall shape. From the Middle Ages to the present, the format of poetry has consisted of words laid out in horizontal lines of uniform typeface, usually set in vertical succession in paragraphs of rectangular shape; and even if, as in Whitman, the poetic line runs horizontally beyond the margin, the printer dutifully pulls in the excess and sets it in the lined space immediately below. Partly to transcend this restricting tradition, John Cage employs a multiple-font typewriter to emulate the typographical variety available to the graphic designer or the preprint scribe, and literary poets from George Herbert to Dylan Thomas and Gregory Corso have written poems to be printed in geometrical shapes, like a vase with indented parabolic sides or a diamond standing on one point. A step beyond this involves setting the letters in nongeometric shapes, such as the vertical lines of rain in Apollinaire's "Il Pleut" or the more unusual and complicated forms in Kenneth Burke's "Flowerishes," or John Hollander's pieces in *Types of Shape* (1969). Another inevitable direction comes from imposing a severe horizontal limitation upon the poetic lines, as A. R. Ammons did by composing a book-length poem on vertical adding machine tape in his *Tape for the Turn of the Year* (1965). However, all these poems still operate within the tradition of lines of poetry and, thus, approximately linear syntax.

Another step beyond involves abolishing the line for the discrete word itself, presented in its printed form for all the suggestiveness it can muster, as in certain scripts for "happenings" that George Brecht has written or the "minimal" poems of Aram Saroyan. From this point the poet can also design his word into an expressive shape, as Liam O'Gallagher, Mary Ellen Solt, Robert Indiana, and Richard Kostelanetz, among others, have done in "pattern poems" or "word-images" or "poems looked *at* not *thru*" that bestow a resonant visual dimension, if not an "ideographic logic" and spatial prosody upon words for a quality, a process, or a thing, such as disintegration or sneezing. Of his purposes in this poetic mode, one practitioner identified, "first, the discovery, or the devising, of expressive shapes for individual words or groups of words that particularly haunt me—to create an image appropriate to a certain word—and, second, the adding of words and letters to archetypal or familiar shapes—literally to verbalize an image. In both respects, the ideal result of the poet's ingenuity should be a word-image whose language and shape are so effectively complementary that the entire picture has a unified integrity and an indelible impact." A move beyond this would eschew the rectangular, two-dimensional page for expressive sculptures of words, as Gerd Stern (or the Frenchman Jean-François Bory) has done, or abolish the word itself for an arrangement of letters or even printed symbols that bear no apparent syntactical relationship to each other. These last pieces are generally classified as "concrete," even if done by card-carrying "poets"; but this kind of work usually defines itself as closer to design than poetry.

As the Yeats-Eliot-Auden conventions became the rites of hackneyed verse, an inevitable departure would be poetic parody, at its best not just for a joke but for richly comic, exaggeratedly ironic effects, as in the works of Armand Schwerner and S. Foster Damon, among others. Damon's *Nightmare Cemetery* (1964), a bleak, often parodic sequence of sonnets, struck the critic Yvor Winters as "a kind of abbreviated *Confidence-Man* in verse." However, the masterpiece in this particular vein is clearly Melvin B. Tolson's *Libretto for the Republic of Liberia* (1953), a fantastic inimitable conglomeration of loaded words written to fulfill Tolson's obligation as poet laureate for the African country's centenary; and among the real achievements of this relatively unknown and, thanks largely to Allen Tate's introduction, usually misunderstood long poem is the scope of its marvelous satire—the political pretentions of the Republic of Liberia (in historical fact, largely a fief of a single American rubber company), the catch-all allusive technique of Ezra Pound, the esoteric footnotes to T. S. Eliot (whose *The Waste Land* made all subsequent footnotes to poetry

CHARACTERISTICS OF AMERICAN POETRY IN 1945, AND SUBSEQUENT REACTIONS TO THE PREDOMINANT STYLE

| Associational Coherence | Cultural Allusiveness | Consistent Prosody | Persona-Narrator | Complex Thought | Formal Diction | Symmetrical Format | Reverent Solemnity |
|---|---|---|---|---|---|---|---|
| Ashbery | Koch | Ginsberg | Lowell (late) | Ginsberg | Antoninus | Ashbery | Tolson |
| Koch | Kunitz | Ashbery | Antoninus | Cage | Ginsberg | Olson | Koch |
| Ignatow | Ashbery | Antoninus | Ginsberg | Wright | Berryman (late) | Hollander | Ginsberg |
| H. Shapiro | Antoninus | Stern | Cage | Roethke | Koch | O'Gallagher | Roethke |
| Ginsberg | Snodgrass | Berrigan | Sexton | Snyder | Ignatow | Stern | Strand |
| Cage | Ignatow | Koch | Plath | Koch | Giorno | Berrigan | Berryman |
| D. Shapiro | Plath | Schwerner | Ignatow | Berrigan | Schwerner | Ginsberg | Stern |
| Antoninus | Snyder | Lamantia | Rexroth | | Stern | Schwerner | Giorno |
| Wagoner | Dickey | Wagoner | Snyder | | | Duncan | D. Shapiro |
| Dugan | Wagoner | Dugan | Dugan | | | Lamantia | Schwerner |
| Damon | Lamantia | | | | | | Damon |
| | Atwood | | | | | | |

This rough chart is by no pretense either comprehensive or definitive. Rather than make accurate classifications, it aims to outline tendencies. Not every poet is included.

either ironic or ludicrous), certain American Negro myths about a close relationship to Africa, and much else.

> The *Höhere* of God's stepchildren
> is beyond the sabotaged world, is beyond
> *das Diktat der Menschenverachtung,*
> *la muerte sobre el esqueleto de la nada,*
> the pelican's breast rent red to feed the young,
> summer's third-class ticket, the *Revue des morts,*
> the skulls trepanned to hold ideas plucked from dung,
> Dives' crumbs in the church of the unchurched,
> absurd life shaking its ass's ears among
> the colors of vowels and Harrar blacks
> with Nessus shirts from Europe on their backs

Along with their footnotes referring to sources both eso-teric and familiar, both classical and contemporary, these lines suggest, as the critic Dan McCall perceived, that "At times Tolson seems to be running wild in the white castle of learning"; and even though some of Tolson's satire may not be entirely intentional, it is precisely such pervasive blas-phemy over so many sacred terrains, along with a general in-scrutability, that makes the *Libretto* a singular contempor-ary masterpiece.

In short, most major poets of the post-WW II period par-ticularly rejected at least one major stylistic trait of the post-Eliot establishment, and these rejections became a cumulative process, as illustrated, with some irony, on the adjacent table. Its decline paralleled the decreasing influence of the New Criticism, founded in part to institutionalize a taste for such verse. Indeed, so powerful was the cumulative impact of such reactions that certain embittered poets rewrote their own artistic traditions, if not repudiated certain early poems, pre-cisely to exclude all traces of that *bête noir* Eliot. What all these rejections of the past decades, abetted by a succession of willed "fresh starts," have accomplished is the creation of a new collective sensibility and artistic situation for American verse, so that a greater plurality of approaches to the en-vironment of poetry—the tradition and techniques of the art and the material of man's experience—are currently, in principle at least, acceptable. Indeed, although no known measure is finally acurate, there seems today more genuine freedom from restricting convention than at any previous time in Anglo-American poetry—an emancipation from constraint similar to that informing contemporary painting and dance. For one thing, there is now, as Harvey Gross notes, "no apparent dominant metrical convention such as obtained in the centuries previous to this one." For another, "coherence" can currently be defined as any arrangement that creates its own persuasiveness; and contemporary prosody, as Gross continues, "is 'organic,' developed out of the subject and stance of the poem, and not an imposed or adopted style." All subjects from mundane to cosmic, from familiar to obscure, from lofty to earthy, are available to poets, as are words from all realms of discourse, and all kinds of syntactical structures from scrupulously discontinuous to outright narrative; moreover, poetry need not be structured in either rectangular shapes or successive lines, organized by linear syntax or associative imagery, or even be written by accredited members of the Church of Poetry; and the line separating poetry from prose has become jagged and fuzzy. "Poetry," writes John Cage, "is not prose by reason of its content or ambiguity but by reason of its allowing musical elements (time, sound) to be introduced into the world of words." (For her own eccentric pieces, Marianne Moore once offered this classic apologia: "The only reason I know for calling my work poetry at all is that there is no other category in which to put it.") It is, I believe, possible for an individual work today to break *all* the old rules and still attain significances familiar to the traditions of poetry.

The lines between one period of art and another cut so deeply that a new poetry and a new scene for poets invariably accompany each other. The major figures of 1920–40 were mostly part-time writers who held regular, nonacademic jobs—Eliot as a publisher, Stevens as an insurance executive, William Carlos Williams as a doctor, Marianne Moore as a librarian and then an editor; only one of their number, John Crowe Ransom, pursued an academic career for his adult life, and his last twenty working years were spent less in the classroom than as the editor of *Kenyon Review*. The poets of the recent period, in contrast, have mostly been university teachers, often billed as "poet-in-residence"; and while some have assumed permanent positions as professors of writing—among them Tolson, Roethke, John Logan, Robert Kelly, Eberhart, Snodgrass, Ammons, and Wilbur—others drift from school to school—Lowell, Kunitz, Levertov, Ignatow, and Dickey. Some important poets have taken doctorates in English to become professors of literature—Simpson, Stafford, Wright, Hoffman, Hollander, Wagoner, and Koch. Those poets who remain outside the academy tend to work in allied literary trades, such as publishing and journalism—Ashbery, Carroll, and Harvey Shapiro; and only one respected contemporary poet has long subsisted, albeit in modest circumstances, entirely on royalties and readings —Allen Ginsberg.

Although the rates paid for poetry have scarcely gone up in recent years—only *The New Yorker* extends three-figure and sometimes even four-figure sums—what has increased spectacularly are, first, the fees offered, mostly by universities, for live readings and guest lectures and, second, the gross number of poets who are asked to perform. Sums as high as, or even over, a thousand dollars are not uncommon; and rumor has it that one respected and talkative poet earned from his trade over fifty thousand dollars in a recent year. Most established poets, I would estimate, have incomes safely in five figures; and between his performing fees and his teaching salary, as well as the anxious and exhausting sessions both jobs demand, many a harassed American poet might suspect that his beneficent society, by offering greater rewards for performing his reliable standards than for creating new songs, is paying him primarily not to write. "Even today," confessed Hayden Carruth, "in this epoch of foundation grants, cushy teaching appointments, reading tours, etc., most of us write out our poems in the worst possible conditions." This unprecedented situation has made more than one poet "on tour" into an ersatz vaudevillian, if not a traveling salesman, enthusiastically delivering his familiar pitch before appreciative but unsophisticated audiences in a succesion of unfamiliar settings. Moreover, it is more by public appearances than by publications that established reputations in poetry are sustained, and several well-known poets, thanks to their popularity as performers, have acquired high reputations that are simply not supported by their verse. For another thing, by now the private patron has all but disappeared from the American poetry scene; but partially replacing him have been a number of native foundations which, under a variety of programs, give grants that have provided considerable leisure time for most major American writers. Indeed, perhaps because poetry has traditionally been the least remunerative of the literary arts, foundations have recently shown particular generosity toward poets, one even offering a year's income, not to write for the theater, but merely to attend enough plays to get, perhaps, inspired.

There is a second, more complicated sociology of American poetry; and this shapes the politics of publication and position, reputation and reward. The scene of American poetry is defined by the proliferation of parochial establishments which jell around various common ties—academic connection, geographical location, sexual persuasion, ethnic or religious or racial origins. Nearly, though not every, significant American poet belongs to one or another group, sometimes less by his loyalty to them than by the group's adherence to him; and what announces the existence of a clique is, first, a discernible network of writers who regularly and publicly praise each other's work, regardless of whether it is excellent or abominable, as well as, second, their blatant penchant for ritualistically either dismissing or ignoring poets outside their circle. One particularly voluble school consists of poets whose paths intersected at Black Mountain College well over a decade ago; to Leslie Fiedler, they comprise "a small circle of friends dedicating books to each other, mythicizing each other from poem to poem." A second constellation connects a number of academics teaching at various schools—Richard Wilbur, Daniel Hoffman, John

Hollander, Donald Hall, et al.; a third consists of Southern gentlemen, usually teachers at Southern colleges, none of whom, except for the late Randall Jarrell, are particularly good or well known; Theodore Roethke was kingpin for "The School of the Pacific Northwest," which also includes David Wagoner, Carolyn Kizer, and William Stafford; a fifth coalesces around the figures of Robert Bly and James Wright, as well as a journal called successively *The Fifties* and *The Sixties*. Yet another could be christened "Lowell's descendants," since all its members at one time or another studied with Robert Lowell and adopted his later "confessional" style— Anne Sexton, Snodgrass, Plath, and Frederick Seidel—while Lowell himself succeeded Delmore Schwartz as poet laureate for the New York literary mob. Poets who appear regularly in *The New Yorker* constitute another establishment, whose chief figures are James Dickey, Elizabeth Bishop, John Updike, and Howard Moss; and what is commonly, though presumptuously, known as the "New York School" comprises Koch, Ashbery, O'Hara, and Berrigan, as well as scores of vociferously parochial younger poets, some of whom were at one time Koch's pupils. And so on and so on.

In sum, this kind of poetry scene encourages stylistic diversity and clearly defined position-taking, as well as competition among informally organized forces, each with its generals, officers, and foot soldiers, all engaged in what James Dickey aptly calls "the pathetic and vicious jostling and literary back-scratching for prizes and favorable notices." In no other literary art, indicatively, is book-reviewing less disinterested and less discriminating—in Lawrence Hart's phrase, "hardly more than an exchange of valentines." (One well-known poetry reviewer once told me that he puffs everything on the grounds that his services are "good for poetry"; another that he reviews only the work of his friends.) Nonetheless, the most reliable measure of ultimate literary success is not the adulation of one's compatriots, whose judgments finally do not count, but recognition by writers connected with other establishments, or by general magazines, or by disaffiliated (as opposed to party-line) anthologists. For instance, the measure of Robert Lowell's incomparable success is not only the persuasive excellence of his poetry and his early friendship with his most promising peers (Jarrell, Schwartz), but also his ascension to masterhood with the original group of Southern gentlemen, the poetry professors, and the New York literary mob as well, in addition to accolades from poets and critics of even other affiliations, such as the young people editing *Salmagundi*, and rewards from all the major prize and fellowship committees, in addition to customary respectful front-page reviews in *The New York Times Book Review*, a cover story from *Time*, and extra publicity from his peace and political activities.

In short, every poetic establishment has a vested interest in the wider recognition of its major figures, just as all teachers of poetry-writing invariably establish an investment in the careers of their pupils; for the acclaim extended to one man enhances the short-term reputations of all those associated with him. On the other hand, the young poet who works either autonomously or in a radically different way is not likely to receive publication in the established presses, let alone fellowships, positions, grants, and other spoils. Finally, however, although the sociology of American poetry greatly influences such transient factors as who gets what fellowship, award, critical notice, or teaching position, once the establishments of the moment disintegrate, or the independent reader or critic ignores the flack of publicity (or perhaps once the writer turns sixty), it is the quality of the poet's work and its impact upon total strangers that earns his ultimate reputation.

No subject earns more discussion than madness when American poets come together; for many of the major recent figures have, to be frank, spent considerable periods of their lives in certified mental institutions. "Sometimes, indeed, it seems," quipped Leslie Fiedler, in a statement that would be libelous, were it not so true, "as if the path which leads back and forth between the classroom and the madhouse is the one which the modern American muse loves especially to tread." Poets reacting against the willed impersonality of Eliot and Auden inevitably made their own experiences as "mentally ill" a subject of their own work—Robert Lowell in "Waking in the Blue," Allen Ginsberg in *Howl*, and Anne Sexton in *To Bedlam and Part-Way Back*. In his poem "Heard in a Violent Ward," the late Theodore Roethke, who found a permanent academic position only when his sympathetic chairman granted automatic leaves, mystically regards himself as heir to a tradition of mad English poets, as he speaks of entering a heaven,

> With the likes of Blake,
> And Christopher Smart,
> And that sweet man, John Clare.

And in a prose piece he tells of "a kind of psychic shorthand when his protagonist is under great stress." To the late poet Delmore Schwartz, himself a sometime inmate, Robert Lowell attributes this couplet that indicatively echoes as it twists two classic lines in Wordsworth:

> We poets in our youth begin in sadness;
> Thereof in the end come despondency and madness.

"Surely," Fiedler continues elsewhere, "it is not the lucidity and logic of Robert Lowell and Theodore Roethke or John Berryman we admired, but their flirtation with incoherence and disorder." The reasons for such high incidence of mental distress, particularly in important poets born between 1913 and 1917, are inevitably more personal than public; yet among the latter possible causes were experience in World War II (sometimes as noncombatants, if not as imprisoned conscientious objectors) and hardships inherent in the profession of poetry, especially before 1950. There was also the powerful symbolic example of Ezra Pound, incarcerated by his country in St. Elizabeth's Hospital. Poets have come to confess their derangements, almost as a badge of honor, while claims are sometimes made on behalf of insanity as a kind of higher sanity; as Roethke himself once wrote, "Disassociation precedes a new state of clarity." The literary public tolerantly, if not generously, accepts such debilities; yet the specific relations between madness and contemporary poetry have hardly been explored in print. Oddly again, while certain previously taboo subjects have become public, others, such as homosexuality, remain all but universally private, the prime exceptions being Paul Goodman and Allen Ginsberg, the latter concluding his "America" with one of the great lines of contemporary poetry,

America I'm putting my queer shoulder to the wheel.

Conversation around the community of poets never ceases to tell of "unpublished gay poems which are really XYZ's best stuff," and this suggests that in the battle for unashamed, "free" expression, there are still some distinct frontiers to be crossed.

Possibility and change are the crucial words for discussing contemporary American poetry; for not only has poetic writing as a whole changed drastically since the end of World War II, but many major poets, particularly older ones, have decidedly explored alternative possibilities in midcareer. Of certain poets now between forty and sixty, the poet-critic Daniel Hoffman has written, "Different as these poets are from one another, each has passed in his own way through a similar progress: early mastery of received modes and forms, the intensification of these traditional materials, then the struggle to free the tongue from accustomed language, the ear from familiar cadences, the eye from habitual ways of seeing, the sensibility from conventional responses to experience." In the end, however, these particular poets, most of whom were recognized in the late forties, have only epitomized the character of their times; for in no other period of literature did poets and their critics alike, as well as other writers and artists, put such a high value upon stylistic development—upon the necessity of replacing old skins around their imagination with new ones—even if the previous style has brought nothing but personal satisfaction and critical success. (This perhaps explains why so many important recent pieces should take as their subject a particular conception of poetry.) Beyond that, at no time before have writers been so sympathetic toward flirtations with artistic impossibility, to the point that a true innovation is often defended less for its intrinsic excellence than as "an interesting thing to do"; and this seems a particularly opportune moment to launch an adventurous poetic involvement. In sum, it is the numerous breakings of old molds for alternative possibilities that constitute the significant stylistic history of post-WW II American poetry, as well as shapes the current "tradition" that promises to inform poetry written in the near future. Although the qualitative measure of recent verse may seem, in close retrospect, less substantial than poetry of 1920–1940 and the present period seems less blessed with indisputable masterpieces, it may be the absence of overbearing contemporary touchstones, as well as the great number and stylistic variousness of good poets, that grants the current moment an atmosphere of deeply felt freedom and possibility.

# Randall Jarrell

## GUNNER

Did they send me away from my cat and my wife
To a doctor who poked me and counted my teeth,
To a line on a plain, to a stove in a tent?
Did I nod in the flies of the schools?

And the fighters rolled into the tracer like rabbits,
The blood froze over my splints like a scab—
Did I snore, all still and grey in the turret,
Till the palms rose out of the sea with my death?

And the world ends here, in the sand of a grave,
All my wars over? . . . It was easy as that!
Has my wife a pension of so many mice?
Did the medals go home to my cat?

# THE DEATH OF THE BALL TURRET GUNNER

From my mother's sleep I fell into the State,
And I hunched in its belly till my wet fur froze.
Six miles from earth, loosed from its dream of life,
I woke to black flak and the nightmare fighters.
When I died they washed me out of the turret with a hose.

# LOSSES

It was not dying: everybody died.
It was not dying: we had died before
In the routine crashes—and our fields
Called up the papers, wrote home to our folks,
And the rates rose, all because of us.
We died on the wrong page of the almanac,
Scattered on mountains fifty miles away;
Diving on haystacks, fighting with a friend,
We blazed up on the lines we never saw.
We died like aunts or pets or foreigners.
(When we left high school nothing else had died
For us to figure we had died like.)

In our new planes, with our new crews, we bombed
The ranges by the desert or the shore,
Fired at towed targets, waited for our scores—
And turned into replacements and woke up
One morning, over England, operational.
It wasn't different: but if we died
It was not an accident but a mistake
(But an easy one for anyone to make).
We read our mail and counted up our missions—
In bombers named for girls, we burned
The cities we had learned about in school—
Till our lives wore out; our bodies lay among
The people we had killed and never seen.
When we lasted long enough they gave us medals;
When we died they said, "Our casualties were low."

They said, "Here are the maps"; we burned the cities.
It was not dying—no, not ever dying;
But the night I died I dreamed that I was dead,
And the cities said to me: "Why are you dying?
We are satisfied, if you are; but why did I die?"

# THE STATE

When they killed my mother it made me nervous;
I thought to myself, It was *right:*
Of course she was crazy, and how she ate!
And she died, after all, in her way, for the State.
But I minded: how queer it was to stare
At one of them not sitting there.

When they drafted Sister I said all night,
"It's healthier there in the fields";
And I'd think, "Now I'm helping to win the War,"
When the neighbors came in, as they did, with my meals.
And I was, I was; but I was scared
With only one of them sitting there.

When they took my cat for the Army Corps
Of Conservation and Supply,
I thought of him there in the cold with the mice
And I cried, and I cried, and I wanted to die.
They were there, and I saw them, and that is my life.
Now there's nothing. I'm dead, and I want to die.

## MAIL CALL

The letters always just evade the hand.
One skates like a stone into a beam, falls like a bird.
Surely the past from which the letters rise
Is waiting in the future, past the graves?
The soldiers are all haunted by their lives.

Their claims upon their kind are paid in paper
That establishes a presence, like a smell.
In letters and dreams they see the world.
They are waiting: and the years contract
To an empty hand, to one unuttered sound—

The soldier simply wishes for his name.

# A LULLABY

For wars his life and half a world away
The soldier sells his family and days.
He learns to fight for freedom and the State;
He sleeps with seven men within six feet.

He picks up matches and he cleans out plates;
Is lied to like a child, cursed like a beast.
They crop his head, his dog tags ring like sheep
As his stiff limbs shift wearily to sleep.

Recalled in dreams or letters, else forgot,
His life is smothered like a grave, with dirt;
And his dull torment mottles like a fly's
The lying amber of the histories.

# THE ORIENT EXPRESS

One looks from the train
Almost as one looked as a child. In the sunlight
What I see still seems to me plain,
I am safe; but at evening
As the lands darken, a questioning
Precariousness comes over everything.

Once after a day of rain
I lay longing to be cold; and after a while
I was cold again, and hunched shivering
Under the quilt's many colors, gray
With the dull ending of the winter day.
Outside me there were a few shapes
Of chairs and tables, things from a primer;
Outside the window
There were the chairs and tables of the world. . . .
I saw that the world
That had seemed to me the plain
Gray mask of all that was strange
Behind it—of all that *was*—was all.

But it is beyond belief.
One thinks, "Behind everything
An unforced joy, an unwilling
Sadness (a willing sadness, a forced joy)
Moves changelessly"; one looks from the train
And there is something, the same thing
Behind everything: all these little villages,
A passing woman, a field of grain,
The man who says good-bye to his wife—
A path through a wood full of lives, and the train

Passing, after all unchangeable
And not now ever to stop, like a heart—

It is like any other work of art.
It is and never can be changed.
Behind everything there is always
The unknown unwanted life.

# A GIRL IN A LIBRARY

An object among dreams, you sit here with your shoes off
And curl your legs up under you; your eyes
Close for a moment, your face moves toward sleep . . .
You are very human.
                        But my mind, gone out in tenderness,
Shrinks from its object with a thoughtful sigh.
This is a waist the spirit breaks its arm on.
The gods themselves, against you, struggle in vain.
This broad low strong-boned brow; these heavy eyes;
These calves, grown muscular with certainties;
This nose, three medium-sized pink strawberries
—But I exaggerate. In a little you will leave:
I'll hear, half squeal, half shriek, your laugh of greeting—
Then, *decrescendo*, bars of that strange speech
In which each sound sets out to seek each other,
Murders its own father, marries its own mother,
And ends as one grand transcendental vowel.

(Yet for all I know, the Egyptian Helen spoke so.)
As I look, the world contracts around you:
I see Brünnhilde had brown braids and glasses
She used for studying; Salome straight brown bangs,
A calf's brown eyes, and sturdy light-brown limbs
Dusted with cinnamon, an apple-dumpling's . . .
Many a beast has gnawn a leg off and got free,
Many a dolphin curved up from Necessity—
The trap has closed about you, and you sleep.
If someone questioned you, *What doest thou here?*
You'd knit your brows like an orangoutang
(But not so sadly; not so thoughtfully)
And answer with a pure heart, guilelessly:

*I'm studying. . . .*
                        If only you were not!
Assignments,
                    recipes,
                            the *Official Rulebook*
*Of Basketball*—ah, let them go; you needn't mind.
The soul has no assignments, neither cooks
Nor referees: it wastes its time.
                                        It wastes its time.
Here in this enclave there are centuries
For you to waste: the short and narrow stream
Of Life meanders into a thousand valleys
Of all that was, or might have been, or is to be.
The books, just leafed through, whisper endlessly . . .
Yet it is hard. One sees in your blurred eyes
The "uneasy half-soul" Kipling saw in dogs'.
One sees it, in the glass, in one's own eyes.
In rooms alone, in galleries, in libraries,
In tears, in searchings of the heart, in staggering joys
We memorize once more our old creation,
Humanity: with what yawns the unwilling
Flesh puts on its spirit, O my sister!

So many dreams! And not one troubles
Your sleep of life? no self stares shadowily
From these worn hexahedrons, beckoning
With false smiles, tears? . . .
                            Meanwhile Tatyana
Larina (gray eyes nickel with the moonlight
That falls through the willows onto Lensky's tomb;
Now young and shy, now old and cold and sure)
Asks, smiling: "But what is she dreaming of, fat thing?"
I answer: She's not fat. She isn't dreaming.
She purrs or laps or runs, all in her sleep;
Believes, awake, that she is beautiful;
She never dreams.
                        Those sunrise-colored clouds
Around man's head—that inconceivable enchantment
From which, at sunset, we come back to life

Of all this, Tanya, she is innocent.
For nineteen years she's faced reality:
They look alike already.
                              They say, man wouldn't be
The best thing in this world—and isn't he?—
If he were not too good for it. But she
—She's good enough for it.
                              And yet sometimes
Her sturdy form, in its pink strapless formal,
Is as if bathed in moonlight—modulated
Into a form of joy, a Lydian mode;
This Wooden Mean's a kind, furred animal
That speaks, in the Wild of things, delighting riddles
To the soul that listens, trusting . . .
                              Poor senseless Life:
When, in the last light sleep of dawn, the messenger
Comes with his message, you will not awake.
He'll give his feathery whistle, shake you hard,
You'll look with wide eyes at the dewy yard
And dream, with calm slow factuality:
"Today's Commencement. My bachelor's degree
In Home Ec., my doctorate of philosophy
In Phys. Ed.
          [Tanya, they won't even *scan*]
To find our graves dug, families dead, selves dying:
Are waiting for me. . . ."
                              Oh, Tatyana,
The Angel comes: better to squawk like a chicken
Than to say with truth, "But I'm a *good* girl,"
And Meet his Challenge with a last firm strange
Uncomprehending smile; and—then, then!—see
The blind date that has stood you up: your life.
(For all this, if it isn't, perhaps, life,
Has yet, at least, a language of its own
Different from the books'; worse than the books'.)
And yet, the ways we miss our lives are life.
Yet . . . yet . . .
               to have one's life add up to *yet!*

You sigh a shuddering sigh. Tatyana murmurs,
"Don't cry, little peasant"; leaves us with a swift
"Good-bye, good-bye . . . Ah, don't think ill of me . . ."
Your eyes open: you sit here thoughtlessly.

I love you—and yet—and yet—I love you.

Don't cry, little peasant. Sit and dream.
One comes, a finger's width beneath your skin,
To the braided maidens singing as they spin;
There sound the shepherd's pipe, the watchman's rattle
Across the short dark distance of the years.
I am a thought of yours: and yet, you do not think . . .
The firelight of a long, blind, dreaming story
Lingers upon your lips; and I have seen
Firm, fixed forever in your closing eyes,
The Corn King beckoning to his Spring Queen.

# THE DIFFICULT RESOLUTION

Night after night the dead moon lit
Mortar and sentry, and the whole strand
Lay stripped of its cottagers, the night's dead
Who escape once more to their habitual
Graves from the terrible life of the island,
To the dreams along whose beaches laps
The owned and amniotic sea.

They know their life, brilliant with the light and play
Riches afford each impulse, the distractions of sunlight
And surf and summer, engaging with the elaborated
Ejaculations of dancers, the laughs of nurses—
Terrible because it is still life: the mother
Thinks, "Enough. I may die"; and the girl speaks
Publicly of love, and means her death.

Under the grave limbs, the accessible grace
Of the new flesh, the cell's old anguish
Works extravagantly: we learn to think,
"My wish unsatisfied, my need unknown;
My intent, and the world's, incommensurable;
And happiness, if there is happiness, inaccessible—
Let me sleep, let me perish!" In the warm darkness
The sleeper whispers at last: "The grave is my mother."

There is the knowledge you and I unlearned.
We heard, a few nights, the unhousing sea,
No womb now of ours; the wind from the darkness
Laughed to us endlessly, a will of the world.
Yesterday's peoples, those storms like an indignation
Of Europe's, implacable with its pressures and anguish—
Over the dark sea and centuries, the strangers coming

To die in the ranges of the empty land—
Who remembers those nameless? The needs and death
Of Yesterday on the bed of straw, by the wall of logs,
Who existed only that you might lavish
Your magnificent and unenduring smile
On the phosphorescence of bathers, the rockets wandering
Up to the cold galaxy—my own face

Looking and unendurable in the young night?
Today, the child lies wet and warm
In his big mother; tomorrow, too, is dumb,
The dry skull of the cold tomb. "Between?"
Between I suffered. "And are content at last
To know no more of that desire, of that intolerable
Anguish: the degradation and the limits of your kind?
That is what you learned from the wind, from the darkness

That was never still, that moved all night
Toward day and its death—star wandering
To other star, a stranger, a new sky?"
No, no! The wind, the night—
Those knew no will to sleep, no hope of death.
Blind strength, the harshness and agony of purpose—
The true, the sure will of that living world

Stretched taut around us like a crazy womb—
I learned that then; I too felt for my instant
The waves of that constriction, the rejecting lips
Wet still with the tides that formed us, with the blind
Determiners of that blind mother: the great beast
Convulsed with its passion for it knows not what,
That gives and takes away and gives and in the end destroys

All that has loved it or has found it bearable;
That weeps—weeps at us, not once for us; that at last
Twists us to pieces, slings us away, merciless with its despair
At us and at itself: the universe we judge.
Remember what you learned then: that you are powerless
Except to know that you are powerless, to learn
Your use and your rejection, all that is destroying you—
And to accept it: the difficult resolution.

# HOPE

*The spirit killeth, but the letter giveth life.*

The week is dealt out like a hand
That children pick up card by card.
One keeps getting the same hand.
One keeps getting the same card.

But twice a day—except on Saturday—
But every day—except on Sunday—
The wheel stops, there is a crack in Time:
With a hiss of soles, a rattle of tin,
My own gray Daemon pauses on the stair,
My own bald Fortune lifts me by the hair.

> *Woe's me! woe's me! In Folly's mailbox*
> *Still laughs the postcard, Hope:*
> *Your uncle in Australia*
> *Has died and you are Pope.*
> *For many a soul has entertained*
> *A Mailman unawares—*
> *And as you cry, Impossible,*
> *A step is on the stairs.*

One keeps getting the same dream
Delayed, marked *Postage Due*,
The bill that one has paid
Delayed, marked *Payment Due*—

Twice a day, in a rotting mailbox,
The white grubs are new.
And Faith, once more, is mine
Faithfully, but Charity
Writes hopefully about a new
Asylum—but Hope is as good as new.

Woe's me! woe's me! In Folly's mailbox
Still laughs the postcard, Hope:
Your uncle in Australia
Has died and you are Pope.
For many a soul has entertained
A Mailman unawares—
And as you cry, Impossible,
A step is on the stairs.

# VARIATIONS

## I

"I lived with Mr. Punch, they said my name was Judy,
I beat him with my rolling-pin, he hit me with his cane.
I ran off with a soldier, he followed in a carriage,
And he drew a big revolver and he shot me through the brain.
But that was his duty, he only did his duty—"

Said Judy, said the Judy, said poor Judy to the string.

"O hear her, just hear her!" the string said softly.
And the string and Judy, they said no more.
Yes, string or Judy, it said no more.
But they hanged Mr. Punch with a six-inch rope,
And "Clap," said the manager; "the play is over."

## II

"I lay like a swan upon the down of Heaven.
When the clouds came the rain grew
Into the rice of my palaces, the great wits
Were the zithers of my garden, I stood among sedge
And held to the peoples the gold staff of God."

Said Grace, said Good, O said the son of God.

The wives and wise, the summer's willows
Nodded and were fed by the wind; when the snow fell
And the wind's steps were pink in the pure winter,
Who spared his charcoal for the son of God,
The vain wind failing at the pass to Hell?

III

"I lived in a room full of bears and porridge,
My mother was dead and my nurse was horrid.
I sat all day on a white china chamber
And I lay all night in my trundle bed.
And she wasn't, she wasn't, O not a bit dead!"

The boy said, the girl said—and Nurse she said:

"I'll stew your ears all day, little hare,
Just as God ate your mother, for you are bad,
Are bad, are bad—" and the nurse is the night
To wake to, to die in: and the day I live,
The world and its life are her dream.


IV

"I was born in a hut, my wit is heavy.
My sister died, they killed my father.
There is no time I was not hungry.
They used me, I am dying.
I stand here among graves."

The white, the yellow, the black man said.

And the world said: Child, you will not be missed.
You are cheaper than a wrench, your back is a road;
Your death is a table in a book.
You had our wit, our heart was sealed to you:
Man is the judgment of the world.

# Delmore Schwartz

## THE HEAVY BEAR WHO GOES WITH ME

*"the withness of the body"*

The heavy bear who goes with me,
A manifold honey to smear his face,
Clumsy and lumbering here and there,
The central ton of every place,
The hungry beating brutish one
In love with candy, anger, and sleep,
Crazy factotum, dishevelling all,
Climbs the building, kicks the football,
Boxes his brother in the hate-ridden city.

Breathing at my side, that heavy animal,
That heavy bear who sleeps with me,
Howls in his sleep for a world of sugar,
A sweetness intimate as the water's clasp,
Howls in his sleep because the tight-rope
Trembles and shows the darkness beneath.
—The strutting show-off is terrified,
Dressed in his dress-suit, bulging his pants,
Trembles to think that his quivering meat
Must finally wince to nothing at all.

That inescapable animal walks with me,
Has followed me since the black womb held,
Moves where I move, distorting my gesture,
A caricature, a swollen shadow,

A stupid clown of the spirit's motive,
Perplexes and affronts with his own darkness,
The secret life of belly and bone,
Opaque, too near, my private, yet unknown,
Stretches to embrace the very dear
With whom I would walk without him near,
Touches her grossly, although a word
Would bare my heart and make me clear,
Stumbles, flounders, and strives to be fed
Dragging me with him in his mouthing care,
Amid the hundred million of his kind,
The scrimmage of appetite everywhere.

# IN THE NAKED BED, IN PLATO'S CAVE

In the naked bed, in Plato's cave,
Reflected headlights slowly slid the wall,
Carpenters hammered under the shaded window,
Wind troubled the window curtains all night long,
A fleet of trucks strained uphill, grinding,
Their freights covered, as usual.
The ceiling lightened again, the slanting diagram
Slid slowly forth.
      Hearing the milkman's chop,
His striving up the stair, the bottle's chink,
I rose from bed, lit a cigarette,
And walked to the window. The stony street
Displayed the stillness in which buildings stand,
The street-lamp's vigil and the horse's patience.
The winter sky's pure capital
Turned me back to bed with exhausted eyes.

Strangeness grew in the motionless air. The loose
Film grayed. Shaking wagons, hooves' waterfalls,
Sounded far off, increasing, louder and nearer.
A car coughed, starting. Morning, softly
Melting the air, lifted the half-covered chair
From underseas, kindled the looking-glass,
Distinguished the dresser and the white wall.
The bird called tentatively, whistled, called,
Bubbled and whistled, so! Perplexed, still wet
With sleep, affectionate, hungry and cold. So, so,
O son of man, the ignorant night, the travail
Of early morning, the mystery of beginning
Again and again,
     while History is unforgiven.

# THE BALLAD OF THE CHILDREN OF THE CZAR

I

The children of the Czar
played with a bouncing ball

In the May morning, in the Czar's garden,
Tossing it back and forth.

It fell among the flowerbeds
Or fled to the north gate.

A daylight moon hung up
In the Western sky, bald white.

Like Papa's face, said Sister,
Hurling the white ball forth.

II

While I ate a baked potato
Six thousand miles apart,

In Brooklyn, in 1916,
Aged two, irrational.

When Franklin D. Roosevelt
Was an Arrow Collar ad.

O Nicholas! Alas! Alas!
My grandfather coughed in your army,

Hid in a wine-stinking barrel,
For three days in Bucharest

Then left for America
To become a king himself.


III

I am my father's father,
You are your children's guilt.

In history's pity and terror
The child is Aeneas again;

Troy is in the nursery,
The rocking horse is on fire.

Child labor! The child must carry
His fathers on his back.

But seeing that so much is past
And that history has no ruth

For the individual,
Who drinks tea, who catches cold,

Let anger be general:
I hate an abstract thing.


IV

Brother and sister bounced
The bounding, unbroken ball,

The shattering sun fell down
Like swords upon their play,

Moving eastward among the stars
Toward February and October.

But the Maywind brushed their cheeks
Like a mother watching sleep,

And if for a moment they fight
Over the bouncing ball

And sister pinches brother
And brother kicks her shins,

Well! The heart of man is known:
It is a cactus bloom.


V

The ground on which the ball bounces
Is another bouncing ball.

The wheeling, whirling world
Makes no will glad.

Spinning in its spotlight darkness,
It is too big for their hands.

A pitiless, purposeless Thing,
Arbitrary and unspent,

Made for no play, for no children,
But chasing only itself.

The innocent are overtaken,
They are not innocent.

They are their father's father,
The past is inevitable.


VI

Now, in another October
Of this tragic star,

I see my second year,
I eat my baked potato.

It is my buttered world,
But, poked by my unlearned hand,

It falls from the highchair down
And I begin to howl.

And I see the ball roll under
The iron gate which is locked.

Sister is screaming, brother is howling,
The ball has evaded their will.

Even a bouncing ball
Is uncontrollable,

And is under the garden wall.
I am overtaken by terror

Thinking of my father's fathers,
And of my own will.

# Daniel Hoffman

## THE CITY OF SATISFACTIONS

As I was travelling toward the city of satisfactions
On my employment, seeking the treasure of pleasure,
Laved in the superdome observation car by Muzak
Soothed by the cool conditioned and reconditioned air,
Sealed in from the smell of the heat and the spines
Of the sere mesquite and the seared windblast of the sand,
It was conjunction of a want of juicy fruit
And the train's slowdown and stopping at a depot
Not listed on the schedule, unnamed by platform sign,
That made me step down on the siding
With some change in hand. The newsstand, on inspection,
Proved a shed of greyed boards shading
A litter of stale rags.
Turning back, I blanched at the Silent Streak: a wink
Of the sun's reflection caught its rear-view window
Far down the desert track. I grabbed the crossbar
And the handcar clattered. Up and down
It pumped so fast I hardly could grab hold it,
His regal head proud despite the bending
Knees, back-knees, back-knees, back-knees propelling.
His eyes bulged beadier than a desert toad's eyes.
His huge hands shrank upon the handlebar,
His mighty shoulders shrivelled and his skin grew
Wrinkled while I watched the while we reeled
Over the mesquite till the train grew larger
And pumping knees, back-knees, we stood still and

Down on us the train bore,
The furious tipping of the levers unabated
Wrenched my sweating eyes and aching armpits,
He leapt on long webbed feet into the drainage
Dryditch and the car swung longside on a siding
Slowing down beside the Pullman diner
Where the napkined waiter held a tray of glasses.
The gamehen steamed crisp-crust behind the glass.
I let go of the tricycle and pulled my askew necktie,
Pushed through the diner door, a disused streetcar,
A Danish half devoured by flies beneath specked glass,
Dirty cups on the counter,
A menu, torn, too coffeestained for choices, told
In a map of rings my cryptic eyes unspelled
Of something worth the digging for right near by
Here just out beyond the two-door shed.
The tracks were gone now but I found a shovel,
Made one, that is, from a rusting oildrum cover,
A scrap of baling wire, a broken crutch,
And down I heaved on the giving earth and rockshards
And a frog drygasped once from a distant gulley
And up I spewed the debris in a range
Of peaks I sank beneath and sweated under till
One lunge sounded the clunk of iron on brass
And furious scratch and pawing of the dryrock
Uncovered the graven chest and the pile of earth downslid
While under a lowering sky, sweatwet, I grasped and wrestled
The huge chest, lunged and jerked and fought it upward
Till it toppled sideways on the sand. I smashed it
Open, and it held a barred box. My nails broke
On the bars that wouldn't open. I smashed it
Open and it held a locked box. I ripped my knuckles
But couldn't wrest that lock off till I smashed it
Open and it held a small box worked
In delicate filigree of silver with
A cunning keyhole. But there was no key.
I pried it, ripped my fingers underneath it
But couldn't get it open till I smashed it
Open and it held a little casket

Sealed tight with twisted wires or vines of shining
Thread. I bit and tugged and twisted, cracked my teeth
But couldn't loose the knot. I smashed it
Open and the top came off, revealing
A tiny casket made of jade. It had
No top, no seam, no turnkey. Thimblesmall
It winked unmoving near the skinbreak
Where steakjuice pulsed and oozed. I thought aroma
Sifted, thinning till the dark horizon
Seemed, and then no longer seemed, a trifle
Sweetened. I knelt before
A piece of desert stone. When I have fitted
That stone into its casket, and replaced
The lid and set that casket in its box,
Fitted the broken top and set that box within
The box it came in and bent back the bars
And put it in the chest, the chest back in the hole,
The peaks around the pit-edge piled back in the pit,
Replaced the baling wire and crutch and oildrum cover
And pushed back through the diner, will the train
Sealed in from the smell of heat and mesquite
Envelop me in Muzak while it swooshes
Past bleak sidings such as I wait on
Nonstop toward the city of satisfactions roaring?
If I could only make this broken top
Fit snug back on this casket

# EXPLORATION

I am who the trail took,
nose of whom I followed,
woodwit I confided in
through thorned-and-briared hallows;
favoring my right side for
clouds the sun had hemmed in.
Behind the North I sought daystar,
bore down highroads hidden
to undiscerning gaze.
My right, my right I turned to
on trails strangely unblazoned
where fistfive forkings burgeoned,
I took my right. Was destined
among deerdroppings on the ridge
or chipmunk stones astrain
or hoofmucks in the swampcabbage
to err? Landmarking birch
selfmultiplied in malice till
woods reared a whitebarred cage
around my spinning eye. The spool
of memory had run out my yarn
and lost the last hank. Found
I the maze I wander in
where my right, trusted hand,
leads round and round a certain copse,
a sudden mound of stone,
an anthill humming in the rocks
an expectant tune?
Lacklearning now my knowledge is
of how to coax recalcitrant
ignition from cold engines,
or mate a fugue in either hand

on spinet or converse
in any tongue but stonecrop signs.
Clouds hump like battling bulls. The firs
lash me with angry tines,
shred my clothes. A windwhipped will
uncompassed, lacking fur or fang,
strange to these parts, yet whom the anthill
anticipating, sang.

# WORDS FOR DR. WILLIAMS

Wouldst thou grace this land with song?
    Well, go yodel your head off.
But if it's poems you want, then take a town
    with mills and chimneys, oil
Slithering on the river toward the falls,
    grit in the air, a man
Just off the night shift turning, tired yet strong
    to watch the girl who hurries
Toward a timeclock step down from the bus—
    slim ankles, one,
Two, and click click click swings past. The sun
    glints on her raincoat. There's
Your muse and hero. Stick around this town
    where people speak American
And love is possible—Your stethoscope
    held to our arteries
In sickness and in health you found some places
    where our own poems grow.

# John Logan

## CYCLE FOR MOTHER CABRINI

### 1.   A Chance Visit to Her Bones

I thank God Mother Cabrini's
Body is subject to laws
Of decay. To me it is
A disservice when flesh

Will not fall from bones
As God for His glory
Sometimes allows. I speak thus
For flesh is my failing:

That it shall fall is my
Salvation. That it shall not
Conquer is my blind hope.
That it shall rise again

Commanding, is my fear.
That it shall rise changed
Is my faith. I think
I can love this saint

Who built high schools
And whose bones I came upon
Today. I laugh a little
At the wax mask that smiles

Surely thru her box of glass:
Artificial faces cannot
Frighten one who remembers
No face is real for long.

Blessed Mother Cabrini
Lives here her saint's life
I said, she sees me all;
I only see her face

Mask, and see her habit
Given form by bones
Which carried about her flesh
Gone now. The bones will rise

To carry changed flesh
And I may walk I
Might walk with her!
Whom I seek to pray to

Some, and strain
To love. Moisten me
With dust from her bones.
I see their shape—help me

Love them help think of
Breast white doves that rise
Over earth-smelling fields
Their wings tremble for her

Birth, as I wait: mine
Is a dry waiting
Her mask stares, she
Stirs—ah

*Her* bones move *me!*

## 2. Recollection

### I

I found your bones that lay
Off the highschool hallway
And drummed them with my need;
They rang and rose and hurried

Me. I bought and set
Your picture in my wallet
And chose a cheap ring,
A piece of junk but something

Your sisters sell; to me
Its feel and pull heavy
On my fingerbone wore
In for a time, the terror

Of your delicate flesh, the scant
Weight within the fragrant
Bones that it seemed turned
To me as to the bright and the unburned

### II

Blessed Mother I know
You met me once in Chicago
I didn't go there
To hunt for saints (or anywhere):

You bowed and smiled at me
Out of a film biography
I don't know why I went
Except perhaps for amusement

And rest; your skill is hid
Behind a sweet and lurid

Piety O queen
Of a Holy wood unseen—

Your eyes and art sent
A deep tiredness apparent
To me as an expected thing
But until I knew unsettling

Because of breathlessness
And hot and blood shocked duress
At my ribs, that sickened me,
And turned the colors of the city.


III

Long years Mother had gone
Before I met you in Tryon
Park although you knew me
At Chicago and eternally.

One time in New York again
Under the wicked regimen
Of grace, I thought to come
To your girls' kingdom

To the middy world of your tomb
By text, principal, and schoolroom.
You know I did not go;
I went another place though:

Can I say what you did
Those days I invalid
At church, ambiguous at its door
Was tried by my confessor;

Without lustre hair
Sprouts at arm's root bitter
Sediment upon the flesh dead
The nail slides from folded

Skin, so shall I be
Till Christ reafford the luxury
By which bodies sing
And souls have their breathing;

Sweet virgin it was you
That left the gay retinue
To cry me grace at its head
Till I like your bones was not dead.


IV

Saint who overlaps
Our lives who knows the mishaps
Of our times the flaws
Of men no longer outlaws

Even; who knows our schools
Our stores our gods and business rules
Saw charts rise and fall
In your chromium hospital—

You helped shape our city
And the city in the sky:
Help me shape your beauty
In this scarred and remade eye.


3.  Mother Cabrini Crosses the Andes


In God's good time we reached the "Cumbre"
which is the topmost height that can be crossed
in the neighborhood of Aconcagua and here we
remained some time.
—St. Francis Xavier Cabrini, *Travels and Letters*
He has made my feet like the feet of harts;
he has set me upon high places.
                    —Gradual from her Mass (Dec. 22)

## I

The tiny saint got the best mule
Though an opera singer was in the party,
And St. Joseph the muleteer was gentle
And helped a lot; providentially,

For the soundest beast leads
And she had never ridden and was jittery—
Tried to guide! Though she learned
Early to be passive to the sea.

Small and weightless as she was
She could have risen to the saddle
Or St. Joseph would have tossed her
Humbly, could she have put

Her foot into his hand
But she could not, ascending
Rather from upon a chair
And set off cowled in furs

Like a monk (her saving comment)
Or Xavier in the mountains of the orient.


## II

And the air in the high Andes
Was thin and lucid as milk
Or fire, or as violets she sailed
In boats in Lombardy,

A child afraid of the water
But sick for the fire and milk
Of the sea's wake and for the souls
That flashed like fish

For the souls that love like milk
And like fire, for the spring soul

That bursts quiet as a violet
And swings upon its thin

Stem to flame at the sun,
Ridiculous as a nun.


III

Had she known the pressure
Here will bleed the skin
Or that the muleteers would be
Too busy to say the Rosary,
That she would fail to jump her mule a-

Cross a crevasse, would fall
Into St. Joseph's arms and
Faint in the snow bank that flanks
The rim (the heights of her cheeks
More pale more glowing than crystal
Vanishing on her habit—eyes

As they opened as soft as furs),
Or had she somehow discovered
She and Mother Chiara
Would spend the evening in a bar
Beside the pampas' edge: she

Would lead the pilgrimage again
Over the high Andes,
Forego the closed cabin
The turn around the horn, would climb
Would rest the party at the Cumbre
Again draw breath and for a moment again

Would turn away forever.


IV

Air shivered in the Andes
As full of color as blood

Or bells, or ice the saboteurs
Left on Lytle Street
When angered by her sick and alien

They opened the mansion pipes;
What was this to her
Who dynamites hearts: rivets,
Quarries, shapes bricks, and built
In Chicago two hospitals
Besides the one they chilled awhile

And burned a little bit.
But they kicked the sisters out
Of Nicaragua—the schoolgirls no trash
These, necks blue as Andes
Snow thin as moons: and hair

Black as the bird-live valleys;
The saint was away on business—
New Orleans orphanage or the Villa
Or the novitiate at old Manresa
On the Hudson. (Or was it the hotel
In Seattle?) And there was trouble in France

Since the archbishop was on the Riviera,
And the priests turned her a cold
Parisian shoulder, but she moved in
At a gilt estate where the sisters
Had to put up sheets over the many mirrors.

Whether they went on their continents
Or ours the austere skirts
Were strangest brushing by the summerhouse
In Rio the intemperate flower parts:
Though here the black was closest
To the holy red that flowed her into God.

In Chicago, upon her martyrdom.
She should have died in Lombardy
Safe from a saint's life and the traveler's

Malady that chilled her and brightened
Her gown, like a bell she jangled in her room
Where she rocked and, died, in a wicker chair.


V

A good mule like god's will and the sea
Does not mind those who disagree
And bore her safely
So that, the stars at easy
Height again, the party
Rested.

But the pampas at night are a sky
Where masses alive and unknown
Are relieved by constellations of bone.


VI

High cold keen the Cumbre air
As the light from the stone and shattering stars

But there is nowhere mountain air
So cold or keen or bright or
Thin as is Francesca's wrist
Humming hyaline
Along the risen limb.

# J. V. Cunningham

## TO MY WIFE

And does the heart grow old? You know
In the indiscriminate green
Of summer or in earliest snow
A landscape is another scene,

Inchoate and anonymous,
And every rock and bush and drift
As our affections alter us
Will alter with the season's shift.

So love by love we come at last,
As through the exclusions of a rhyme,
Or the exactions of a past,
To the simplicity of time,

The antiquity of grace, where yet
We live in terror and delight
With love as quiet as regret
And love like anger in the night.

## TO THE READER

Time will assuage.
Time's verses bury
Margin and page
In commentary,

For gloss demands
A gloss annexed
Till busy hands
Blot out the text,

And all's coherent.
Search in this gloss
No text inherent:
The text was loss.

The gain is gloss.

# DOCTOR DRINK

### I

In the thirtieth year of life
I took my heart to be my wife,

And as I turn in bed by night
I have my heart for my delight.

No other heart may mine estrange
For my heart changes as I change,

And it is bound, and I am free,
And with my death it dies with me.

### II    INTERVIEW WITH DOCTOR DRINK

I have a fifth of therapy
In the house, and transference there.
Doctor, there's not much wrong with me,
Only a sick rattlesnake somewhere

In the house, if it be there at all,
But the lithe mouth is coiled. The shapes
Of door and window move. I call.
What is it that pulls down the drapes,

Disheveled and exposed? Your rye
Twists in my throat: intimacy
Is like hard liquor. Who but I
Coil there and squat, and pay your fee?

75

## III

*Lip* was a man who used his head.
He used it when he went to bed
With his friend's wife, and with his friend,
With either sex at either end.


## IV    EPITAPH FOR SOMEONE OR OTHER

Naked I came, naked I leave the scene,
And naked was my pastime in between.


## V

All in due time: love will emerge from hate,
And the due deference of truth from lies.
If not quite all things come to those who wait
They will not need them: in due time one dies.


## VI

Dear child whom I begot,
Forgive me if my page
Hymns not your helpless age,
For you are mine, and not:
Mine as sower and sown,
But in yourself your own.


## VII

Life flows to death as rivers to the sea,
And life is fresh and death is salt to me.


## VIII

On a cold night I came through the cold rain
And false snow to the wind shrill on your pane
With no hope and no anger and no fear:
Who are you? and with whom do you sleep here?

# Robert Lowell

## MR. EDWARDS AND THE SPIDER

I saw the spiders marching through the air,
Swimming from tree to tree that mildewed day
In latter August when the hay
Came creaking to the barn. But where
The wind is westerly,
Where gnarled November makes the spiders fly
Into the apparitions of the sky,
They purpose nothing but their ease and die
Urgently beating east to sunrise and the sea;

What are we in the hands of the great God?
It was in vain you set up thorn and briar
In battle array against the fire
And treason crackling in your blood;
For the wild thorns grow tame
And will do nothing to oppose the flame;
Your lacerations tell the losing game
You play against sickness past your cure.
How will the hands be strong? How will the heart
   endure?

A very little thing, a little worm,
Or hourglass-blazoned spider, it is said,
Can kill a tiger. Will the dead
Hold up his mirror and affirm
To the four winds the smell

And flash of his authority? It's well
If God who holds you to the pit of hell,
Much as one holds a spider, will destroy,
Baffle and dissipate your soul. As a small boy

On Windsor Marsh, I saw the spider die
When thrown into the bowels of fierce fire:
There's no long struggle, no desire
To get up on its feet and fly—
It stretches out its feet
And dies. This is the sinner's last retreat;
Yes, and no strength exerted on the heat
Then sinews the abolished will, when sick
And full of burning, it will whistle on a brick.

But who can plumb the sinking of that soul?
Josiah Hawley, picture yourself cast
Into a brick-kiln where the blast
Fans your quick vitals to a coal—
If measured by a glass,
How long would it seem burning! Let there pass
A minute, ten, ten trillion; but the blaze
Is infinite, eternal: this is death,
To die and know it. This is the Black Widow,
    death.

# THE QUAKER GRAVEYARD IN NANTUCKET

### I

A brackish reach of shoal off Madaket—
The sea was still breaking violently and night
Had steamed into our North Atlantic Fleet,
When the drowned sailor clutched the drag-net. Light
Flashed from his matted head and marble feet,
He grappled at the net
With the coiled, hurdling muscles of his thighs:
The corpse was bloodless, a botch of reds and whites,
Its open, staring eyes
Were lustreless dead-lights
Or cabin-windows on a stranded hulk
Heavy with sand. We weight the body, close
Its eyes and heave it seaward whence it came,
Where the heel-headed dogfish barks its nose
On Ahab's void and forehead; and the name
Is blocked in yellow chalk,
Sailors, who pitch this portent at the sea
Where dreadnoughts shall confess
Its hell-bent deity,
When you are powerless
To sand-bag this Atlantic bulwark, faced
By the earth-shaker, green, unwearied, chaste
In his steel scales: ask for no Orphean lute
To pluck life back. The guns of the steeled fleet
Recoil and then repeat
The hoarse salute.

### II

Whenever winds are moving and their breath
Heaves at the roped-in bulwarks of this pier,

The terns and sea-gulls tremble at your death
In these home waters. Sailor, can you hear
The Pequod's sea wings, beating landward, fall
Headlong and break on our Atlantic wall
Off 'Sconset, where the yawing S-boats splash
The bellbuoy, with ballooning spinnakers,
As the entangled, screeching mainsheet clears
The blocks: off Madaket, where lubbers lash
The heavy surf and throw their long lead squids
For blue-fish? Sea-gulls blink their heavy lids
Seaward. The winds' wings beat upon the stones,
Cousin, and scream for you and the claws rush
At the sea's throat and wring it in the slush
Of this old Quaker graveyard where the bones
Cry out in the long night for the hurt beast
Bobbing by Ahab's whaleboats in the East.


III

All you recovered from Poseidon died
With you, my cousin, and the harrowed brine
Is fruitless on the blue beard of the god,
Stretching beyond us to the castles in Spain,
Nantucket's westward haven. To Cape Cod
Guns, cradled on the tide,
Blast the eelgrass about a waterclock
Of bilge and backwash, roil the salt and sand
Lashing earth's scaffold, rock
Our warships in the hand
Of the great God, where time's contrition blues
Whatever it was these Quaker sailors lost
In the mad scramble of their lives. They died
When time was open-eyed,
Wooden and childish; only bones abide
There, in the nowhere, where their boats were tossed
Sky-high, where mariners had fabled news
Of IS, the whited monster. What it cost
Them is their secret. In the monster's slick
I see the Quakers drown and hear their cry:

'If God himself had not been on our side,
If God himself had not been on our side,
When the Atlantic rose against us, why,
Then it had swallowed us up quick.'


IV

This is the end of the whaleroad and the whale
Who spewed Nantucket bones on the thrashed swell
And stirred the troubled waters to whirlpools
To send the Pequod packing off to hell:
This is the end of them, three-quarters fools,
Snatching at straws to sail
Seaward and seaward on the turntail whale,
Spouting out blood and water as it rolls,
Sick as a dog to these Atlantic shoals:
*Clamavimus*, O depths. Let the sea-gulls wail

For water, for the deep where the high tide
Mutters to its hurt self, mutters and ebbs.
Waves wallow in their wash, go out and out,
Leave only the death-rattle of the crabs,
The beach increasing, its enormous snout
Sucking the ocean's side.
This is the end of running on the waves;
We are poured out like water. Who will dance
The mast-lashed master of Leviathans
Up from this field of Quakers in their unstoned graves?


V

When the whale's viscera go and the roll
Of its corruption overruns this world
Beyond tree-swept Nantucket and Wood's Hole
And Martha's Vineyard, Sailor, will your sword
Whistle and fall and sink into the fat?
In the great ash-pit of Jehoshaphat
The bones cry for the blood of the white whale,
The fat flukes arch and whack about its ears,

The death-lance churns into the sanctuary, tears
The gun-blue swingle, heaving like a flail,
And hacks the coiling life out: it works and drags
And rips the sperm-whale's midriff into rags,
Gobbets of blubber spill to wind and weather,
Sailor, and gulls go round the stoven timbers
Where the morning stars sing out together
And thunder shakes the white surf and dismembers
The red flag hammered in the mast-head. Hide,
Our steel, Jonas Messias, in Thy side.


VI   OUR LADY OF WALSINGHAM

There once the penitents took off their shoes
And then walked barefoot the remaining mile;
And the small trees, a stream and hedgerows file
Slowly along the munching English lane,
Like cows to the old shrine, until you lose
Track of your dragging pain.
The stream flows down under the druid tree,
Shiloah's whirlpools gurgle and make glad
The castle of God. Sailor, you were glad
And whistled Sion by that stream. But see:

Our Lady, too small for her canopy,
Sits near the altar. There's no comeliness
At all or charm in that expressionless
Face with its heavy eyelids. As before,
This face, for centuries a memory,
*Non est species, neque decor,*
Expressionless, expresses God: it goes
Past castled Sion. She knows what God knows,
Not Calvary's Cross nor crib at Bethlehem
Now, and the world shall come to Walsingham.


VII

The empty winds are creaking and the oak
Splatters and splatters on the cenotaph,

The boughs are trembling and a gaff
Bobs on the untimely stroke
Of the greased wash exploding on a shoal-bell
In the old mouth of the Atlantic. It's well;
Atlantic, you are fouled with the blue sailors,
Sea-monsters, upward angel, downward fish:
Unmarried and corroding, spare of flesh
Mart once of supercilious, wing'd clippers,
Atlantic, where your ball-trap guts its spoil
You could cut the brackish winds with a knife
Here in Nantucket, and cast up the time
When the Lord God formed man from the sea's slime
And breathed into his face the breath of life,
And blue-lung'd combers lumbered to the kill.
The Lord survives the rainbow of His will.

# SKUNK HOUR

*(For Elizabeth Bishop)*

Nautilus Island's hermit
heiress still lives through winter in her Spartan
  cottage;
her sheep still graze above the sea.
Her son's a bishop. Her farmer
is first selectman in our village,
she's in her dotage.

Thristing for
the hierarchic privacy
of Queen Victoria's century,
she buys up all
the eyesores facing her shore,
and lets them fall.

The season's ill—
we've lost our summer millionaire,
who seemed to leap from an L. L. Bean
catalogue. His nine-knot yawl
was auctioned off to lobstermen.
A red fox stain covers Blue Hill.

And now our fairy
decorator brightens his shop for fall,
his fishnet's filled with orange cork,
orange, his cobbler's bench and awl,
there is no money in his work,
he'd rather marry.

One dark night,
my Tudor Ford climbed the hill's skull,

I watched for love-cars. Lights turned down,
they lay together, hull to hull,
where the graveyard shelves on the town . . .
My mind's not right.

A car radio bleats,
'Love, O careless Love . . .' I hear
my ill-spirit sob in each blood cell,
as if my hand were at its throat . . .
I myself am hell,
nobody's here—

only skunks, that search
in the moonlight for a bite to eat.
They march on their soles up Main Street:
white stripes, moonstruck eyes' red fire
under the chalk-dry and spar spire
of the Trinitarian Church.

I stand on top
of our back steps and breathe the rich air—
a mother skunk with her column of kittens
    swills the garbage pail.
She jabs her wedge-head in a cup
of sour cream, drops her ostrich tail,
and will not scare.

# TO DELMORE SCHWARTZ

*(Cambridge 1946)*

We couldn't even keep the furnace lit!
Even when we had disconnected it,
the antiquated
refrigerator gurgled mustard gas
through your mustard-yellow house,
and spoiled our long maneuvered visit
from T. S. Eliot's brother, Henry Ware. . . .

Your stuffed duck craned toward Harvard from my trunk:
its bill was a black whistle, and its brow
was high and thinner than a baby's thumb;
its webs were tough as toenails on its bough.
It was your first kill; you had rushed it home,
pickled in a tin wastebasket of rum—
it looked through us, as if it'd died dead drunk.
You must have propped its eyelids with a nail,
and yet it lived with us and met our stare,
Rabelaisian, lubricious, drugged. And there,
perched on my trunk and typing-table,
it cooled our universal
*Angst* a moment, Delmore. We drank and eyed
the chicken-hearted shadows of the world.
Underseas fellows, nobly mad,
we talked away our friends. "Let Joyce and Freud,
the Masters of Joy,
be our guests here," you said. The room was filled
with cigarette smoke circling the paranoid,
inert gaze of Coleridge, back
from Malta—his eyes lost in flesh, lips baked and black.
Your tiger kitten, *Oranges,*

cartwheeled for joy in a ball of snarls.
You said:
*"We poets in our youth begin in sadness;*
*thereof in the end come despondency and madness;*
Stalin has had two cerebral hemorrhages!"
The Charles
River was turning silver. In the ebb-
light of morning, we stuck
the duck
-'s web-
foot, like a candle, in a quart of gin we'd killed.

# John Berryman

## THE BALL POEM

What is the boy now, who has lost his ball,
What, what is he to do? I saw it go
Merrily bouncing, down the street, and then
Merrily over—there it is in the water!
No use to say 'O there are other balls':
An ultimate shaking grief fixes the boy
As he stands rigid, trembling, staring down
All his young days into the harbour where
His ball went. I would not intrude on him,
A dime, another ball, is worthless. Now
He senses first responsibility
In a world of possessions. People will take balls,
Balls will be lost always, little boy,
And no one buys a ball back. Money is external.
He is learning, well behind his desperate eyes,
The epistemology of loss, how to stand up
Knowing what every man must one day know
And most know many days, how to stand up.
And gradually light returns to the street,
A whistle blows, the ball is out of sight,
Soon part of me will explore the deep and dark
Floor of the harbour . . . I am everywhere,
I suffer and move, my mind and my heart move
With all that move me, under the water
Or whistling, I am not a little boy.

# DREAM SONGS

IV

Filling her compact & delicious body
with chicken páprika, she glanced at me
twice.
Fainting with interest, I hungered back
and only the fact of her husband & four other people
kept me from springing on her

or falling at her little feet and crying
'You are the hottest one for years of night
Henry's dazed eyes
have enjoyed, Brilliance.' I advanced upon
(despairing) my spumoni. —Sir Bones: is stuffed,
de world, wif feeding girls.

—Black hair, complexion Latin, jewelled eyes
downcast . . . The slob beside her   feasts . . . What
    wonders is
she sitting on, over there?
The restaurant buzzes. She might as well be on Mars.
Where did it all go wrong? There ought to be a law
    against Henry.
—Mr. Bones: there is.

Westward, hit a low note, for a roarer lost
across the Sound but north from Bremerton,
hit a way down note.
And never cadenza again of flowers, or cost.
Him who could really do that cleared his throat
& staggered on.

The bluebells, pool-shallows, saluted his over-needs,
while the clouds growled, heh-heh, & snapped, & crashed.

No stunt he'll ever unflinch once more will fail
(O lucky fellow, eh Bones?)—drifted off upstairs,
downstairs, somewheres.
No more daily, trying to hit the head on the nail:
thirstless: without a think in his head:
back from wherever, with it said.

Hit a high long note, for a lover found
needing a lower into friendlier ground
to bug among worms no more
around um jungles where ah blurt 'What for?'
Weeds, too, he favoured as   most men don't favour men.
The Garden Master's gone.

It was wet & white & swift and where I am
we don't know. It was dark and then
it isn't.
I wish the barker would come. There seems to be to eat
nothing. I am unusually tired.
I'm alone too.

If only the strange one with so few legs would come,
I'd say my prayers out of my mouth, as usual.
Where are his notes I loved?
There may be horribles; it's hard to tell.
The barker nips me but somehow I feel
he too is on my side.

I'm too alone. I see no end. If we could all
run, even that would be better. I am hungry.
The sun is not hot.
It's not a good position I am in.
If I had to do the whole thing over again
I  wouldn't.

## XXIX

There sat down, once, a thing on Henry's heart
só heavy, if he had a hundred years
& more, & weeping, sleepless, in all them time
Henry could not make good.
Starts again always in Henry's ears
the little cough somewhere, an odour, a chime.

And there is another thing he has in mind
like a grave Sienese face a thousand years
would fail to blur the still profiled reproach of. Ghastly,
with open eyes, he attends, blind.
All the bells say: too late. This is not for tears;
thinking.

But never did Henry, as he thought he did,
end anyone and hacks her body up
and hide the pieces, where they may be found.
He knows: he went over everyone, & nobody's missing.
Often he reckons, in the dawn, them up.
Nobody is ever missing.

LXXV

Turning it over, considering, like a madman
Henry put forth a book.
No harm resulted from this.
Neither the menstruating     stars (nor man) was moved
at once.
Bare dogs drew closer for a second look

and performed their friendly operations there.
Refreshed, the bark rejoiced.
Seasons went and came.
Leaves fell, but only a few.
Something remarkable about this
unshedding bulky bole-proud blue-green moist

thing made by savage & thoughtful
surviving Henry
began to strike the passers from despair
so that sore on their shoulders old men hoisted
six-foot sons and polished women called
small girls to dream awhile toward the flashing & bursting
    tree!

## CCXVI

'Scads a good eats', dere own t'ree cars, the 'teens
(until of them shall be asked one thing, they romp or
   doze)
have got it made;
no prob. was ever set them, their poor ol' jerks
of parents *loved* them, with deep-freeze, & snacks
would keep a Hindu family-group alive.

Well, so they're liars & gluttons & cowards: so what?
. . . It's the Land of Plenty, maybe about to sigh.
Why shouldn't they terrify
with hegemony Dad (stupido Dad) and teach'?
(The tanks of the elders roll, in exercise, on the German
   plain.)
Even if their sense is to (swill &) die

why don't they join us, pal, as Texas did
(the oil-mailed arrogant butt), and learn how to speak
modestly, & with exactness, and
. . . like a sense of the country, man? Come off it.
   Powers,
the fêted traitor, became so in hours,
and the President, ignorant, didn't even lie.

# Theodore Roethke

OPEN HOUSE

My secrets cry aloud.
I have no need for tongue.
My heart keeps open house,
My doors are widely swung.
An epic of the eyes
My love, with no disguise.

My truths are all foreknown,
This anguish self-revealed.
I'm naked to the bone,
With nakedness my shield.
Myself is what I wear:
I keep the spirit spare.

The anger will endure,
The deed will speak the truth
In language strict and pure.
I stop the lying mouth:
Rage warps my clearest cry
To witless agony.

# THE WAKING

I wake to sleep, and take my waking slow.
I feel my fate in what I cannot fear.
I learn by going where I have to go.

We think by feeling. What is there to know?
I hear my being dance from ear to ear.
I wake to sleep, and take my waking slow.

Of those so close beside me, which are you?
God bless the Ground! I shall walk softly there,
And learn by going where I have to go.

Light takes the Tree; but who can tell us how?
The lowly worm climbs up a winding stair;
And, lovely, learn by going where to go.

Great Nature has another thing to do
To you and me; so take the lively air,
And, lovely, learn by doing where to go.

This shaking keeps me steady. I should know.
What falls away is always. And is near.
I wake to sleep, and take my waking slow.
I learn by going where I have to go.

# ELEGY FOR JANE

*My Student, Thrown by a Horse*

I remember the neckcurls, limp and damp as tendrils;
And her quick look, a sidelong pickerel smile;
And how, once startled into talk, the light syllables leaped
   for her,
And she balanced in the delight of her thought,
A wren, happy, tail into the wind,
Her song trembling the twigs and small branches.
The shade sang with her;
The leaves, their whispers turned to kissing;
And the mold sang in the bleached valleys under the rose.

Oh, when she was sad, she cast herself down into such a
   pure depth,
Even a father could not find her:
Scraping her cheek against straw;
Stirring the clearest water.

My sparrow, you are not here,
Waiting like a fern, making a spiny shadow.
The sides of wet stones cannot console me,
Nor the moss, wound with the last light.

If only I could nudge you from this sleep,
My maimed darling, my skittery pigeon.
Over this damp grave I speak the words of my love:
I, with no rights in this matter,
Neither father nor lover.

# WORDS FOR THE WIND

I

Love, love, a lily's my care,
She's sweeter than a tree.
Loving, I use the air
Most lovingly: I breathe;
Mad in the wind I wear
Myself as I should be,
All's even with the odd,
My brother the vine is glad.

Are flower and seed the same?
What do the great dead say?
Sweet Phoebe, she's my theme:
She sways whenever I sway.
"O love me while I am,
You green thing in my way!"
I cried, and the birds came down
And made my song their own.

Motion can keep me still:
She kissed me out of thought
As a lovely substance will;
She wandered; I did not:
I stayed, and light fell
Across her pulsing throat;
I stared, and a garden stone
Slowly became the moon.

The shallow stream runs slack;
The wind creaks slowly by;
Out of a nestling's beak

Comes a tremulous cry
I cannot answer back;
A shape from deep in the eye—
That woman I saw in a stone—
Keeps pace when I walk alone.


II

The sun declares the earth;
The stones leap in the stream;
On a wide plain, beyond
The far stretch of a dream,
A field breaks like the sea;
The wind's white with her name,
And I walk with the wind.

The dove's my will today.
She sways, half in the sun:
Rose, easy on a stem,
One with the sighing vine,
One to be merry with,
And pleased to meet the moon.
She likes wherever I am.

Passion's enough to give
Shape to a random joy:
I cry delight: I know
The root, the core of a cry.
Swan-heart, arbutus-calm,
She moves when time is shy:
Love has a thing to do.

A fair thing grows more fair;
The green, the springing green
Makes an intenser day
Under the rising moon;
I smile, no mineral man;
I bear, but not alone,
The burden of this joy.

III

Under a southern wind,
The birds and fishes move
North, in a single stream;
The sharp stars swing around;
I get a step beyond
The wind, and there I am,
I'm odd and full of love.

Wisdom, where is it found?—
Those who embrace, believe.
Whatever was, still is,
Says a song tied to a tree.
Below, on the ferny ground,
In rivery air, at ease,
I walk with my true love.

What time's my heart? I care.
I cherish what I have
Had of the temporal:
I am no longer young
But the winds and waters are;
What falls away will fall;
All things bring me to love.

IV

The breath of a long root,
The shy perimeter
Of the unfolding rose,
The green, the altered leaf,
The oyster's weeping foot,
And the incipient star—
Are part of what she is.
She wakes the ends of life.

Being myself, I sing
The soul's immediate joy.

Light, light, where's my repose?
A wind wreathes round a tree.
A thing is done: a thing
Body and spirit know
When I do what she does:
Creaturely creature, she!—

I kiss her moving mouth,
Her swart hilarious skin;
She breaks my breath in half;
She frolicks like a beast;
And I dance round and round,
A fond and foolish man,
And see and suffer myself
In another being, at last.

# THE DREAM

## I

### I

I met her as a blossom on a stem
Before she ever breathed, and in that dream
The mind remembers from a deeper sleep:
Eye learned from eye, cold lip from sensual lip.
My dream divided on a point of fire;
Light hardened on the water where we were;
A bird sang low; the moonlight sifted in;
The water rippled, and she rippled on.

### II

She came toward me in the flowing air,
A shape of change, encircled by its fire.
I watched her there, between me and the moon;
The bushes and the stones danced on and on;
I touched her shadow when the light delayed;
I turned my face away, and yet she stayed.
A bird sang from the center of a tree;
She loved the wind because the wind loved me.

### III

Love is not love until love's vulnerable.
She slowed to sigh, in that long interval.
A small bird flew in circles where we stood;
The deer came down, out of the dappled wood.
All who remember, doubt. Who calls that strange?
I tossed a stone, and listened to its plunge.
She knew the grammar of least motion, she
Lent me one virtue, and I live thereby.

## IV

She held her body steady in the wind;
Our shadows met, and slowly swung around;
She turned the field into a glittering sea;
I played in flame and water like a boy
And I swayed out beyond the white seafoam;
Like a wet log, I sang within a flame.
In that last while, eternity's confine,
I came to love, I came into my own.

# THE LOST SON

At Woodlawn I heard the dead cry:
I was lulled by the slamming of iron,
A slow drip over stones,
Toads brooding wells.
All the leaves stuck out their tongues;
I shook the softening chalk of my bones,
Saying,
Snail, snail, glister me forward,
Bird, soft-sigh me home,
Worm, be with me.
This is my hard time.

Fished in an old wound,
The soft pond of repose;
Nothing nibbled my line,
Not even the minnows came.

Sat in an empty house
Watching shadows crawl,
Scratching.
There was one fly.

Voice, come out of the silence.
Say something.
Appear in the form of a spider
Or a moth beating the curtain.

Tell me:
Which is the way I take;
Out of what door do I go,
Where and to whom?

Dark hollows said, lee to the wind,
The moon said, back of an eel,
The salt said, look by the sea,
Your tears are not enough praise,
You will find no comfort here,
In the kingdom of bang and blab.

Running lightly over spongy ground,
Past the pasture of flat stones,
The three elms,
The sheep strewn on a field,
Over a rickety bridge
Toward the quick-water, wrinkling and rippling.

Hunting along the river,
Down among the rubbish, the bug-riddled foliage,
By the muddy pond-edge, by the bog-holes,
By the shrunken lake, hunting, in the heat of summer.

The shape of a rat?
       It's bigger than that.
       It's less than a leg
       And more than a nose,
       Just under the water
       It usually goes.

Is it soft like a mouse?
Can it wrinkle its nose?
Could it come in the house
On the tips of its toes?

Take the skin of a cat
And the back of an eel,
Then roll them in grease,—
That's the way it would feel.

It's sleek as an otter
With wide webby toes

Just under the water
It usually goes.


II   THE PIT

Where do the roots go?
    Look down under the leaves.
Who put the moss there?
    These stones have been here too long.
Who stunned the dirt into noise?
    Ask the mole, he knows.
I feel the slime of a wet nest.
    Beware Mother Mildew.
Nibble again, fish nerves.


III   THE GIBBER

At the wood's mouth,
By the cave's door,
I listened to something
I had heard before.

Dogs of the groin
Barked and howled,
The sun was against me,
The moon would not have me.

The weeds whined,
The snakes cried,
The cows and briars
Said to me: Die.

What a small song. What slow clouds. What dark water.
Hath the rain a father? All the caves are ice. Only the snow's
    here.
I'm cold. I'm cold all over. Rub me in father and mother.
Fear was my father, Father Fear.
His look drained the stones.

What gliding shape
Beckoning through halls,
Stood poised on the stair,
Fell dreamily down?

From the mouths of jugs
Perched on many shelves,
I saw substance flowing
That cold morning.

Like a slither of eels
That watery cheek
As my own tongue kissed
My lips awake.

Is this the storm's heart? The ground is unstilling itself.
My veins are running nowhere. Do the bones cast out their
    fire?
Is the seed leaving the old bed? These buds are live as birds.
Where, where are the tears of the world?
Let the kisses resound, flat like a butcher's palm;
Let the gestures freeze; our doom is already decided.
All the windows are burning! What's left of my life?
I want the old rage, the lash of primordial milk!
Goodbye, goodbye, old stones, the time-order is going,
I have married my hands to perpetual agitation,
I run, I run to the whistle of money.

Money money money
Water water water

How cool the grass is.
Has the bird left?
The stalk still sways.
Has the worm a shadow?
What do the clouds say?

These sweeps of light undo me.
Look, look, the ditch is running white!

I've more veins than a tree!
Kiss me, ashes, I'm falling through a dark swirl.


IV   THE RETURN

The way to the boiler was dark,
Dark all the way,
Over slippery cinders
Through the long greenhouse.

The roses kept breathing in the dark.
They had many mouths to breathe with.
My knees made little winds underneath
Where the weeds slept.

There was always a single light
Swinging by the fire-pit,
Where the fireman pulled out roses,
The big roses, the big bloody clinkers.

Once I stayed all night.
The light in the morning came slowly over the white
Snow.
There were many kinds of cool
Air.
Then came steam.

Pipe-knock.

Scurry of warm over small plants.
Ordnung! ordnung!
Papa is coming!

A fine haze moved off the leaves;
Frost melted on far panes;
The rose, the chrysanthemum turned toward the light.
Even the hushed forms, the bent yellowy weeds
Moved in a slow up-sway.

It was beginning winter,
An in-between time,
The landscape still partly brown:
The bones of weeds kept swinging in the wind,
Above the blue snow.

It was beginning winter,
The light moved slowly over the frozen field,
Over the dry seed-crowns,
The beautiful surviving bones
Swinging in the wind.

Light traveled over the wide field;
Stayed.
The weeds stopped swinging.
The mind moved, not alone,
Through the clear air, in the silence.

Was it light?
Was it light within?
Was it light within light?
Stillness becoming alive,
Yet still?

A lively understandable spirit
Once entertained you.
It will come again.
Be still.
Wait.

# IN A DARK TIME

In a dark time, the eye begins to see,
I meet my shadow in the deepening shade;
I hear my echo in the echoing wood—
A lord of nature weeping to a tree.
I live between the heron and the wren,
Beasts of the hill and serpents of the den.

What's madness but nobility of soul
At odds with circumstance? The day's on fire!
I know the purity of pure despair,
My shadow pinned against a sweating wall.
That place among the rocks—is it a cave,
Or winding path? The edge is what I have.

A steady storm of correspondences!
A night flowing with birds, a ragged moon,
And in broad day the midnight come again!
A man goes far to find out what he is—
Death of the self in a long, tearless night,
All natural shapes blazing unnatural light.

Dark, dark my light, and darker my desire.
My soul, like some heat-maddened summer fly,
Keeps buzzing at the sill. Which I is *I*?
A fallen man, I climb out of my fear.
The mind enters itself, and God the mind,
And one is One, free in the tearing wind.

# JOURNEY TO THE INTERIOR

I

In the long journey out of the self,
There are many detours, washed-out interrupted raw places
Where the shale slides dangerously
And the back wheels hang almost over the edge
At the sudden veering, the moment of turning.
Better to hug close, wary of rubble and falling stones.
The arroyo cracking the road, the wind-bitten buttes, the
    canyons,
Creeks swollen in midsummer from the flash-flood roaring
    into the narrow valley.
Reeds beaten flat by wind and rain,
Grey from the long winter, burnt at the base in late summer.
—Or the path narrowing,
Winding upward toward the stream with its sharp stones,
The upland of alder and birchtrees,
Through the swamp alive with quicksand,
The way blocked at last by a fallen fir-tree,
The thickets darkening,
The ravines ugly.

II

I remember how it was to drive in gravel,
Watching for dangerous down-hill places, where the wheels
    whined beyond eighty—
When you hit the deep pit at the bottom of the swale,
The trick was to throw the car sideways and charge over the
    hill, full of the throttle.
Grinding up and over the narrow road, spitting and roaring.
A chance? Perhaps. But the road was part of me, and its
    ditches,

And the dust lay thick on my eyelids,—Who ever wore
goggles?—
Always a sharp turn to the left past a barn close to the
roadside,
To a scurry of small dogs and a shriek of children,
The highway ribboning out in a straight thrust to the North,
To the sand dunes and fish flies, hanging, thicker than moths,
Dying brightly under the street lights sunk in coarse concrete,
The towns with their high pitted road-crowns and deep
gutters,
Their wooden stores of silvery pine and weather-beaten red
courthouses,
An old bridge below with a buckled iron railing, broken by
some idiot plunger;
Underneath, the sluggish water running between weeds,
broken wheels, tires, stones.
And all flows past—
The cemetery with two scrubby trees in the middle of the
prairie,
The dead snakes and muskrats, the turtles gasping in the
rubble,
The spikey purple bushes in the winding dry creek bed—
The floating hawks, the jackrabbits, the grazing cattle—
I am not moving but they are,
And the sun comes out of a blue cloud over the Tetons
While, farther away, the heat-lightning flashes.
I rise and fall in the slow sea of a grassy plain,
The wind veering the car slightly to the right,
Whipping the line of white laundry, bending the cottonwoods
apart,
The scraggy wind-break of a dusty ranch-house.
I rise and fall, and time folds
Into a long moment;
And I hear the lichen speak,
And the ivy advance with its white lizard feet—
On the shimmering road,
On the dusty detour.

I see the flower of all water, above and below me, the never
   receding,
Moving, unmoving in a parched land, white in the moonlight:
The soul at a still-stand,
At ease after rocking the flesh to sleep,
Petals and reflections of petals mixed on the surface of a
   glassy pool,
And the waves flattening out when the fishermen drag their
   nets over the stones.

In the moment of time when the small drop forms, but does
   not fall,
I have known the heart of the sun,—
In the dark and light of a dry place,
In a flicker of fire brisked by a dusty wind.
I have heard, in a drip of leaves,
A slight song,
After the midnight cries.
I rehearse myself for this:
The stand at the stretch in the face of death,
Delighting in surface change, the glitter of light on waves,
And I roam elsewhere, my body thinking,
Turning toward the other side of light,
In a tower of wind, a tree idling in air,
Beyond my own echo,
Neither forward nor backward,
Unperplexed, in a place leading nowhere.

As a blind man, lifting a curtain, knows it is morning,
I know this change:
On one side of silence there is no smile;
But when I breathe with the birds,
The spirit of wrath becomes the spirit of blessing,
And the dead begin from their dark to sing in my sleep.

# Stanley Kunitz

## OPEN THE GATES

Within the city of the burning cloud,
Dragging my life behind me in a sack,
Naked I prowl, scourged by the black
Temptation of the blood grown proud.

Here at the monumental door,
Carved with the curious legend of my youth,
I brandish the great bone of my death,
Beat once therewith and beat no more.

The hinges groan: a rush of forms
Shivers my name, wrenched out of me.
I stand on the terrible threshold, and I see
The end and the beginning in each other's arms.

# THE SCIENCE OF THE NIGHT

I touch you in the night, whose gift was you,
My careless sprawler,
And I touch you cold, unstirring, star-bemused,
That are become the land of your self-strangeness.
What long seduction of the bone has led you
Down the imploring roads I cannot take
Into the arms of ghosts I never knew,
Leaving my manhood on a rumpled field
To guard you where you lie so deep
In absent-mindedness,
Caught in the calcium snows of sleep?

And even should I track you to your birth
Through all the cities of your mortal trial,
As in my jealous thought I try to do,
You would escape me—from the brink of earth
Take off to where the lawless auroras run,
You with your wild and metaphysic heart.
My touch is on you, who are light-years gone.
We are not souls but systems, and we move
In clouds of our unknowing
                              like great nebulae.
Our very motives swirl and have their start
With father lion and with mother crab.

Dreamer, my own lost rib,
Whose planetary dust is blowing
Past archipelagoes of myth and light,
What far Magellans are you mistress of
To whom you speed the pleasure of your art?
As through a glass that magnifies my loss
I see the lines of your spectrum shifting red,

The universe expanding, thinning out,
Our worlds flying, oh flying, fast apart.

From hooded powers and from abstract flight
I summon you, your person and your pride.
Fall to me now from outer space,
Still fastened desperately to my side;
Through gulfs of streaming air
Bring me the mornings of the milky ways
Down to my threshold in your drowsy eyes;
And by the virtue of your honeyed word
Restore the liquid language of the moon,
That in gold mines of secrecy you delve.
Awake!
      My whirling hands stay at the noon,
Each cell within my body holds a heart
And all my hearts in unison strike twelve.

## FATHER AND SON

Now in the suburbs and the falling light
I followed him, and now down sandy road
Whiter than bone-dust, through the sweet
Curdle of fields, where the plums
Dropped with their load of ripeness, one by one.
Mile after mile I followed, with skimming feet,
After the secret master of my blood,
Him, steeped in the odor of ponds, whose indomitable love
Kept me in chains. Strode years; stretched into bird;
Raced through the sleeping country where I was young,
The silence unrolling before me as I came,
The night nailed like an orange to my brow.

How should I tell him my fable and the fears,
How bridge the chasm in a casual tone,
Saying, "The house, the stucco one you built,
We lost. Sister married and went from home,
And nothing comes back, it's strange, from where she goes.
I lived on a hill that had too many rooms:
Light we could make, but not enough of warmth,
And when the light failed, I climbed under the hill.
The papers are delivered every day;
I am alone and never shed a tear."

At the water's edge, where the smothering ferns lifted
Their arms, "Father!" I cried, "Return! You know
The way. I'll wipe the mudstains from your clothes;
No trace, I promise, will remain. Instruct
Your son, whirling between two wars,
In the Gemara of your gentleness,
For I would be a child to those who mourn
And brother to the foundlings of the field

And friend of innocence and all bright eyes.
O teach me how to work and keep me kind."

Among the turtles and the lilies he turned to me
The white ignorant hollow of his face.

# THE DARK AND THE FAIR

A roaring company that festive night;
The beast of dialectic dragged his chains,
Prowling from chair to chair in the smoking light,
While the snow hissed against the windowpanes.

Our politics, our science, and our faith
Were whiskey on the tongue; I, being rent
By the fierce divisions of our time, cried death
And death again, and my own dying meant.

Out of her secret life, that griffin-land
Where ivory empires build their stage, she came,
Putting in mine her small impulsive hand,
Five-fingered gift, and the palm not tame.

The moment clanged: beauty and terror danced
To the wild vibration of a sister-bell,
Whose unremitting stroke discountenanced
The marvel that the mirrors blazed to tell.

A darker image took this fairer form
Who once, in the purgatory of my pride,
When innocence betrayed me in a room
Of mocking elders, swept handsome to my side,

Until we rose together, arm in arm,
And fled together back into the world.
What brought her now, in the semblance of the warm,
Out of cold spaces, damned by colder blood?

That furied woman did me grievous wrong,
But does it matter much, given our years?

We learn, as the thread plays out, that we belong
Less to what flatters us than to what scars;

So, freshly turning, as the turn condones,
For her I killed the propitiatory bird,
Kissing her down. Peace to her bitter bones,
Who taught me the serpent's word, but yet the word.

# GOOSE POND

Goose Pond's imaginable snows,
The fall of twenty years at once,
Like subtler moons reflect the rose
Decompositions of the sun.

A feather tumbling from a cloud
Scrolls thunders of the natural law;
The cattails rattle; cinnamon fern
Raises rag banners towards the thaw,

And early-footed ghost flowers scour
Through willow-dapplings to a cave
Where secrecy grows fur. Self burns
At the pulpits where Jack-preachers rave!

Now a sulky weather dogs the heart,
There is no bottom to the day,
The water lily's Chinese stalk
Drags heavy, as the white-lipped boy

Climbs from detritus of his birth,
The rusted hoop, the broken wheels,
The sunken boat of little worth,
Past balconies of limber eels

Until, along that marshy brink,
The springy trails devoid of plan,
He meets his childhood beating back
To find what furies made him man.

# THE APPROACH TO THEBES

In the zero of the night, in the lipping hour,
Skin-time, knocking-time, when the heart is pearled
And the moon squanders its uranian gold,
She taunted me, who was all music's tongue,
Philosophy's and wilderness's breed,
Of shifting shape, half jungle-cat, half-dancer,
Night's woman-petaled, lion-scented rose,
To whom I gave, out of a hero's need,
The dolor of my thrust, my riddling answer,
Whose force no lesser mortal knows. Dangerous?
Yes, as nervous oracles foretold
Who could not guess the secret taste of her:
Impossible wine! I came into the world
To fill a fate; am punished by my youth
No more. What if dog-faced logic howls
Was it art or magic multiplied my joy?
Nature has reasons beyond true or false.
We played like metaphysic animals
Whose freedom made our knowledge bold
Before the tragic curtain of the day:
I can bear the dishonor now of growing old.

Blinded and old, exiled, diseased, and scorned—
The verdict's bitten on the brazen gates,
For the gods grant each of us his lot, his term.
Hail to the King of Thebes!—my self, ordained
To satisfy the impulse of the worm,
Bemummied in those famous incestuous sheets,
The bloodiest flags of nations of the curse,
To be hung from the balcony outside the room
Where I encounter my most flagrant source.
Children, grandchildren, my long posterity,

To whom I bequeath the spiders of my dust,
Believe me, whatever sordid tales you hear,
Told by physicians or mendacious scribes,
Of beardless folly, consanguineous lust,
Fomenting pestilence, rebellion, war,
I come prepared, unwanting what I see,
But tied to life. On the royal road to Thebes
I had my luck, I met a lovely monster,
And the story's this: I made the monster me.

# MY SURGEONS

My surgeons are a savage band,
Surely their patient is ill-fated.
Their tricks are coarse: the small sweet hand
I seized was wax, or amputated.
With the humiliated swollen-footed
And the lost persecuted their traps are baited.

Deftly they opened the brain of a child,
And it was full of flying dreams;
Father was prowling in a field
With speckled tongue and a collar of flame.
They labeled it "Polluted Streams,"
The body floating with the name.

They studied a prostrate fever-chart
With unmitigating eyes; one said,
"Bohemian germs, *Weltschmerz*, bad art
And Spanish fly. Off with his head."
Another, "Fascist. His boot is filled with blood."
They cut me up till I was red.

Lastly they squeezed out of my veins
The bright liquor of sympathy;
I lost the touch of souls, the reins
On white revenge, and I was free
Of pity, a solid man of snow.
But in the night to whom could I go?

Lie down with me, dear girl, before
My butcher-boys begin to rave.
"No hope for persons any more,"
They cry, "on either side of the grave."
Tell them I say the heart forgives
The world. Yes, I believe. In love.

# REVOLVING MEDITATION

How much I disapprove of it!
How little I love it!
Though, contrariwise,
Can there be
Anything half as dear?
God knows I've had my joys,
Tasted the honey on the branch
And picked a sprig or two
Of accidental laurel
Along the way;
But why do I wake at the sound,
In the middle of the night,
Of the tread of the Masked Man
Heavy on the stairs,
And from the street below
The lamentation of the wounded glove?
Agh! I am sometimes weary
Of this everlasting search
For the drama in a nutshell,
The opera of the tragic sense,
Which I would gladly be rid of.
A shameless keyhole god
Keeps spying on my worst,
Incontinently glued
To the obscene dumb show
Of the debasers of currency
In the private cabinet,
The dealers of soiled cards
At their desperate game ...
And the double-dealers,
The ambiguous ones with their smeared
Faces, the acrobatic dancers—

Those who stood
Naked with me,
Adorable, adored,
On the magnet-head
Of the same inexorable pin.
Why should I be bothered with it?
Imagination cries
That in the grand accountancy
What happens to us is false;
Imagination makes,
Out of what stuff it can,
An action fit
For a more heroic stage
Than body ever walked on.
I have learned,
Trying to live
With this perjured quid of mine,
That the truth is not in the stones,
But in the architecture;
Equally, I am not deceived
By the triumph of the stuffing
Over the chair.
If I must build a church,
Though I do not really want one,
Let it be in the wilderness
Out of nothing but nail-holes.
I listen, I am always listening,
In fear that something might get by,
To the grammar of the public places,
But I fly towards Possibility,
In the extravagantly gay
Surprise of a journey,
Careless that I am bound
To the flaming wheel of my bones,
Preferring to hear, as I
Am forced to hear,
The voice of the solitary
Who makes others less alone,
The dialogue of lovers,

And the conversation of two worms
In the beam of a house,
Their mouths filled with sawdust.

# THREE FLOORS

Mother was a crack of light
And a gray eye peeping;
I made believe by breathing hard
That I was sleeping.

Sister's doughboy on last leave
Had robbed me of her hand;
Downstairs at intervals she played
*Warum* on the baby grand.

Under the roof a wardrobe trunk
Whose lock a boy could pick
Contained a red Masonic hat
And a walking stick.

Bolt upright in my bed that night
I saw my father flying.
The wind was walking on my neck,
The window-panes were crying.

IV

# Charles Olson

## THE KINGFISHERS

I

What does not change / is the will to change

He woke, fully clothed, in his bed. He
remembered only one thing, the birds, how
when he came in, he had gone around the rooms
and got them back in their cage, the green one first,
she with the bad leg, and then the blue,
the one they had hoped was a male

Otherwise? Yes, Fernand, who had talked
                         lispingly of Albers & Angkor Vat.
He had left the party without a word.
                      How he got up, got into his coat,
I do not know. When I saw him, he was
                    at the door, but it did not matter,
he was already sliding along the wall of the night, losing himself
in some crack of the ruins. That it should have
                been he who said, "The kingfishers!
who cares
for their feathers
now?"

His last words had been, "The pool is slime." Suddenly everyone,
ceasing their talk, sat in a row around him, watched
they did not so much hear, or pay attention, they
wondered, looked at each other, smirked, but listened,
he repeated and repeated, could not go beyond his thought
"The pool    the kingfishers' feathers were wealth    why
did the export stop?"

It was then he left

II

I thought of the E on the stone, and of what Mao said
la lumiere"
        but the kingfisher
de l'aurore"
        but the kingfisher flew west
est devant nous!
        he got the color of his breast
        from the heat of the setting sun!

The features are, the feebleness of the feet
        (syndactylism of the 3rd & 4th digit)
the bill, serrated, sometimes a pronounced beak, the wings
where the color is, short and round, the tail
inconspicuous.

But not these things were the factors. Not the birds.
The legends are
legends. Dead, hung up indoors, the kingfisher
will not indicate a favoring wind,
or avert the thunderbolt. Nor, by its nesting,
still the waters, with the new year, for seven days.
It is true, it does nest with the opening
        year, but not on the waters.
It nests at the end of a tunnel bored by itself in a bank. There,
six or eight white and translucent eggs are laid, on fishbones
not on bare clay, on bones thrown up in pellets by the birds.

        On these rejectamenta
(as they accumulate they form a cup-shaped
        structure) the young are born.
And, as they are fed and grow, this
        nest of excrement and decayed fish becomes
        a dripping, fetid mass
Mao concluded:
        nous devons
        nous lever
        et agir!

III

When the attentions change / the jungle
leaps in

                even the stones are split
                            they rive

Or,
enter
that other conqueror we more naturally recognize
he so resembles ourselves

But the E
cut so rudely on that oldest stone
sounded otherwise,
was differently heard

as, in another time, were treasures used:

(and, later, much later, a fine ear thought
a scarlet coat)

            "of green feathers     feet, beaks and eyes
            of gold

            "animals likewise,
            resembling snails

            "a large wheel, gold,
                            with figures of unknown four-foots,
            and worked with tufts of leaves, weight
            3800 ounces

            "last, two birds, of thread and featherwork, the quills
            gold, the feet
            gold, the two birds perched on two reeds
            gold, the reeds arising from two embroidered mounds,
            one yellow, the other
            white.

            "And from each reed hung
            seven feathered tassels.

In this instance, the priests
(in dark cotton robes, and dirty,
their dishevelled hair matted with blood, and flowing wildly
over their shoulders)
rush in among the people, calling on them
to protect their gods

And all now is war
where so lately there was peace,
and the sweet brotherhood, the use
of tilled fields.

IV

Not one death but many,
not accumulation but change, the feed-back proves,

                                        the feed-back is
the law

        Into the same river no man steps twice
        When fire dies air dies
        No one remains, nor is, one

Around an appearance, one common model, we grow up
many. Else how is it,
if we remain the same,
we take pleasure now
in what we did not take pleasure before? love
contrary objects, admire and / or find fault? use
other words, feel other passions, have
nor figure, appearance, disposition, tissue
the same?

        To be in different states without a change
        is not a possibility

We can be precise. The factors are
in the animal and / or the machine the factors are
communication and / or control, both involve
the message. And what is the message? The message is
a discrete or continuous sequence of measurable
                                        events distributed in time

is the birth of air, is
the birth of water, is
a state between
the origin and
the end, between
birth and the beginning of
another fetid nest

is change, presents
no more than itself

And the too strong grasping of it,
when it is pressed together and condensed,
loses it

This very thing you are

    2

    They buried their dead in a sitting posture
    serpent   cane   razor   ray of the sun

    And she sprinkled water on the head of the child, crying
    "Cioa-coatl! Cioa-coatl!"
    with her face to the west

    Where the bones are found, in each personal heap
    with what each enjoyed, there is always
    the Mongolian louse

The light is in the east. Yes. And we must rise, act. Yet
in the west, despite the apparent darkness (the whiteness
which covers all), if you look, if you can bear, if you can,
                                          long enough

          as long as it was necessary for him, my guide
          to look into the yellow of that longest-lasting rose

so you must, and, in that whiteness, into that face,
                          with what candor, look

and, considering the dryness of the place
    the long absence of an adequate race

        (of the two who first came, each a conquistador,
                          one healed, the other
        tore the eastern idols down, toppled
        the temple walls, which, says the excuser
        were black from human gore)

hear
hear, where the dry blood talks
    where the old appetite walks

              la piu saporita et migliore
              che si possa truovar al mondo

where it hides, look
in the eye how it runs
in the flesh / chalk

       but under these petals
       in the emptiness
       regard the light, contemplate
       the flower

whence it arose

       with what violence benevolence is bought
       what cost in gesture justice brings
       what wrongs domestic rights involve
       what stalks
       this silence

what pudor pejorocracy affronts
how awe, night-rest and neighborhood can rot
what breeds where dirtiness is law
what crawls
below

    3

       I am no Greek, hath not th'advantage.
       And of course, no Roman:
       he can take no risk that matters,
       the risk of beauty least of all.

       But I have my kin, if for no other reason than
       (as he said, next of kin) I commit myself, and,
       given my fredom, I'd be a cad
       if I didn't. Which is most true.

       It works out this way, despite the disadvantage.
       I offer, in explanation, a quote:
       si j'ai du goût, ce n'est guères
       que pour la terre et les pierres

       Despite the discrepancy (an ocean    courage    age)
       this is also true: if I have any taste
       it is only because I have interested myself
       in what was slain in the sun

I pose you your question:

shall you uncover honey / where maggots are?

I hunt among stones

# Louis Zukofsky

**POEM BEGINNING "THE"**

1 The
2 Voice of Jesus I. Rush singing
3                              in the wilderness
4 A boy's best friend is his mother,
5 It's your mother all the time.
6 Residue of Oedipus-faced wrecks
7 Creating out of the dead,—
8 From the candle flames of the souls of
        dead mothers
9 Vide the legend of thin Christ sending her
        out of the temple,—
10 Books from the stony heart, flames rapping
        the stone,
11 Residue of self-exiled men
12 By the Tyrrhenian.
13                    Paris.
14 But everywhere only the South Wind, the
        sirocco, the broken Earth-face.
15 The broken Earth-face, the age demands an
        image of its life and contacts,
16 Lord, lord, not that we pray, are sure of
        the question,
17 But why are our finest always dead?

18 And why, Lord, this time, is it Mauberly's
        Luini in porcelain, why is it Chelifer,
19 Why is it Lovat who killed Kangaroo,
20 Why Stephen Daedalus with the cane of
        ash,
21 But why les neiges?
22 And why, if all of Mary's Observations
        have been made
23 Have not the lambs become more sapient
        drinking of the spring;
24 Kerith is long dry, and the ravens that
        brought the prophet bread
25 Are dust in the waste-land of a raven-
        winged evening.
26 And why if the waste land has been explored,
        travelled over, circumscribed,
27 Are there only wrathless skeletons exhumed
        new planted in its sacred wood,
28 Why—heir, long dead,—Odysseus, wan-
        dering of ten years
29 Out-journeyed only by our Stephen, bibbing
        of a day,
30 O why is that to Hecuba as Hecuba to he!
31 You are cra-a-zee on the subject of babies,
        says she,
32 That is because somehow our authors have been
        given a woman's intuition.
33 Il y a un peu trop de femme in this South Wind.
34 And on the cobblestones, bang, bang, bang,
        myself like the wheels—
35 The tram passes singing
36 O do you take this life as your lawful wife,
37                  I do!
38 O the Time is 5
39         I do!
40 O the Time is 5
41         I do!
42 O do you take these friends as your loves
        to wive,

43 O the Time is 5
44　　　　　I do!

45 For it's the hoo-doos, the somethin' voo-doos
46 And not Kings onelie, but the wisest men
47 Graue Socrates, what says Marlowe?
48 For it was myself seemed held
49 Beating—beating—
50 Body trembling as over an hors d'oeuvres—
51
52 And the dream ending—Dalloway! Dalloway—
53 The blind portals opening, and I awoke!

54 Let me be
55 Not by art have we lived,
56 Not by graven images forbidden to us
57 Not by letters I fancy,
58 Do we dare say
59 With Spinoza grinding lenses, Rabbaisi,
60 After living on Cathedral Parkway?

SECOND MOVEMENT: INTERNATIONAL EPISODE

61 This is the aftermath
62 When Peter Out and I discuss the theatre.
63 Evenings, our constitutional.
64 We both strike matches, both in unison,
65　　　　　to light one pipe, my own.
66 'Tis, 'tis love, that makes the world go
　　　　round and love is what I dream.
67 Peter is polite and I to me am almost as
　　　　polite as Peter.
68 Somehow, in Germany, the Jew goat-song
　　　　is unconvincing—
69　How the brain forms its vision think-
　　　　ing incessantly of the things,
70 Not the old Greeks anymore,—
71　the things themselves a shadow world
　　　　scarce shifting the incessant
　　　　thought—

72  Time, time the goat were an offering,
73  Eh, what show do we see tonight, Peter?
74  "Il Duce: I feel God deeply."
75    Black shirts—black shirts—some power
          is so funereal.

76  Lion-heart, frate mio, and so on in two
          languages
77  the thing itself a shadow world.
78  Goldenrod
79  Of which he is a part,
80  Sod
81  He hurried over
82  Underfoot,
83  Make now
84  His testament of sun and sky
85  With clod
86  To root what shoot
87  It sends to run the sun,
88  The sun-sky blood.
89  My loves there is his mystery beyond
          your loves.
90  Uncanny are the stars,
91  His slimness was as evasive
92  And his grimness was not yours,
93  Do you walk slowly the halls of the heavens,
94  Or saying that you do, lion-hearted not ours,
95  Hours, days months, past from us and gone,
96  Lion-heart not looked upon, walk with the
          stars.
97  Or have these like old men acknowledged
98  No kin but that grips of death,
99  Of being dying only to live on with them
100 Entirely theirs,
101 And so quickly grown that we on earth like
          stems raised dark
102 Feel only the lull, heave, phosphor
          change, death, the
103 One follow, the other, the end?

104 Our candles have been buried beneath these
         waters,
105 Their lights are his,
106 Ship-houses on the waters he might have lived
         near.
107 Steady the red light and it makes no noise
         whatever.
108 Damn it! they have made capital of his flesh
         and bone.
109 What, in revenge, can dead flesh and bone
         make capital?
110 And his heart is dry
111 Like the teeth of a dead camel
112 But his eyes no longer blink
113 Not even as a blind dog's.

114 With the blue night shadows on the sand
115 May his kingdom return to him,
116 The Bedouin leap again on his *asilah*,
117 The expanse of heaven hang upon his shoulder
118 As an embroidered texture,
119 Behind him on his saddle sit the night
120 Sing into his ear:

121 Swifter than a tiger to his prey,
122 Lighter than the storm wind, dust or spray,
123 The Bedouin bears the Desert-Night,
124 Big his beard and young with life,
125 Younger yet his gay, wild wife
126          The Desert-Night.
127 Some new trappings for his steed,
128 All the stars in dowry his meed
129          From the Desert-Night.

130 I've changed my mind, Zukofsky,
131 How about some other show—
132 "The Queen of Roumania," "Tilbury,"
         "The West-Decline,"

133 "Hall's Mills," "The Happy Quetzal-
            coatl,"
134 "Near Ibsen," "Dancing with H.R.H.,"
            "Polly Wants a New Fur Coat,"
135 "The Post Office"—
136 Speaking of the post office, the following
            will handicap you for the position,
137   my dear Peter,
138 Your weight less than one hundred
            twenty-five pounds,
139 One half of a disabled veteran, and
            probably
140   the whole of an unknown soldier,
141 That's indomitaeque morti for you.

142 Is it true what you say, Zukofsky,
143 Sorry to say, My Peter Out.

144 "Tear the Codpiece Off, A Musical
            Comedy,"
145 Likewise, "Panting for Pants,"
146 "The Dream That Knows No Waking."


THIRD MOVEMENT: IN CAT MINOR

147 Hard, hard the cat-world.
148 On the stream Vicissitude
149 Our milk flows lewd.

150 We'll cry, we'll cry,
151 We'll cry the more
152 And wet the floor,
153 Megrow, megrow,
154 Around around,
155 The only sound
156 The prowl, our prowl,
157 Of gentlemen cats
158 With paws like spats

159 Who weep the nights

160 Till the nights are gone—
161 —And r-r-run—the Sun!


FOURTH MOVEMENT: MORE "RENAISSANCE"

162 Is it the sun you're looking for,
163 Drop in at Askforaclassic, Inc.,
164 Get yourself another century,
165 A little frost before sundown,
166 It's the times don'chewknow,
167 And if you're a Jewish boy, then be your
    Plato's Philo.


168 Engprof, thy lectures were to me
169  Like those roast flitches of red boar
170 That, smelling, one is like to see
171  Through windows where the steam's galore
172  Like our own "Cellar Door."


173 On weary bott'm long wont to sit,
174  Thy graying hair, thy beaming eyes,
175 Thy heavy jowl would make me fit
176  For the Pater that was Greece,
177  The siesta that was Rome.
178 Lo! from my present—say not—itch
179  How statue-like I see thee stand
180 Phi Beta Key within thy hand!
181  Professor—from the backseats which
182 Are no man's land!


183 Poe,
184 Gentlemen, don'chewknow,
185 But never wrote an epic.


FIFTH MOVEMENT: AUTOBIOGRAPHY

186 Speaking about epics, mother,
187 How long ago is it since you gathered
    mushrooms,

188 Gathered mushrooms while you mayed.
189 It is your mate, my father, boating.
190 A stove burns like a full moon in a desert night.
191 Un in hoyze is kalt. You think of a new
            grave,
192 In the fields, flowers.
193 Night on the bladed grass, bayonets dewed.
194 It is your mate, my father, boating.
195 Speaking about epics, mother,—
196 Down here among the gastanks, ruts,
            cemetary-tenements—
197 It is your Russia that is free.
198 And I here, can I say only—
199        "So then an egoist can never embrace
              a party
200        Or take up with a party?
201        Oh, yes, only he cannot let himself
202        Be embraced or taken up by the party."
203 It is your Russia that is free, mother.
204 Tell me, mother.

205 Winged wild geese, where lies the passage.
206 In far away lands lies the passage.
207 Winged wild geese, who knows the pathway?
208 Of the winds, asking, we shall say:
209 Wind of the South and wind of the North
210 Where has our sun gone forth?
211 Naked, twisted, scraggly branches,
212 And dark, gray patches through the branches,
213 Ducks with puffed-up, fluttering feathers
214 On a cobalt stream.
215 And faded grass that's slowly swaying.
216 A barefoot shepherd boy
217 Striding in the mire:
218 Swishing indifferently a peeled branch
219 On jaded sheep.
220 An old horse strewn with yellow leaves
221 By the edge of the meadow
222 Draws weakly with humid nostrils

223 The moisture of the clouds.
224 Horses that pass through inappreciable
         woodland,
225 Leaves in their manes tangled, mist, au-
         tumn green,
226 Lord, why not give these bright brutes—
         your good land—
227 Turf for their feet always, years for their mien.
228 See how each peer lifts his head, others follow,
229 Mate paired with mate, flanks coming full
         they crowd,
230 Reared in your sun, Lord, escaping each hollow
231 Where lift-struck we stand, utter their praise
         aloud.
232 Very much Chance, Lord, as when you first
         made us,
233 You might forget them, Lord, preferring what
234 Being less lovely where sadly we fuss?
235 Weed out these horses as tho they were not?
236 Never alive in brute delicate trembling
237 Song to your sun, against autumn assembling.

238 If horses could but sing Bach, mother,—
239 Remember how I wished it once—
240 Now I kiss you who could never sing Bach,
         never read Shakespeare.

241 In Manhattan here the Chinamen are yellow
         in the face, mother,
242 Up and down, up and down our streets they
         go yellow in the face,
243 And why is it the representatives of your,
         my, race are always hankering for
         food, mother?
244 We, on the other hand, eat so little.
245 Dawn't you think Trawtsky rawthaw a
         darrling,
246 I ask our immigrant cousin querulously.
247 Naw! I think hay is awlmawst a Tchekoff.

248 But she has more color in her cheeks than
               the Angles—Angels—mother,—
249 They have enough, though. We should
               get some more color, mother.
250 If I am like them in the rest, I should
               resemble them in that, mother,
251 Assimilation is not hard,
252 And once the Faith's askew
253 I might as well look Shagetz just as much
               as Jew.
254 I'll read their Donne as mine,
255 And leopard in their spots
256 I'll do what says their Coleridge,
257 Twist red hot pokers into knots.
258 The villainy they teach me I will execute
259 And it shall go hard with them,
260 For I'll better the instruction,
261 Having learned, so to speak, in their
               colleges.
262    It is engendered in the eyes
263    With gazing fed, and fancy dies
264    In the cradle where it lies
265    In the cradle where it lies
266 I, Señora, am the Son of the Respected
               Rabbi,
267 Israel of Saragossa,
268 Not that the Rabbis give a damn,
269 Keine Kadish wird man sagen.


HALF-DOZENTH MOVEMENT: FINALE, AND AFTER

270 Under the cradle the white goat stands, mother,
271 What will the goat be saddled with, mother?
272             Almonds, raisins
273 What will my heart be bartering, mother,
274             Wisdom, learning.
275 Lullaby, lullaby, lullaby, lullaby.
276 These are the words of the prophet, mother,
277 Likely to save me from Tophet, mother—

278 What will my heart be burning to, mother,
279         Wisdom, learning.
280 By the cat and the well, I swear, my
        Shulamite!
281 In my faith, in my hope, and in my love.
282 I will cradle thee, I will watch thee,
283 Sleep and dream thou, dear my boy!
284   (Presses his cheek against her mouth.)
285 I must try to fare forth from here.
286 I do not forget you,
287 I am just gone out for to-night,
288 The Royal Stag is abroad,
289 I am gone out hunting,
290 The leaves have lit by the moon.
291 Even in their dirt, the Angles like Angels
        are fair,
292 Brooks Nash, for instance, faisant un petit
        bruit, mais très net,
293 Saying, He who is afraid to do that should
        be denied the privilege,
294 And where the automobile roads with the
        gasoline shine,
295 Appropriately the katydid—
296 Ka-ty did. . . . Ka-ty didn't. . . .

297 Helen Gentile,
298 And did one want me; no.
299 But wanted me to take one? yes.
300 And should I have kissed one? no.
301 That is, embraced one first
302 And holding closely one, then kissed one?
        yes.
303 Angry against things' iron I ring
304 Recalcitrant prod and kick.
305 Oh, Baedekera Schönberg, you here
306         dreaming of the relentlessness of motion
307 As usual,
308 One or two dead in the process what does it
      matter.

309 Our God immortal such Life as is our God,
310 Bei dein Zauber, by thy magic I embrace
       thee,
311 Open Sesame, Ali Baba, I, thy firefly, little
       errant star, call here,
312 By thy magic I embrace thee.


313 O my son Sun, my son, my son Sun!
       would God
314 I had died for thee, O Sun, my son, my
       son!


315 I have not forgotten you, mother,—
316 It is a lie—Aus meinen grossen leiden mach ich
       die kleinen lieder,
317 Rather they are joy, against nothingness joy—
318 By the wrack we shall sing our Sun-song
319 Under our feet will crawl
320 The shadows of dead worlds
321 We shall open our arms wide,
322 Call out of pure might—
323 Sun, you great Sun, our Comrade,
324 From eternity to eternity we remain true to you,
325 A myriad years we have been,
326 Myriad upon myriad shall be.
327 How wide our arms are,
328 How strong,
329 A myriad years we have been,
330 Myriad upon myriad shall be.

# John Cage

## DIARY: HOW TO IMPROVE THE WORLD (YOU WILL ONLY MAKE MATTERS WORSE) 1965

This text is a mosaic of ideas, statements, words, and stories. It is also a diary. For each day, I determined by chance operations how many parts of the mosaic I would write and how many words there would be in each. The number of words per day was to equal, or, by the last statement written, to exceed one hundred words.

I used an IBM Selectric typewriter to print my text. I used twelve different type faces, letting chance operations determine which face would be used for which statement. So, too, the left marginations were determined, the right marginations being the result of not hyphenating words and at the same time keeping the number of characters per line forty-three or less. The present typography follows the original chance-determined plan.

I.      Continue; I'll discover where you
                sweat (Kierkegaard).     We are getting
                    rid of ownership, substituting use.
        Beginning with ideas.     Which ones can we
                    take?     Which ones can we give?
        *Disappearance of power politics.*     Non-
                    measurement.     *Japanese, he said: we*
                    *also hear with our feet.*     *I'd quoted*
        *Busoni: Standing between musician and*
        *music is notation.*     *Before I'd given the*
        *history: chance operations, indeterminacy.*
            *I'd cited the musics of India: notation*
            *of them's after the fact.*     *I'd spoken of*

        *direct musical action (since it's*
*ears, not interposing eyes).* 2:00 A. M.,
                Jensen said, "Even if you didn't like
            the results (Lindsay, etc.), we hope
        you liked the telling of it." Telling
            (?) of it! We were there while it was
happening! *II. Minimum ethic: Do what*
                *you said you'd do. Impossible?*
                *Telephone. No answer?* My idea was
    that if they wanted to fight (human
                        nature and all that), they should
do it in the Antarctic, rest of us
            gambling on daily outcome: proceeds for
                    world welfare. Instead they're
                    cooperative down there, exchanging
            data, being friendly. April '64: U.S.
                    State Department man gave Honolulu
                    talk—"global village whether we
        like it or not"—, cited fifty-five
                    services which are global in extent.
                Mountain range dividing Oahu, formerly
                crenelated (crenelations for self-
                    protection while shooting arrows),
        is now tunneled, permitting population
            circulation. Wars etc. part of dying
                political-economic structures. Social
            work equals increasing number of
global services. **III. AS McLUHAN SAYS,**
                **EVERYTHING HAPPENS AT ONCE.    IMAGE IS**
**NO LONGER STREAM FALLING OVER ROCKS,**
            **GETTING FROM ORIGINAL TO FINAL PLACE;**
    **IT'S AS TENNEY EXPLAINED: A VIBRATING**
                    **COMPLEX, ANY ADDITION OR SUBTRACTION**
**OF COMPONENT(S), REGARDLESS OF APPARENT**
        **POSITION(S) IN THE TOTAL SYSTEM,**
            **PRODUCING ALTERATION, A DIFFERENT MUSIC.**


*153*

**FULLER: AS LONG AS ONE HUMAN BEING IS
HUNGRY, THE ENTIRE HUMAN RACE IS
HUNGRY.**   City planning's obsolete.   What's
needed is global planning so Earth
may stop stepping like octopus on its
own feet.   Buckminster Fuller uses his
head: comprehensive design science;
inventory of world resources.   Conversion:
the mind turns around, no longer
facing in its direction.   Utopia?
Self-knowledge.   Some will make it,
with or without LSD.   The others?   Pray
for acts of God, crises, power
failures, no water to drink.   *IV.   We
see symmetrically: canoe on northern
Canadian lake, stars in midnight sky
repeated in water, forested shores
precisely mirrored.   Our hearing's
asymmetrical: noticed sounds surprise us,
echoes of shouts we make transform our
voices, straight line of sound from us to
shore's followed by echo's slithering
around the lake's perimeter.   When I
said, "Fifty-five global services,"
California Bell Telephone man replied
(September '65), "It's now sixty-one."*
The seasons (creation, preservation,
destruction, quiescence): this was
experience and resultant idea (no
longer is: he flies to Rio).   What shall
we wear as we travel about?   A summer suit
with or without long underwear?   What
about Stein's idea: People are the way
their land and air is?   **V.**   When I said
that culture was changing from

Renaissance to what it is now (McLuhan),
Johns objected to what he said was
an oversimplification.    But Johns was
speaking according to our non-
Renaissance experience: total field, non-
focused multiplicity.    **We are, are we not,**
**socially speaking, in a situation of**
**the old dying and the new coming into**
**being?    For the old—paying bills,**
**seeking for power—take the attitude**
**of play: games.    For the new—doing what**
**isn't necessary, "moving sand from one**
**part of the beach to another"**
**(Buckminster Fuller)—take the**
**religious attitude: cerebration.    (It**
**celebrates.) The people have left.**
**The cat and kittens were taken to the**
**SPCA.    The house is full of fleas.    VI.**
They say totally determined music and
indeterminate music sound the same.    I
visited Hamada.    Getting up from
the wheel, he said, "I'm not interested
in results; just going on.    Art's in
process of coming into its own: life.
*The lake is undefined.    The land around*
*rests upon it obscuring its shape, shape*
*that needs to remain unrevealed.    Sung.*
*"Floating world."    Rain, curtain of wind-*
*swept lake's surface beyond: second view*
*(there are others, he tells me, one with*
*mists rising).    Yesterday it was stillness*
*and reflections, groups of bubbles.    An*
*American garden: water, not sand,*
*vegetation, not stones.    Thunder.*
**Without intending to, I'm going from lake**
**to lake.    Saltair.    Salt Lake.    VII.**

Hugh Nibley.     I hadn't seen him since
               high school days.     I asked him what
he thought about other planets and
                 sentient populations.     Yes, he said,
throughout the universe: it's Mormon
doctrine.     We'd said good-bye.     I opened
               the door of the car, picked up my
   attache' case and everything in it fell
       out on the grass and the gutter.     His
                    comment: Something memorable always
happens.     Things we were going to do are
now being done by others.     They were, it
              seems, not in our minds to do (were we
     or they out of our minds?) but simply
ready to enter any open mind, any mind
         disturbed enough not to have an idea in
        it.     *VIII.     The daily warmth we
     experience, my father said, is not
     transmitted by Sun to Earth but is what
              Earth does in response to Sun.
              Measurements, he said, measure
       measuring means.*     Bashô: Matsutake ya
                 shiranu ko no ha no hebaritsuku.
   The leaf of some unknown tree sticking
     on the mushroom (Blythe).     Mushroom does
not know that leaf is sticking on it
     (Takemitsu).     Project: Discover way to
translate Far Eastern texts so western men
                 can read orientally.
       Communication?     Bakarashi!     Words
              without syntax, each word
       polymorphic.     He wanted me to agree that
the piano tuner and the piano maker have
     nothing to do with it (the composition).
The younger ones had said: Whoever makes
         the stretcher isn't separate from the

painting.    (It doesn't stop there
either.)    IX.    **LOOKING IN ALL DIRECTIONS
NOT JUST ONE DIRECTION.**    Housing
(Fuller) will be, like telephoning, a
service.    Only circumstance to stop your
living there: someone's there already
               (it's busy).    Thus we'll learn to
desire emptiness.    Not being able to say,
"This is mine," we'll want when we
inquire to get no response at all.    4:00
               P. M. throughout the world.    Whether
               we like it or not (is what he said)
it's happening to us.    **Advertisements are
all good; the news is all bad (McLuhan).
But how we receive bad news can change:
we're glad to hear unemployment's
increasing.    Soon, all that will be
               required of us will be one hour's
work per year (Fuller).**    X.    *They ask what
the purpose of art is.    Is that how
things are?    Say there were a thousand
   artists and one purpose, would one
artist be having it and all the nine
         hundred and ninety-nine others be
missing the point?*    **Arcata Bottom sign
         said: Experiment endlessly and keep
         humble.**    "Write to Center for the Study
               of Democratic Institutions; they'll
         know about the global services."    I
   did.    They answered they knew nothing,
               suggested writing to State Department.
Books one formerly needed were hard to
               locate.    Now they're all out in
         paperback.    Society's changing.
         Relevant information's hard to come
   by.    Soon it'll be everywhere, unnoticed.

XI.     **ELECTRONICS.**      Day comes, the day we
            die.     *There's less and less to do:*
      *circumstances do it for us.     Earth.*

               Old reasons for doing things no
            longer exist.     (Sleep whenever.     Your
work goes on being done.     You and it no
            longer have a means of separation.)
                  *We had the chance to do it*
                  *individually.     Now we must do it*
                  *together: globally.     War will not be*
            *group conflict: it'll be murder, pure*
                        *and simple, individually conceived.*

         Curiosity, awareness.     They returned to
            the fact we all need to eat to explain
their devotion to money rather than music.

               When I spoke of the equation, work
            equals money equals virtue, they
            interrupted me (they didn't let me say
that nowadays there's no equation),
      saying, "How can you speak of money and
virtue in the same breath?"     XII.     **WHERE**
            **THERE DOESN'T SEEM TO BE ANY SPACE,**
               **KNOW WE NO LONGER KNOW WHAT SPACE IS.**
               **HAVE FAITH SPACE IS THERE, GIVING ONE**
         **THE CHANCE TO RENOVATE HIS WAY OF**
               **RECOGNIZING IT, NO MATTER THE MEANS,**
                     **PSYCHIC, SOMATIC, OR MEANS**
               **INVOLVING EXTENSIONS OF EITHER.**
People still ask for definitions, but
                  it's quite clear now that nothing
                     can be defined.     Let alone art, its
      purpose etc.     We're not even sure of
carrots (whether they're what we think
            they are, how poisonous they are, who
grew them and under what circumstances).

                        **SHE WAS INDIGNANT WHEN I SUGGESTED**

**THE USE OF AN APHRODISIAC.      WHY?**
                    **NATURALLY SHE CONSIDERS TV A WASTE OF**
         **TIME.**     XIII.      The purpose of one
activity is no longer separate from the
               purpose of any other activity.      All
                    activities fuse in one purpose which
is (cf. Huang-Po Doctrine of Universal
                         Mind) no purpose.       Imitate the
Ganges' sands, becoming indifferent to
      perfume, indifferent to filth.

*Influence.      Where does it come from?*
*Responsibility?      Sick ones now are*
                    *heartsick.      Narcissi, they became*
            *entranced with emotions, purposes,*
      *mystified by living in the twentieth*
      *century.      We've invented something else,*
                    *not the wheel.      We extended nervous*
*systems.      McLuhan: Agenbite of Outwit*
*(Location, Spring '63).      (The inability of*
                    *people to be inactive.      As Satie said:*
                    *If I don't smoke, someone else will in*
                         *my place.      Audience participation,*
            *active passivity.)*      XIV.      Since the
Spirit's omnipresent, there's a difference
            in things but no difference in spirit.
               McLuhan was able to say "The medium is
                    the message" because he started from
no concern with content.      Or choose
                         quantity, not quality (we get
                         quality willy-nilly) : i.e. we'd like
                  to stay alive, the changes that are
      taking place are so many and so
      interesting.      Composition'll have, he
               said, less and less to do with what
                    happens.      Things happen more
      quickly.      One of the signs you'll get

that'll tell you things are going well is
that you and everyone else you know will
be inhabiting lightweight Dymaxion
houses, disengaged from ownership and
from violated Earth spot (read
Fuller).  **XV.**  **Smiling, she said, let
the old ones walk out: there's not
much to be done about them in any case.**
**Distractions?**  **Interruptions?**  **Welcome
them.**  **They give you the chance to
know whether you're disciplined.**  **That
way you needn't bother about sitting
cross-legged in the lotus position.**
**Phonetics.**  *He was a physicist and a
computer-composer in his spare time.
Why was he so stupid?  Because he was
of the opinion that the only thing
that will engage the intellect is the
measurement of relations between things?
When told that his mind could change,
his response was, "How?  Why?"*  Conflict
won't be between people and people but
between people and things.  In this
conflict let's try to arrange matters so
the outcome as in philosophy will
never be decisive.  Treat redwoods, for
instance, as entities that have at
least a chance to win.  **XVI.**  **He
wanders through markets as though
they were forests and he an exploring
botanist (throws nothing away).**  **Lake.
Take what you're working on with
you, if, that is, you have
something to do.**  **Gaps.**  **What a pity
that she should feel obliged to take
matters in her own hands!**  **(There's**

**practically no kitchen, he says, and**
             **it's already been figured out that**
     **money's being saved.)     Mexico.**
              Europeans are still up against it.
They seem to require a center of
             interest.     They understand tragedy but
life itself (and any art that's like it)
    puzzles them, seems unsatisfactory.
                  We're starved for entertainment
              (thanking the two women).     XVII.     **By**
    becoming angry I simply altered my
    biochemistry, bringing about a two-hour
         recovery.     Meanwhile circumstances
    continued characterized by habit.     *Going*
*in different directions we get instead of*
       *separation a sense of space.*     **Music as**
                **discourse (jazz) doesn't work.     If**
                  **you're going to have a discussion,**
     **have it and use words.     (Dialogue is**
                  **another matter.)     Acts and facts.**
    **Straw that breaks the camel's back:**
    **their saying No (they advertise they'll**
              **say Yes).**     *Principles?     Then all's*
            *intolerable.     No principles (which*
         *doesn't mean we fail to become*
    *furious).     So?     We swim, drowning now*
    *and then.     I must write and tell him*
              *about beauty, the urgency to avoid*
            *it.*     XVIII.     Hearing of past actions
    (politics, economics), people soon
    won't be able to imagine how such
          things could've happened.     Fusing
              politics with economics prepared
    disappearance of both.     Still
       invisible.     **Arriving, realizing we**
              **never departed.     He mentioned heads**

on the ceiling.    Seeing them, noticed
him too.    Fusion of credit card with
passport.    Means of making one's voice
heard:    refusal to honor credit card.
End of the month?    That too may be
changed: the measurement of time,
what season it is, whether it's
night or day.    In any case, no bills,
just added information.    **"Take it easy,
but take it."**    What'll we do?    (Before
lunch.)    "Wing it."    **XIX.    Wanting list of
current global services, how'll I get
it?    Long costly correspondences?
(Pentagon advises telephoning.)    I'll
write to the President (of the U.S.), to
the Secretary (of State of the U.S.).
Time passing, I'll ask those I
encounter whether they've any
information.    (McLuhan hadn't any.)
I'll write to Fuller.    Should have done
that in the first place (Pope Paul,
Lindsay: Take note).**    Amateur (used to
say, "Don't touch it!") now speaks of
audience participation, feels something,
anything, is needed, would help.    Develop
panopticity of mind (Listen).    **WHAT'LL
HAPPEN WHEN INTELLIGENCE IS RECOGNIZED
AS A GLOBAL RESOURCE (FULLER)?
POLITICAL ORGANIZATIONS—GIVING UP
INVOLVEMENT WITH PLAY (PARTNERS,
OPPONENTS), INVOLVEMENT WITH UNATTAINABLE
GOALS (VICTORIES, TRUTHS,
FREEDOMS)—WILL SIMPLY FADE OUT OF THE
PICTURE.    IMAGE COMING UP IS THAT OF
THE UTILITIES (GAS, ELECTRICITY,
TELEPHONES): UNQUESTIONABLE, EMOTIONALLY**

**UNAROUSING.    XX.    What is a drawing?**
**No one knows any longer.    Something**
**that doesn't require that you wait**
**while you're making it for it to dry?**
               **Something on paper?    Museum director**
               **said (Tobey, Schwitters), "It's a**
**question of emphasis."    Thanksgiving.**

**Art.**    Transportation plan (eventually at no
               monetary cost, conveyances recognized
for what they are: extensions of each human
   being and his luggage): short distances
                   costly (to taxi for one block is a
                       luxury), long trips cheap as dirt
(crossing continents, oceans).    Effect of
                   videophone on travel?    That we'll
               stay home, settling like gods for
               impressions we'll give of being
   everywhere at once?    *XXI.    Everywhere*
           *where economics and policitics obtain*
       *(everywhere?), policy is dog eat dog.*
           *Take taxi tolls between cities.    Those*
*in one town higher than those in the*
           *other.    Driver going from one to the*
   *other must drive home alone.    Relaxation*
                   *of rules, ties (Take marriage), is*
       *indicated.*    Now that we've got the
four-lane roads, we won't have any use for
them.    (Good for roller-skating, he said.)
                   Refuse value judgments.    Since
   **time lags were inordinately long,**
           **change's now welcome.**    Advertising's
           discredited itself.    When they
   advertise something, we avoid it.
*There's nothing we really need to do that*
                   *isn't dangerous.    Eighth Street*
       *artists knew this years ago: constantly*

spoke of risk.     But what's meant by risk?

Lose something?     Property, life?

Principles?     The way to lose our

principles is to examine them, to give

them an airing.     XXII.     Heaven's no

longer paved with gold (changes in

church architecture).     Heaven's a motel.

She changed part of the loft: wall-to-wall

carpeting, mobile TV.     No conflicts.

Twenty-two telephone calls were made

by Betty Zeiger "disrupting efficiency

of federal agencies . . . dedicated to

pursuit of peace."     State Department

said Hawaii speaker was a woman.

Fifty-five (now sixty-one) global services

are in area of humanities "beyond

mere provision of food/shelter."     Not

technological services.     State Department:

Global village developed from

"Literary Villages" (plan for the

betterment of life in India).     "We are

packages of leaking water."     "The next

water you drink may be your own."

XXIII.     LET'S CALL IT THE

COLLECTIVE CONSCIOUSNESS (WE'VE GOT

THE COLLECTIVE UNCONSCIOUS).     THE

QUESTION IS: WHAT ARE THE THINGS

EVERYONE NEEDS REGARDLESS OF LIKES

AND DISLIKES?     BEGINNING OF ANSWER:

WATER, FOOD, SHELTER, CLOTHING,

ELECTRICITY, AUDIO-VISUAL

COMMUNICATION, TRANSPORTATION.     FORM

OF ANSWER: GLOBAL UTILITIES NETWORK.     Do

not fear that as the globe gets utility

organized your daily life will not

remain (or become as the case may be)

disorganized, characterized by chaos,
illuminated anarchically.    You'll
have nothing to do; so what will you
do?    A lifelong university
(Fuller)?    In the lobby after La
Monte Young's music stopped,
Geldzahler said: It's like being in a
womb; now that I'm out, I want to get
back in.    I felt differently and so did
Jasper Johns: we were relieved to be
released.    XXIV.    Knowing-seeing,
conforming with reality.    *Anscombe's*
*a feminist, insists on wearing pants.*
*Obliged to lecture dressed in a*
*dress, she took one with her,*
*changed into it, lectured, changed back,*
*walked home (teaching all the time) in*
*pants.    As was said, "When will you*
*undress yourself of your ideas?"    No*
*escape.*    Billy Klüver said decision
of judge in South America (e.g.) is
taken as precedent by judge in Sweden.
Brown's work (Life Against Death) is
prophetic (also de Kooning's remark: we no
longer have tragedy; the situation an
individual may be in is only pathetic):
society as a mass is what needs
psychoanalysis.    (Thus polymorphous
perversity, necessity of Utopia.)    Looking
at billions, unlike Nehru, we must
treat them as one person.    **XXV.    SHE**
**SAYS LIFE IS LIKE A BLANK WALL,**
**IMPASSIBLE.    CORRECT DEDUCTION: SHE IS**
**IN LOVE.    Klüver: ITU lists many**
**international agreements re Morse code,**
**telegrams, telephones, radio, television,**

emergency signals, meteorological
information, frequencies and powers
of stations, means to prevent
static.      "How would it be if these
agreements didn't exist?"      (ITU asks.)
"No press-news, no pictures in the
papers, no exchanged radio programs, no
static-free radio reception, no
meteorological prognoses, no storm
warnings, no security at sea, in air."

*Klüver reports: ITU (International*
*Telecommunication Union) was*
*established in 1865 (nine years*
*older than UPU—post—and seventeen*
*older than railroad agreements).*  XXVI.

The truth is that everything causes
everything else.      We do not speak therefore
of one thing causing another.      There
are no secrets.      It's just we thought they
said dead when they said bread.      Or
that we weren't tuned in when
transmission took place.      Being
told about global services, Barnett
Newman emphasized the importance of
the arts.      Society has tape
recorders, radio broadcasts, and also
copyright laws (which it considers
extending).      (Gets in its own way.)      Get
rid of copyright (this text is
copyright).      We're making
nonspecialist interpenetrations.
Automation.      Alteration of global
society through electronics so that world
will go round by means of united
intelligence rather than by means of
divisive intelligence (politics,

economics).     Say this idea has no basis
in fact but arose through brushing of
            misinformation.     No sweat.     It arose
                (the idea exists, is fact).     XXVII.
Do not imagine there aren't many things
                to do.     We need for instance an
            utterly wireless technology.     Just as
Fuller domes (dome within dome,
    translucent, plants between) will give
                impression of living in no home at
            all (outdoors), so all technology
            must move toward way things were
        before man began changing them:
    identification with nature in her manner
of operation, complete mystery.     Fuller
                prophecy at end of Tomkins profile
        of him editorially (New Yorker)
                eliminated.     Subject: global
network for electrical power (including
            China who'd participate in a spirit
of practicality).     Fuller's remarks
        considered laughable in view of
                November blackout.     (We need another
    blackout, one that isn't so pleasant,
one that'll suggest using our heads the
way Fuller uses his.)     XXVIII.     We've
                poisoned our food, polluted our air
            and water, killed birds and cattle,
            eliminated forests, impoverished,
            eroded the earth.     We're unselfish,
        skilful: we include in our acts to
        perform—we've had a rehearsal—
    the last one.     What would you call it?
            Nirvana?     "Not only was instant
    universal voice communication forecast
        by David Sarnoff, but also instant

television, instant newspapers, instant
                        magazines and instant visual
telephone service . . . the development of
                such global communications system
                        would link people everywhere . . . for
        reorientation toward a 'one-world
        concept of mass communications in an
                era marked by the emergence of a
                        universal language, a universal
        culture and a universal common
                        market.' "     **XXIX.    POPULATION.**
Art's obscured the difference between
                art and life.    Now let life obscure
                        the difference between life and art.
                                Fuller's life is art: comprehensive
                design science, inventory of world
                        resources (if enough mined copper
                exists, re-use it, don't mine more:
                        same with ideas).    World needs
        arranging.    It'll be like living a
                        painting by Johns: Stars and
                Stripes'll be utilities, our daily
lives the brushstrokes.    *McLuhan: Work's*
        *obsolete.    Why?    Work's partial*
        *involvement in activity.    Activity is*
*now necessarily total involvement (cf.*
        *work of artists, work not involved in*
        *profit).    Why total involvement?*
                *Electronics.    Why everything-at-once?*
*The way we-things are.    Yathabhutam.*
                **Where there's a history of**
        **organization (art), introduce disorder.**
        **Where there's a history of**
                        **disorganization (world society),**
                **introduce order.    These directives are**
**no more opposed to one another than**

mountan's opposed to spring

weather.    "How can you believe this when
            you believe that?"    How can I not?
Long life.

# John Giorno

**RAINBOW FIRE**

<table>
<tr><td>The wild</td><td>Icarus</td></tr>
<tr><td>"forest</td><td>is an asteroid</td></tr>
<tr><td>of darkness"</td><td>Icarus is an asteroid,</td></tr>
<tr><td>The wild</td><td></td></tr>
<tr><td>"forest of darkness"</td><td>For lasting</td></tr>
<tr><td>running through</td><td>For lasting</td></tr>
<tr><td></td><td>multi-colored</td></tr>
<tr><td>San Francisco</td><td>multi-colored</td></tr>
<tr><td>Bay</td><td>flames</td></tr>
<tr><td>San Francisco Bay</td><td></td></tr>
<tr><td>is the stopping</td><td>In one</td></tr>
<tr><td>station</td><td>that took place</td></tr>
<tr><td>is the stopping station</td><td>In one that took place</td></tr>
<tr><td>for hundreds</td><td>at about</td></tr>
<tr><td>of thousands</td><td>4:30 A.M.</td></tr>
<tr><td></td><td>at about 4:30 A.M.,</td></tr>
<tr><td>According</td><td>a tall,</td></tr>
<tr><td>to a Japanese</td><td>red-haired</td></tr>
<tr><td>legend</td><td>member</td></tr>
<tr><td>According</td><td></td></tr>
<tr><td>to a Japanese legend,</td><td>A priest</td></tr>
<tr><td>the almost</td><td>in Brooklyn</td></tr>
<tr><td>daily</td><td>A priest in Brooklyn</td></tr>
<tr><td>earthquakes</td><td>acted quickly</td></tr>
<tr><td>here</td><td>yesterday</td></tr>
<tr><td></td><td>acted quickly yesterday</td></tr>
</table>

running through
three Mekong
Delta provinces
three Mekong Delta
provinces
and long regarded
as the Viet Cong's

to put out
flames
engulfing
a 12-year-old
altar boy
engulfing
a 12-year-old altar boy

and the thing
it does
and the thing it does
every 19 years
every 19 years
is pass
close
to Earth

and long regarded
as the Viet Cong's
strongest
fortress
strongest fortress
in South
Vietnam

"We think
California
"We think California
will slide
into the sea
will slide into the sea,

to put out
flames

a celestial
rock
a celestial rock
a half-mile
in diameter
a half-mile
in diameter,

flames
with brilliant everchanging
with brilliant
everchanging hues
hues,

whose surplice
had brushed
whose surplice had brushed
against
a candle
against a candle
and caught fire
and caught
fire.

is pass close
to Earth
on its 409-day
orbit
on its 409-day orbit
around
the sun
around the sun.

place
the equivalent
place the equivalent

for hundreds
of thousands
of birds
of birds
on the Pacific
flyway
on the Pacific flyway.

The police
said
The police said
the Rev. Joseph
McGroarty
the Rev. Joseph McGroarty,
53 years old
53 years old,
rushed
to the altar boy
rushed to the altar boy
James O'Mahoney,
of 3422 Farragut Road,

in South Vietnam,
was reported
today
was reported today
blazing
from end
to end
blazing
from end to end,

Icarus
attempted
Icarus attempted
to fly
to fly
with the help

of 1 to 2
tablespoons
of 1 to 2 tablespoons
of RAINBOW
FIRE

a tall,
red-haired member
of the Tactical
Patrol
Force
of the Tactical
Patrol Force
was seen
cracking
a student
was seen cracking
a student
across
the skull
across the skull
with his nightstick
with his nightstick.

of RAINBOW FIRE
on a single
sheet
on a single sheet
of newspaper
of newspaper,

there will be
violent
there will be violent
earthquakes
earthquakes,

The rolling
thunder

James O'Mahoney,
of 3422 Farragut Road,
and tried
to rip off
and tried to rip off
the youth's
burning
surplice

the almost daily
earthquakes here
are the result
of stirrings
are the result
of stirrings
by a giant
catfish

with the help
of a pair
of wings
of a pair of wings
supplied him
by his father
Daedalus

there will be
violent
there will be violent
change
change
in all of
in all of society
society

by a giant catfish
that lurks

The rolling thunder
of 500-pound
bombs
of 500-pound bombs
was clearly
heard
was clearly heard
in the capital
in the capital

Sirhan
Bishara
Sirhan
Sirhan Bishara Sirhan
is a member

the youth's
burning surplice,
a thin
white
a thin white,
waist-length

vestment
waist-length
vestment,
and black
cassock
and black cassock.

is a member
of the Rosicrucian
order
of the Rosicrucian order,
an occult
fraternal
organization

supplied him

beneath
the islands
that lurks
beneath the islands.

and maybe even
Atlantis
and maybe even Atlantis
will rise
will rise."

Another
room
Another room
houses
houses
gorgeous,
silken
robes
gorgeous,
silken robes
of the rulers
of the rulers

fold
securely
fold securely
to enclose
the powder
to enclose the powder

an occult
fraternal organization
which expounds
a philosophy
which expounds
a philosophy
based
on study

by his father
Daedalus,
but was drowned
but was drowned owing
owing
to his approaching
too near

Bleeding
Bleeding,
the student
fell
the student fell
to the ground
to the ground.

to his approaching
too near
the sun
the sun,

Don says
Icarus
Don says Icarus
may even
collide
may even collide
with Earth
with Earth

forcing
the guerrillas
forcing the guerrillas
to flee
into the open
to flee into the open.

Dr. Suyehiro,
the son

of metaphysics

The priest's
own surplice
The priest's own surplice
caught fire
caught
fire.

most of them
The Kaftans
most of them the Kaftans
which the sultans wore
which the sultans
wore.

The U.S.
destroyer
Strong
The U.S. destroyer
Strong
was ordered
to stand
offshore

said that a cuttlefish
of an extraordinary size
usually
found
usually found
only in remote
depths
only in remote depths
had been caught
in shallow
water

As he lay
there

of a seismologist
Dr. Suyehiro,
the son of a seismologist,
said that a cuttlefish
of an extraordinary
size

At its closest
At its closest,
it comes
within
it comes within
3,951,000
3,951,000
miles
of us
miles of us,

and place
on burning
logs
and place
on burning logs
in the fireplace
or campfire
in the fireplace
or campfire.

Father
McGroarty
Father McGroarty
pulled
the boy
pulled the boy
to the marble
floor
to the marble floor
and rolled him
around

As he lay there,
in sight
of several
newsmen
and students

and rolled him
around
to put out
the fire
to put out the fire,
the police said
the police said.

was ordered
to stand offshore
and shell
guerrillas
and shell guerrillas
as they hauled
their munitions

based on study
of metaphysics
and development
and development
of "psychic
powers"
of "psychic powers."
The giant
cuttlefish
The giant cuttlefish,
it is thought
it is thought,
may have
sensed
may have sensed
the imminence
of last week's

which melted
the wax
which melted the wax
with which
the wings
with which the wings
were fastened
were fastened.

had been caught
in shallow water
near Aburatsubo
near Aburatsubo
two days
before
two days before
the big quake
on May 16
the big quake
on May 16.

auto
junkyards
auto junkyards,
hamburger
stands
hamburger stands,
motels
in sight
of several newsmen
and students,
a second
uniformed
policeman
a second uniformed
policeman
bent over him

quake

    as they hauled
    their munitions
    onto beaches
from fire-threatened
    caches
from fire-threatened caches
    in the forest
    in the forest.

    For best
    color effects
For best color effects
    let the flames
    subside
    somewhat

These singular
    pulses
These singular pulses,
    recurring
recurring every
every 1.3372795
1.3372795 seconds
    seconds,

the imminence
of last week's
    quake
    and sought
    refuge
and sought refuge
    in waters
    away
in waters away
from its usual
    habitat

Handsome
Handsome,
blonde
and blue-eyed
blonde and blue-eyed,
Baty
had waited
Baty had waited
for the police
on the altar
steps

motels,
small
factories
small factories,
billboards
billboards,
gas
stations
gas stations

bent over him
and struck him
and struck him
with his nightstick
with his nightstick.

let the flames
subside somewhat
before
placing
before placing
RAINBOW FIRE

Hundreds
of flower
people
Hundreds

for the police
on the altar steps
in the center
of about
100 friends
of about 100 friends
all claiming
to be
Don Baty
all claiming
to be Don Baty.

RAINBOW FIRE
on the burning
on the burning logs
logs.

are observable
for about
a minute
are observable
for about a minute,
vanish
for some
three minutes

as a pendant,
and inside
the bowl
and inside the bowl
is a live
Rainbow
Fish
is a live
Rainbow Fish.

from its usual habitat
close
to the epicenter

of flower people
flocked
to Sugar
Loaf
flocked
to Sugar Loaf
near Boulder,
Colo.

A necklace
with a miniature
A necklace
with a miniature
fish
bowl
fish bowl
as a pendant

The youth
was taken
The youth was taken
by stretcher
by stretcher
from the campus

The priest
then slapped out
The priest
then slapped out
the flames
the flames
on his own
vestments
on his own vestments.

from the campus
by volunteer
medical
personnel

close to the epicenter
of the tremor
of the tremor.

near Boulder,
Colo.,
because
they said
because they said,
the asteroid
was going
to smash
the asteroid
was going to smash
into our planet
into our planet.

by volunteer
medical personnel.

The colors
last
The colors last
as long
as the logs
burn
as long as
the logs burn.

vanish
for some
three minutes,
then reappear
then reappear.

# Dan Graham

## VARIANT FOR *POSSIBILITIES OF POETRY* FROM SCHEMATA CONCEIVED IN 1966

Schema for a set of poems whose component pages are specifically published as individual poems in various magazines. As the data for every variant is self-referential, each poem-page is to be set in its final form by the editor of the publication where it is to appear, the exact data in each particular instance to correspond to the fact(s) of its published appearance. (These categories are arbitrary, and others may be substituted by the editor to conform to length or other contingencies.)

1. Using any arbitrary schematic (such as the example published here) produces a large, finite permutation of specific, discrete poems.

2. If a given variant-poem is attempted to be set up by the editor following the logic step-by-step (linearly), it would be found impossible to compose a completed version of the poem as each of the component lines of exact data requiring completion (in terms of specific numbers and percentages) would be contingently determined by every other number and percentage which itself in turn would be determined by the other numbers or percentages, *ad infinitum*.

3. It would be possible to 'compose' the entire set of permutationally possible poems and to select the applicable variant(s) with the aid of a computer which could 'see' the ensemble instantly.

(number of) adjectives
(number of) adverbs
(percentage of) area not occupied by type
(percentage of) area occupied by type
(number of) columns
(number of) conjunctions
(number of) depression of type into surface of page
(number of) gerunds
(number of) infinitives
(number of) letters of alphabet
(number of) lines
(number of) mathematical symbols
(number of) nouns
(number of) numbers
(number of) participles
(perimeter of) page
(weight of) paper sheet
(type) paper stock
(thinness of) paper stock
(number of) prepositions
(number of) pronouns
(number of point) size type
(name of) typeface
(number of) words
(number of) words capitalized
(number of) words italicized
(number of) words not capitalized
(number of) words not italicized

37 adjectives
0 adverbs
87.40% area not occupied by type
12.60% area occupied by type
2 columns
0 conjunctions
0 mms. depression of type into surface of page
0 gerunds
0 infinitives
24 letters of alphabet
28 lines
11 mathematical symbols
36 nouns
49 numbers
7 participles
5⅜″ × 8″ page
Dondell paper sheet
uncoated offset paper stock
.0039″ paper stock
6 prepositions
0 pronouns
10 point size type
Aster typeface
60 words
2 words capitalized
0 words italicized
58 words not capitalized
60 words not italicized

# EXCLUSION PRINCIPLE

1,000,000,000,000,000,000,000,000,000.00000000 miles to edge of known universe
100,000,000,000,000,000,000,000,000.00000000 miles to edge of galaxy (Milky Way)
3,573,000,000.00000000 miles to edge of solar system (Pluto)
205.00000000 miles to Washington, D.C.
2.85000000 miles to Times Square, New York City
.38600000 miles to Union Square subway stop
.11820000 miles to corner of 14th Street and First Avenue
.00367000 miles to front door of Apartment 1D, 153 First Avenue
.00021600 miles to typewriter paper page
.00000700 miles to lens of glasses
.00000098 miles to cornea from retinal wall

1966

V

# W. D. Snodgrass

## APRIL INVENTORY

The green catalpa tree has turned
All white; the cherry blooms once more.
In one whole year I haven't learned
A blessed thing they pay you for.
The blossoms snow down in my hair;
The trees and I will soon be bare.

The trees have more than I to spare.
The sleek, expensive girls I teach,
Younger and pinker every year,
Bloom gradually out of reach.
The pear tree lets its petals drop
Like dandruff on a tabletop.

The girls have grown so young by now
I have to nudge myself to stare.
This year they smile and mind me how
My teeth are falling with my hair.
In thirty years I may not get
Younger, shrewder, or out of debt.

The tenth time, just a year ago,
I made myself a little list
Of all the things I'd ought to know;
Then told my parents, analyst,

And everyone who's trusted me
I'd be substantial, presently.

I haven't read one book about
A book or memorized one plot.
Or found a mind I didn't doubt.
I learned one date. And then forgot.
And one by one the solid scholars
Get the degrees, the jobs, the dollars.

And smile above their starchy collars.
I taught my classes Whitehead's notions;
One lovely girl, a song of Mahler's.
Lacking a source-book or promotions,
I showed one child the colors of
A luna moth and how to love.

I taught myself to name my name,
To bark back, loosen love and crying;
To ease my woman so she came,
To ease an old man who was dying.
I have not learned how often I
Can win, can love, but choose to die.

I have not learned there is a lie
Love shall be blonder, slimmer, younger;
That my equivocating eye
Loves only by my body's hunger;
That I have poems, true to feel,
Or that the lovely world is real.

While scholars speak authority
And wear their ulcers on their sleeves,
My eyes in spectacles shall see
These trees procure and spend their leaves.
There is a value underneath
The gold and silver in my teeth.

Though trees turn bare and girls turn wives,
We shall afford our costly seasons;
There is a gentleness survives
That will outspeak and has its reasons.
There is a loveliness exists,
Preserves us. Not for specialists.

# A FLAT ONE

Old Fritz, on this rotating bed
For seven wasted months you lay
Unfit to move, shrunken, gray,
No good to yourself or anyone
But to be babied—changed and bathed and fed.
      At long last, that's all done.

Before each meal, twice every night,
We set pads on your bedsores, shut
Your catheter tube off, then brought
The second canvas-and-black-iron
Bedframe and clamped you in between them, tight,
      Scared, so we could turn

You over. We washed you, covered you,
Cut up each bite of meat you ate;
We watched your lean jaws masticate
As ravenously your useless food
As thieves at hard labor in their chains chew
      Or insects in the wood.

Such pious sacrifice to give
You all you could demand of pain:
Receive this haddock's body, slain
For you, old tyrant; take this blood
Of a tomato, shed that you might live.
      You had that costly food.

You seem to be all finished, so
We'll plug your old recalcitrant anus
And tie up your discouraged penis
In a great, snow-white bow of gauze.

We wrap you, pin you, and cart you down below,
        Below, below, because

    Your credit has finally run out.
    On our steel table, trussed and carved,
    You'll find this world's hardworking, starved
    Teeth working in your precious skin.
The earth turns, in the end, by turn about
        And opens to take you in.

    Seven months gone down the drain; thank God
    That's through. Throw out the four-by-fours,
    Swabsticks, the thick salve for bedsores,
    Throw out the diaper pads and drug
Containers, pile the bedclothes in a wad,
        And rinse the cider jug

    Half-filled with the last urine. Then
    Empty out the cotton cans,
    Autoclave the bowls and spit pans,
    Unhook the pumps and all the red
Tubes—catheter, suction, oxygen;
        Next, wash the empty bed.

    —All this Dark Age machinery
    On which we had tormented you
    To life. Last, we collect the few
    Belongings: snapshots, some odd bills,
Your mail, and half a pack of Luckies we
        Won't light you after meals.

    Old man, these seven months you've lain
    Determined—not that you would live—
    Just to not die. No one would give
    You one chance you could ever wake
From that first night, much less go well again,
        Much less go home and make

    Your living; how could you hope to find

A place for yourself in all creation?—
Pain was your only occupation.
And pain that should content and will
A man to give it up, nerved you to grind
      Your clenched teeth, breathing, till

Your skin broke down, your calves went flat.
And your legs lost all sensation. Still,
You took enough morphine to kill
A strong man. Finally, nitrogen
Mustard: you could last two months after that;
      *It* would kill you then.

Even then you wouldn't quit.
Old soldier, yet you must have known
Inside the animal had grown
Sick of the world, made up its mind
To stop. Your mind ground on its separate
      Way, merciless and blind,

Into these last weeks when the breath
Would only come in fits and starts
That puffed out your sections like the parts
Of some enormous, damaged bug.
You waited, not for life, not for your death,
      Just for the deadening drug

That made your life seem bearable.
You still whispered you would not die.
Yet in the nights I heard you cry
Like a whipped child; in fierce old age
You whimpered, tears stood on your gun-metal
      Blue cheeks shaking with rage

And terror. So much pain would fill
Your room that when I left I'd pray
That if I came back the next day
I'd find you gone. You stayed for me—

Nailed to your own rapacious, stiff self-will.
  You've shook loose, finally.

  They'd say this was a worthwhile job
  Unless they tried it. It is mad
  To throw our good lives after bad;
  Waste time, drugs, and our minds, while strong
Men starve. How many young men did we rob
  To keep you hanging on?

  I can't think we did *you* much good.
  Well, when you died, none of us wept.
  You killed for us, and so we kept
  You, because we need to earn our pay.
No. We'd still have to help you try. We would
  Have killed for you today.

# THE EXAMINATION

Under the thick beams of that swirly smoking light,
    The black robes are clustering, huddled in together.
Hunching their shoulders, they spread short, broad sleeves
    like night-
        Black grackles' wings; then they reach bone-yellow
            leather-

y fingers, each to each. And are prepared. Each turns
    His single eye—or since one can't discern their eyes,
That reflective, single, moon-pale disc which burns
    Over each brow—to watch this uncouth shape that lies

Strapped to their table. One probes with his ragged nails
    The slate-sharp calf, explores the thigh and the lean thews
Of the groin. Others raise, red as piratic sails,
    His wing, stretching, trying the pectoral sinews.

One runs his finger down the whet of that cruel
    Golden beak, lifts back the horny lids from the eyes,
Peers down in one bright eye malign as a jewel,
    And steps back suddenly. "He is anaesthetized?"

"He is. He is. Yes. Yes." The tallest of them, bent
    Down by the head, rises: "This drug possesses powers
Sufficient to still all gods in this firmament.
    This is Garuda who was fierce. He's yours for hours.

"We shall continue, please." Now, once again, he bends
    To the skull, and its clamped tissues. Into the cran-
ial cavity, he plunges both of his hands
    Like obstetric forceps and lifts out the great brain,

Holds it aloft, then gives it to the next who stands
    Beside him. Each, in turn, accepts it, although loath,

Turns it this way, that way, feels it between his hands
    Like a wasp's nest or some sickening outsized growth.

They must decide what thoughts each part of it must think;
    They tap at, then listen beside, each suspect lobe;
Next, with a crow's quill dipped into India ink,
    Mark on its surface, as if on a map or globe,

Those dangerous areas which need to be excised.
    They rinse it, then apply antiseptics to it;
Now silver saws appear which, inch by inch, slice
    Through its ancient folds and ridges, like thick suet.

It's rinsed, dried, and daubed with thick salves. The smoky
    saws
    Are scrubbed, resterilized, and polished till they gleam.
The brain is repacked in its case. Pinched in their claws,
    Glimmering needles stitch it up, that leave no seam.

Meantime, one of them has set blinders to the eyes,
    Inserted light packing beneath each of the ears
And calked the nostrils in. One, with thin twine, ties
    The genitals off. With long wooden-handled shears,

Another chops pinions out of the scarlet wings.
    It's hoped that with disuse he will forget the sky
Or, at least, in time, learn, among other things,
    To fly no higher than his superiors fly.

Well; that's a beginning. The next time, they can split
    His tongue and teach him to talk correctly, can give
Him opinions on fine books and choose clothing fit
    For the integrated area where he'll live.

Their candidate may live to give them thanks one day.
    He will recover and may hope for such success
He might return to join their ranks. Bowing away,
    They nod, whispering, "One of ours; one of ours. Yes.
        Yes."

# Sylvia Plath

## THE COLOSSUS

I shall never get you put together entirely,
Pieced, glued, and properly jointed.
Mule-bray, pig-grunt and bawdy cackles
Proceed from your great lips.
It's worse than a barnyard.

Perhaps you consider yourself an oracle,
Mouthpiece of the dead, or of some god or other.
Thirty years now I have laboured
To dredge the silt from your throat.
I am none the wiser.

Scaling little ladders with gluepots and pails of lysol
I crawl like an ant in mourning
Over the weedy acres of your brow
To mend the immense skull-plates and clear
The bald, white tumuli of your eyes.

A blue sky out of the Oresteia
Arches above us. O father, all by yourself
You are pithy and historical as the Roman Forum.
I open my lunch on a hill of black cypress.
Your fluted bones and acanthine hair are littered

In their old anarchy to the horizon-line.
It would take more than a lightning-stroke

To create such a ruin.
Nights, I squat in the cornucopia
Of your left ear, out of the wind,

Counting the red stars and those of plum-colour.
The sun rises under the pillar of your tongue.
My hours are married to shadow.
No longer do I listen for the scrape of a keel
On the blank stones of the landing.

# SUICIDE OFF EGG ROCK

Behind him the hotdogs split and drizzled
On the public grills, and the ochreous salt flats,
Gas tanks, factory stacks—that landscape
Of imperfections his bowels were part of—
Rippled and pulsed in the glassy updraught.
Sun struck the water like a damnation.
No pit of shadow to crawl into,
And his blood beating the old tattoo
I am, I am, I am. Children
Were squealing where combers broke and the spindrift
Ravelled wind-ripped from the crest of the wave.
A mongrel working his legs to a gallop
Hustled a gull flock to flap off the sandspit.

He smouldered, as if stone-deaf, blindfold,
His body beached with the sea's garbage,
A machine to breathe and beat forever.
Flies filing in through a dead skate's eyehole
Buzzed and assailed the vaulted brainchamber.
The words in his book wormed off the pages.
Everything glittered like blank paper.

Everything shrank in the sun's corrosive
Ray but Egg Rock on the blue wastage.
He heard when he walked into the water

The forgetful surf creaming on those ledges.

# ELM

*For Ruth Fainlight*

I know the bottom, she says. I know it with my great tap
   root:
It is what you fear.
I do not fear it: I have been there.

Is it the sea you hear in me,
Its dissatisfactions?
Or the voice of nothing, that was your madness?

Love is a shadow.
How you lie and cry after it.
Listen: these are its hooves: it has gone off, like a horse.

All night I shall gallop thus, impetuously,
Till your head is a stone, your pillow a little turf,
Echoing, echoing.

Or shall I bring you the sound of poisons?
This is rain now, this big hush.
And this is the fruit of it: tin-white, like arsenic.

I have suffered the atrocity of sunsets.
Scorched to the root
My red filaments burn and stand, a hand of wires.

Now I break up in pieces that fly about like clubs.
A wind of such violence
Will tolerate no bystanding: I must shriek.

The moon, also, is merciless: she would drag me
Cruelly, being barren.
Her radiance scathes me. Or perhaps I have caught her.

I let her go. I let her go
Diminished and flat, as after radical surgery.
How your bad dreams possess and endow me.

I am inhabited by a cry.
Nightly it flaps out
Looking, with its hooks, for something to love.

I am terrified by this dark thing
That sleeps in me;
All day I feel its soft, feathery turnings, its malignity.

Clouds pass and disperse.
Are those the faces of love, those pale irretrievables?
Is it for such I agitate my heart?

I am incapable of more knowledge.
What is this, this face
So murderous in its strangle of branches?—

Its snaky acids kiss.
It petrifies the will. These are the isolate, slow faults
That kill, that kill, that kill.

# TULIPS

The tulips are too excitable, it is winter here.
Look how white everything is, how quiet, how snowed-in.
I am learning peacefulness, lying by myself quietly
As the light lies on these white walls, this bed, these hands.
I am nobody; I have nothing to do with explosions.
I have given my name and my day-clothes up to the nurses
And my history to the anaesthetist and my body to surgeons.

They have propped my head between the pillow and the
   sheet-cuff
Like an eye between two white lids that will not shut.
Stupid pupil, it has to take everything in.
The nurses pass and pass, they are no trouble,
They pass the way gulls pass inland in their white caps,
Doing things with their hands, one just the same as another,
So it is impossible to tell how many there are.

My body is a pebble to them, they tend it as water
Tends to the pebbles it must run over, smoothing them gently.
They bring me numbness in their bright needles, they bring
   me sleep.
Now I have lost myself I am sick of baggage—
My patent leather overnight case like a black pillbox,
My husband and child smiling out of the family photo;
Their smiles catch onto my skin, little smiling hooks.

I have let things slip, a thirty-year-old cargo boat
Stubbornly hanging on to my name and address.
They have swabbed me clear of my loving associations.
Scared and bare on the green plastic-pillowed trolley
I watched my tea-set, my bureaus of linen, my books

Sink out of sight, and the water went over my head.
I am a nun now, I have never been so pure.

I didn't want any flowers, I only wanted
To lie with my hands turned up and be utterly empty.
How free it is, you have no idea how free—
The peacefulness is so big it dazes you,
And it asks nothing, a name tag, a few trinkets.
It is what the dead close on, finally; I imagine them
Shutting their mouths on it, like a Communion tablet.

The tulips are too red in the first place, they hurt me.
Even through the gift paper I could hear them breathe
Lightly, through their white swaddlings, like an awful baby.
Their redness talks to my wound, it corresponds.
They are subtle: they seem to float, though they weigh me down,
Upsetting me with their sudden tongues and their colour,
A dozen red lead sinkers round my neck.

Nobody watched me before, now I am watched.
The tulips turn to me, and the window behind me
Where once a day the light slowly widens and slowly thins,
And I see myself, flat, ridiculous, a cut-paper shadow
Between the eye of the sun and the eyes of the tulips,
And I have no face, I have wanted to efface myself.
The vivid tulips eat my oxygen.

Before they came the air was calm enough,
Coming and going, breath by breath, without any fuss.
Then the tulips filled it up like a loud noise.
Now the air snags and eddies round them the way a river
Snags and eddies round a sunken rust-red engine.
They concentrate my attention, that was happy
Playing and resting without committing itself.

The walls, also, seem to be warming themselves.
The tulips should be behind bars like dangerous animals;
They are opening like the mouth of some great African cat,

And I am aware of my heart: it opens and closes
Its bowl of red blooms out of sheer love of me.
The water I taste is warm and salt, like the sea,
And comes from a country far away as health.

# THE APPLICANT

First, are you our sort of a person?
Do you wear
A glass eye, false teeth or a crutch,
A brace or a hook,
Rubber breasts or a rubber crotch,

Stitches to show something's missing? No, no? Then
How can we give you a thing?
Stop crying.
Open your hand.
Empty? Empty. Here is a hand

To fill it and willing
To bring teacups and roll away headaches
And do whatever you tell it.
Will you marry it?
It is guaranteed

To thumb shut your eyes at the end
And dissolve of sorrow.
We make new stock from the salt.
I notice you are stark naked.
How about this suit—

Black and stiff, but not a bad fit.
Will you marry it?
It is waterproof, shatterproof, proof
Against fire and bombs through the roof.
Believe me, they'll bury you in it.

Now your head, excuse me, is empty.
I have the ticket for that.

Come here, sweetie, out of the closet.
Well, what do you think of *that*?
Naked as paper to start

But in twenty-five years she'll be silver,
In fifty, gold.
A living doll, everywhere you look.
It can sew, it can cook,
It can talk, talk, talk.

It works, there is nothing wrong with it.
You have a hole, it's a poultice.
You have an eye, it's an image.
My boy, it's your last resort.
Will you marry it, marry it, marry it.

# LADY LAZARUS

I have done it again.
One year in every ten
I manage it—

A sort of walking miracle, my skin
Bright as a Nazi lampshade,
My right foot

A paperweight,
My face a featureless, fine
Jew linen.

Peel off the napkin
O my enemy.
Do I terrify?—

The nose, the eye pits, the full set of teeth?
The sour breath
Will vanish in a day.

Soon, soon the flesh
The grave cave ate will be
At home on me

And I a smiling woman.
I am only thirty.
And like the cat I have nine times to die.

This is Number Three.
What a trash
To annihilate each decade.

What a million filaments.
The peanut-crunching crowd
Shoves in to see

Them unwrap me hand and foot—
The big strip tease.
Gentlemen, ladies

These are my hands
My knees.
I may be skin and bone,

Nevertheless, I am the same, identical woman.
The first time it happened I was ten.
It was an accident.

The second time I meant
To last it out and not come back at all.
I rocked shut

As a seashell.
They had to call and call
And pick the worms off me like sticky pearls.

Dying
Is an art, like everything else.
I do it exceptionally well.

I do it so it feels like hell.
I do it so it feels real.
I guess you could say I've a call.

It's easy enough to do it in a cell.
It's easy enough to do it and stay put.
It's the theatrical

Comeback in broad day
To the same place, the same face, the same brute
Amused shout:

'A miracle!'
That knocks me out.
There is a charge

For the eyeing of my scars, there is a charge
For the hearing of my heart—
It really goes.

And there is a charge, a very large charge
For a word or a touch
Or a bit of blood

Or a piece of my hair or my clothes.
So, so, Herr Doktor.
So, Herr Enemy.

I am your opus,
I am your valuable,
The pure gold baby

That melts to a shriek.
I turn and burn.
Do not think I underestimate your great concern.

Ash, ash—
You poke and stir.
Flesh, bone, there is nothing there—

A cake of soap,
A wedding ring,
A gold filling.

Herr God, Herr Lucifer
Beware
Beware.

Out of the ash
I rise with my red hair
And I eat men like air.

# DADDY

You do not do, you do not do
Any more, black shoe
In which I have lived like a foot
For thirty years, poor and white,
Barely daring to breathe or Achoo.

Daddy, I have had to kill you.
You died before I had time—
Marble-heavy, a bag full of God,
Ghastly statue with one grey toe
Big as a Frisco seal

And a head in the freakish Atlantic
Where it pours bean green over blue
In the waters off beautiful Nauset.
I used to pray to recover you.
Ach, du.

In the German tongue, in the Polish town
Scraped flat by the roller
Of wars, wars, wars.
But the name of the town is common.
My Polack friend

Says there are a dozen or two.
So I never could tell where you
Put your foot, your root,
I never could talk to you.
The tongue stuck in my jaw.

It stuck in a barb wire snare.
Ich, ich, ich, ich,

I could hardly speak.
I thought every German was you.
And the language obscene

An engine, an engine
Chuffing me off like a Jew.
A Jew to Dachau, Auschwitz, Belsen.
I began to talk like a Jew.
I think I may well be a Jew.

The snows of the Tyrol, the clear beer of Vienna
Are not very pure or true.
With my gypsy ancestress and my weird luck
And my Taroc pack and my Taroc pack
I may be a bit of a Jew.

I have always been scared of *you*,
With your Luftwaffe, your gobbledygoo.
And your neat moustache
And your Aryan eye, bright blue.
Panzer-man, panzer-man, O You—

Not God but a swastika
So black no sky could squeak through.
Every woman adores a Fascist,
The boot in the face, the brute
Brute heart of a brute like you.

You stand at the blackboard, daddy,
In the picture I have of you,
A cleft in your chin instead of your foot
But no less a devil for that, no not
Any less the black man who

Bit my pretty red heart in two.
I was ten when they buried you.
At twenty I tried to die
And get back, back, back to you.
I thought even the bones would do.

But they pulled me out of the sack,
And they stuck me together with glue.
And then I knew what to do.
I made a model of you,
A man in black with a Meinkampf look

And a love of the rack and the screw.
And I said I do, I do.
So daddy, I'm finally through.
The black telephone's off at the root,
The voices just can't worm through.

If I've killed one man, I've killed two—
The vampire who said he was you
And drank my blood for a year,
Seven years, if you want to know.
Daddy, you can lie back now.

There's a stake in your fat black heart
And the villagers never liked you.
They are dancing and stamping on you.
They always knew it was you.
Daddy, daddy, you bastard, I'm through.

# Brother Antoninus

## IN SAVAGE WASTES

> *A monk ran into a party of handmaids of the Lord
> on a certain journey. Seeing them he left the road
> and gave them a wide berth. But the Abbess said
> to him: If you were a perfect monk, you would
> not even have looked close enough to see that we
> were women.*
>
> —Verba Seniorum

A hermit who has lived a long time in the desert
experiences great dearth of spirit, and one night,
exhausted, falls asleep over his prayers. He is
awakened by a knock at the door, and opening it
beholds two nuns. They explain that they are on
pilgrimage and have become separated from their
company, and beg him shelter for the night. He
graciously shows them into his cell, and prepares
to spend the night outside so that they may have
its privacy to themselves. However, once inside
they lock the door and throwing off their habits
reveal themselves as naked succubi. They cast a
spell over him, and seduce him, and there is not
a shred of sensory excitation which they do not
stimulate within him and gratify.

In the morning the monk wakes up and realizes
he has dreamed. There is no sign either of pil-
grims or succubi, nor any evidence of the dis-

orders so real to him during the night. The monk leaves his desert cell and begins to make his way back to the world. As he goes he meets a young man, vaguely familiar to him, who is newly dressed in a monk's habit and is entering the desert to become a solitary. The young monk seems to recognize him and calls him by name; kneeling before him he asks his blessing. Then he says to him: "Tell me, Father, what is the greatest blessing and the greatest curse of the spiritual life?" The monk replies: "Sleep. In sleep we dream. In dreams we betray ourselves. In betrayal we discover ourselves. In self-discovery we lose our innocence. In loss of innocence we gain knowledge. In knowledge we gain wisdom. In wisdom we recover innocence. God be with you." With these words the monk leaves the young man, whom he now recognizes as himself, and reenters the world.


I too, O God, as you very well know,
Am guilty.

And the desert gorges, those hacked
Untendered waste-worlds of the soul—

What buzzard's eye from its sun-skewered height
Has peered such places,
Pierced such deeps?

The gullies of death, the engorged
Arroyos, badlands of the hackling heart,
The scups of perversity.

I too, I too, as You very well know . . .

Where the kites are shrieking
There reeks the carcass.

213

Where the treasure is sunk
There cowers the heart.
Having done such things in the green wood
What will I do in the dry?

Guilt-stretched the night.
Choked in the abstract dimension
I see the eyes of my lust.

Have pity on me, have pity on me,
At least you my friends,
For God hath touched me.

For the light is lost.
Great darknesses drop over the waste.
The hostile stars burn green as cat's eyes
In their depth of dread.
There is not an owl on the greasewood,
There is not a saw-whet on the creosote bush
To keep a man company.

I too, O God, as You very well know,
Am guilty.

For I sought and found not,
I searched, but was not successful.
When I failed, You drew back the veil,
And I am in terror.

In terror,
Who gazed in the poisonous pool.
In dread,
Who sucked of its jet.
Am sick and am sick
Who have seen to myself,
Begging forgiveness of my own self,
In what I have done.

For if You, O God, can pardon a man,
Should himself be less merciful?

Let me forgive myself of my terrible sins
That I may have peace.

Let me have mercy on myself
Or I will hang myself on a juniper tree
To wipe out my guilt.

There will be flints and grits forever in my bed.
There will be cinders in my mush.

I am burned black.
I am back from a bitter journey.
I have cruised hell.

Let me forgive myself
That thought to be a saint
And am proved a monster.

That thought to be righteous and good,
And am proved vile.

That thought myself to be the Christ
And am found the Devil.

Windless, the air dead, the night hot.
Can I find, in fact, the friendliness of a human face?

Forgive me, O God, that my heart should hold such horrors.

The vast desert stars.
The waterless ridges.
The vacant gullies.

When I am proved out
I will come back to my people
And confess my crimes.

For I will make friends of the sinner
And comfort him in his plight.
I will pick the evildoer up from the ground

That he may take heart from his evil
And hunger the good.

I will bless the bad,
That he may be brought from madness,
May be made whole.

Speechless the stars.
No word in the wind.
The hell of nature defiled
Shuts her dread face.

For there is no man that is righteous
But carries somewhere in his salty heart
A worse villainy.

Never a man without his vices.
If any man doubts it
He has not sunk to the whoredom of his heart,
Nor tongued his own flesh.

Our loves betray us.
We give ourselves to God
And in our faithlessness
Play strumpet to the devil.

Thus it is that my hate is scribbled about my mouth
And my lust rings my eyes.

My guilt is blistered upon my hands.
They have prized blood.
They are dabbed with sin.

O my God, my God, what can I say
Except that Thou hast touched me?

In sleep, in deep slumber,
In the raw desert night,
Thou didst send Thy holy devils

There to accost me.
As Thy terrible henchmen
They did show me me.

What visions of vastness on the moon-sunken wastes?
So dry is the night the dust-devils wander,
They whisper me out.

I will go back once more to the city of man,
Will abase myself before the sinner
For he is cleaner than I.

At least he never has claimed to be good,
Nor supposed himself righteous.

At least he does not swear by Thy truth
And live by his lies.

At least he does not bless with the one hand
While he horribly defiles with the other.

Forgive me, dear Christ, and make me as Thyself,
Who knew Thy true Self.

Hot night. The crude desert stars. The devouring distances.
There is not a coyote's howl to quaver the darkness.
There is not the scuttle of a deermouse nor the slow drag of
  a serpent.
There is not the mutter of a single leaf
So heavy hangs the air.

O my soul, my soul, what deaths, what pits, what savageries,
  what wastes!

If I could touch so much as a piece of human dung
That some hapless wanderer dropped by a yucca
I should consider myself not friendless.

But my thoughts return upon me

And I dare not sleep,
For I am in dread of my dreams.

Therefore in the morning will I go forth
And return to the ways of man.

I will seek God henceforth in the shameful human face.
I will serve God in the wretched human act.
I will savour God in the salt of human tears.

In the body's corruptness will He be revealed to me,
In the postures of defloration,
In the deeds of wrath.

Where the murderer strangles his hope,
Where the thief plunders his heart,
Where the ogler gloats and gloats on his own self
And gloating profanes.

Out of these, out of these, will Thy peace shine forth
If I show pity.

No day? No dawn? No water? No wet?
A drop of grace for my parched tongue,
One drop would suffice me.

Forgive me, that my heart was vicious.
In my viciousness of heart
I coupled the bitch.

But in the spate of such hardness
Thou didst come to redeem me.
Hadst Thou not discovered my sin to myself
Thou couldst never have touched me to forgive me.
Therefore blessed is my sin.

I will seek out a human face that I may know pity.
That I might betray and be forgiven.
That I might be betrayed and forgive.

I will seek love in the face of a man
And pity in the eyes of a woman.

I will seek faith in the brow of a child.

I will return to my mother,
To the breasts of her that nursed me,
To the lap of her that bore me.

And I will find my father.
He will bless my head.
He will forgive me.

Therefore will I be whole again,
And be made new again,
And again be made as a child.

For the night is dark.
But off in the east I see low light.
I smell the dawn.

And will find my God in the thwarted love that breaks
   between us!

VI

# Allen Ginsberg

## AMERICA

America I've given you all and now I'm nothing.
America two dollars and twentyseven cents January 17, 1956.
I can't stand my own mind.
America when will we end the human war?
Go fuck yourself with your atom bomb.
I don't feel good don't bother me.
I won't write my poem till I'm in my right mind.
America when will you be angelic?
When will you take off your clothes?
When will you look at yourself through the grave?
When will you be worthy of your million Trotskyites?
America why are your libraries full of tears?
America when will you send your eggs to India?
I'm sick of your insane demands.
When can I go into the supermarket and buy what I need
    with my good looks?
America after all it is you and I who are perfect not the next
    world.
Your machinery is too much for me.
You made me want to be a saint.
There must be some other way to settle this argument.
Burroughs is in Tangiers I don't think he'll come back it's
    sinister.
Are you being sinister or is this some form of practical joke?
I'm trying to come to the point.
I refuse to give up my obsession.

America stop pushing I know what I'm doing.

America the plum blossoms are falling.

I haven't read the newspapers for months, everyday somebody goes on trial for murder.

America I feel sentimental about the Wobblies.

America I used to be a communist when I was a kid I'm not sorry.

I smoke marijuana every chance I get.

I sit in my house for days on end and stare at the roses in the closet.

When I go to Chinatown I get drunk and never get laid.

My mind is made up there's going to be trouble.

You should have seen me reading Marx.

My psychoanalyst thinks I'm perfectly right.

I won't say the Lord's Prayer.

I have mystical visions and cosmic vibrations.

America I still haven't told you what you did to Uncle Max after he came over from Russia.

I'm addressing you.

Are you going to let your emotional life be run by Time Magazine?

I'm obsessed by Time Magazine.

I read it every week.

Its cover stares at me every time I slink past the corner candystore.

I read it in the basement of the Berkeley Public Library.

It's always telling me about responsibility. Businessmen are serious. Movie producers are serious. Everybody's serious but me.

It occurs to me that I am America.

I am talking to myself again.

Asia is rising against me.

I haven't got a chinaman's chance.

I'd better consider my national resources.

My national resources consist of two joints of marijuana millions of genitals an unpublishable private literature that goes 1400 miles an hour and twentyfive-thousand mental institutions.

I say nothing about my prisons nor the millions of
    underprivileged who live in my flowerpots under the light
    of five hundred suns.
I have abolished the whorehouses of France, Tangiers is the
    next to go.
My ambition is to be President despite the fact that I'm a
    Catholic.


America how can I write a holy litany in your silly mood?
I will continue like Henry Ford my strophes are as individual
    as his automobiles more so they're all different sexes.
America I will sell you strophes $2500 apiece $500 down on
    your old strophe
America free Tom Mooney
America save the Spanish Loyalists
America Sacco & Vanzetti must not die
America I am the Scottsboro boys.
America when I was seven momma took me to Communist
    Cell meetings they sold us garbanzos a handful per ticket
    a ticket costs a nickel and the speeches were free everybody
    was angelic and sentimental about the workers it was all
    so sincere you have no idea what a good thing the party was
    in 1935 Scott Nearing was a grand old man a real mensch
    Mother Bloor made me cry I once saw Israel Amter plain.
    Everybody must have been a spy.
America you don't really want to go to war.
America it's them bad Russians.
Them Russians them Russians and them Chinamen. And them
    Russians.
The Russia wants to eat us alive. The Russia's power mad.
    She wants to take our cars from out our garages.
Her wants to grab Chicago. Her needs a Red Readers' Digest.
    Her wants our auto plants in Siberia. Him big bureaucracy
    running our fillingstations.
That no good. Ugh. Him make Indians learn read. Him need
    big black niggers. Hah. Her make us all work sixteen hours
    a day. Help.
America this is quite serious.
America this is the impression I get from looking in the
    television set.

225

America is this correct?

I'd better get right down to the job.

It's true I don't want to join the Army or turn lathes in precision parts factories, I'm nearsighted and psychopathic anyway.

America I'm putting my queer shoulder to the wheel.

# A SUPERMARKET IN CALIFORNIA

What thoughts I have of you tonight, Walt Whitman, for I walked down the sidestreets under the trees with a headache self-conscious looking at the full moon.

In my hungry fatigue, and shopping for images, I went into the neon fruit supermarket, dreaming of your enumerations!

What peaches and what penumbras! Whole families shopping at night! Aisles full of husbands! Wives in the avocados, babies in the tomatoes!—and you, Garcia Lorca, what were you doing down by the watermelons?

I saw you, Walt Whitman, childless, lonely old grubber, poking among the meats in the refrigerator and eyeing the grocery boys.

I heard you asking questions of each: Who killed the pork chops? What price bananas? Are you my Angel?

I wandered in and out of the brilliant stacks of cans following you, and followed in my imagination by the store detective.

We strode down the open corridors together in our solitary fancy tasting artichokes, possessing every frozen delicacy, and never passing the cashier.

Where are we going, Walt Whitman? The doors close in an hour. Which way does your beard point tonight?

(I touch your book and dream of our odyssey in the supermarket and feel absurd.)

Will we walk all night through solitary streets? The trees add shade to shade, lights out in the houses, we'll both be lonely.

Will we stroll dreaming of the lost America of love past blue automobiles in driveways, home to our silent cottage?

Ah, dear father, graybeard, lonely old courage-teacher, what America did you have when Charon quit poling his ferry and you got out on a smoking bank and stood watching the boat disappear on the black waters of Lethe?

BERKELEY, 1955

# WICHITA VORTEX SUTRA

I

Turn Right Next Corner
            *The Biggest Little Town in Kansas*
                        *Macpherson*
Red sun setting flat plains west streaked
            with gauzy veils, chimney mist spread
            around christmas-tree bulbed refineries—aluminum
            white tanks squat beneath
            winking signal towers' bright plane-lights,
                        orange gas flares
            beneath pillows of smoke, flames in machinery—
                        transparent towers at dusk

*In advance of the Cold Wave*
            *Snow is spreading eastward to*
                        *the Great Lakes*
      News Broadcast & old clarinets
            Watertower dome Lighted on the flat plain
                  car radio speeding acrost railroad tracks—

Kansas! Kansas! Shuddering at last!
            PERSON appearing in Kansas!
            angry telephone calls to the University
            Police dumbfounded leaning on
                        their radiocar hoods
            While Poets chant to Allah in the roadhouse Showboat!
Blue eyed children dance and hold thy Hand O aged Walt
            who came from Lawrence to Topeka to envision
                  Iron interlaced upon the city plain—
      Telegraph wires strung from city to city O Melville!
                  Television brightening thy *rills of Kansas lone*
I come,
            lone man from the void, riding a bus
            hypnotized by red tail lights on the straight
                        space road ahead—
      & the Methodist minister with cracked eyes
                        leaning over the table

                    quoting Kierkegaard 'death of God'
                                    a million dollars
            in the bank   owns all West Wichita
                                        come to Nothing!
                    Prajnaparamita Sutra over coffee—Vortex
            of telephone radio aircraft assembly frame ammunition
            petroleum nightclub Newspaper streets illuminated by Bright
                                            EMPTINESS—

            Thy sins are forgiven, Wichita!
                            Thy lonesomeness annulled, O Kansas dear!
                                    as the western Twang prophesied
                    thru banjo, when lone cowboy walked the railroad track
                            past an empty station toward the sun
                        sinking giant-bulbed orange down the box canyon—
                    Music strung over his back
                        and empty handed   singing on this planet earth
                                    I'm a lonely Dog, O Mother!
            Come, Nebraska, sing & dance with me—
                    Come lovers of Lincoln and Omaha,
                                    hear my soft voice at last
            As Babes need the chemical touch of flesh in pink infancy
                    lest they die Idiot returning to Inhuman—
                                                Nothing—
            So, tender lipt adolescent girl, pale youth,
                                    give me back my soft kiss
                    Hold me in your innocent arms,
                            accept my tears as yours to harvest
                            equal     in nature to the Wheat
                        that made your bodies' muscular bones
                            broad shouldered, boy bicept—
                        from leaning on cows & drinking Milk
                                            in Midwest Solitude—
            No more fear of tenderness, much delight in weeping, ecstasy
                    in singing, laughter rises that confounds
                            staring Idiot mayors
                                and stony politicians eyeing
                                Thy breast,
                                    O Man of America, be born!
            Truth breaks through!
                    How big is the prick of the President?
                    How big is Cardinal Viet-Nam?
            How little the prince of the F.B.I., unmarried all these years!
                    How big are all the Public Figures?
            What kind of flesh hangs, hidden behind their Images?

                                          Approaching Salina,
Prehistoric excavation, *Apache Uprising*
                              in the drive-in theater
        Shelling Bombing Range     mapped in the distance,
        Crime Prevention Show, sponsor Wrigley's Spearmint
        Dinosaur Sinclair advertisement, glowing green—
South 9th Street lined with poplar & elm branch
                spread over evening's tiny headlights—
Salinas Highschool's brick darkens Gothic
                        over a night-lit door—
What wreaths of naked bodies, thighs and faces,
                small hairy bun'd vaginas,
                silver cocks, armpits and breasts
                moistened by tears
                        for 20 years, for 40 years?
Peking Radio surveyed by Luden's Coughdrops
                Attacks on the Russians & Japanese,
Big Dipper leaning above the Nebraska border,
                handle down to the blackened plains,
        telephone-pole ghosts crossed
                        by roadside, dim headlights—
        dark night, & giant T-bone steaks,
                and in *The Village Voice*
        New Frontier Productions present
                Camp Comedy: *Fairies I Have Met.*
Blue highway lamps strung along the horizon east at Hebron
                Homestead National Monument near Beatrice—

Language, language
        black Earth-circle in the rear window,
                no cars for miles along highway
        beacon lights on oceanic plain
        language, language
                over Big Blue River
                chanting *La Illaha El* ('*lill*) *Allah Who*
                revolving my head to my heart like my mother
                chin abreast at Allah
                        Eyes closed, blackness
vaster than midnight prairies,
                Nebraskas of solitary Allah,
                        Joy, I am I
                        the lone One singing to myself
                                God come true—
                        Thrills of fear,

*231*

nearer than the vein in my neck—?
What if I opened my soul to sing to my absolute self
      Singing as the car crash chomped thru blood & muscle
                                 tendon skull?
      What if I sang, and loosed the chords of fear brow?
          What exquisite noise wd
                    shiver my car companions?
      I am the Universe tonite
              riding in all my Power riding
chauffeured thru my self by a long haired saint with eyeglasses
What if I sang till Students knew I was free
    of Viet-Nam, trousers, free of my own meat,
   free to die in my thoughtful shivering Throne?
         freer than Nebraska, freer than America,
              May I disappear
          in magic Joy-smoke! Pouf! reddish Vapor,
Faustus vanishes weeping & laughing
     under stars on Highway 77 between Beatrice & Lincoln—
    "Better not to move but let things be" Reverend Preacher?
         We've all already disappeared!


Space highway open, entering Lincoln's ear
    ground to a stop Tracks Warning
              Pioneer Boulevard—
   William Jennings Bryan sang
   *Thou shalt not crucify mankind upon a cross of Gold!*
           O Baby Doe! Gold's
   Department Store hulks o'er 10th Street now
 —an unregenerate old flop who didn't want to be a monkey
now's the Highest Perfect Wisdom dust
     and Lindsay's cry
    survives compassionate in the Highschool Anthology—
a giant dormitory brilliant on the evening plain
             drifts with his memories—
There's a nice white door over there
         for me O dear!    on Zero Street.
*February 15, 1966*


II

Face the Nation
Thru Hickman's rolling earth hills
     icy winter
         grey sky    bare trees lining the road

South to Wichita
   you're in the Pepsi Generation  Signum enroute
Aiken Republican on the radio    60,000
   Northvietnamese troops now infiltrated but over 250,000
   South Vietnamese  armed men
       our Enemy—
         Not Hanoi our enemy
         Not China our enemy
           The Viet Cong!
      MacNamara made a "bad guess"
"Bad Guess" chorused the Reporters?
   Yes, no more than a Bad Guess, in 1962
       "8000 American Troops handle the
        Situation"
        Bad Guess
  in 1956, 80% of the
    Vietnamese people would've voted for Ho Chi Minh
    wrote Ike  years later  *Mandate for Change*
       A bad guess in the Pentagon
And the Hawks were guessing all along
       Bomb China's 200,000,000
       cried Stennis from Mississippi
       I guess it was 3 weeks ago
  Holmes Alexander in Albuquerque Journal
    Provincial newsman
     said I guess we better begin to do that Now.
     his typewriter clacking in his aged office
     on a side street  under Sandia Mountain?
     Half the world away from China
Johnson got some bad advice  Republican Aiken sang
to the Newsmen over the radio
   The General guessed they'd stop infiltrating the South
    if they bombed the North—
     So I guess they bombed!
  Pale Indochinese boys came thronging thru the jungle
     in increased numbers
     to the scene of TERROR!
While the triangle-roofed Farmer's Grain Elevator
  sat quietly by the side of the road
    along the railroad track
  American Eagle beating its wings over Asia
    million dollar helicopters
    a billion dollars worth of Marines
     who loved *Aunt Betty*

Drawn from the shores and farms shaking
from the high schools to the landing barge
blowing the air thru their cheeks with fear
in *Life* on Television
Put it this way on the radio
Put it this way in television language
Use the words
language, language:
"A bad guess"

Put it this way in headlines
Omaha World Herald— *Rusk says Toughness*
*Essential for Peace*
Put it this way
Lincoln Nebraska morning Star—
*Vietnam War Brings Prosperity*
Put it *this* way
Declared MacNamara,    speaking language
Asserted Maxwell Taylor
General, Consultant to White House
Vietcong losses leveling up three five zero zero
per month
Front page testimony February '66
Here in Nebraska same as Kansas same known in Saigon
in Peking, in Moscow, same known
by the youths of Liverpool three five zero zero
the latest quotation in the human meat market—
Father I cannot tell a lie!


A black horse bends its head to the stubble
beside the silver stream winding thru the woods
by an antique red barn on the outskirts of Beatrice—
Quietness, quietness
over this countryside
except for unmistakable signals on radio
followed by the honkytonk tinkle
of a city piano
to calm the nerves of taxpaying housewives of a Sunday morn.
Has anyone looked in the eyes of the dead?
U.S. Army recruiting service sign *Careers With A Future*
Is anyone living to look for future forgiveness?
Water hoses frozen on the street, the
Crowd gathered to see a strange happening garage—
Red flames on Sunday morning
in a quiet town!

Has anyone looked in the eyes of the wounded?
Have we seen but paper faces, Life Magazine?
Are screaming faces made of dots,
electric dots on Television—
fuzzy decibels registering
the mammal voiced howl
from the outskirts of Saigon to console model picture tubes
in Beatrice, in Hutchinson, in El Dorado
in historic Abilene
O inconsolable!

Stop, and eat more flesh.
"We will negotiate anywhere anytime"
said the giant President
Kansas City Times 2/14/66: "Word reached U.S. authorities that
Thailand's leaders feared that in Honolulu Johnson might have
tried to persuade South Vietnam's rulers to ease their stand against
negotiating with the Viet Cong.
American officials said these fears were groundless and Hum-
phrey was telling the Thais so."
A.P. dispatch
The last week's paper is Amnesia.
Three five zero zero is numerals
Headline language poetry, nine decades after Democratic Vistas
and the Prophecy of the Good Grey Poet
Our nation "of the fabled damned"
or else . . .
Language, language
Ezra Pound the Chinese Written Character for truth
defined as man standing by his word
Word picture:        forked creature
Man
standing by a box, birds flying out
representing mouth speech
Ham Steak please waitress, in the warm cafe.
Different from a bad guess.
The war is language
language abused
for Advertisement,
language used
like magic for power on the planet:
Black Magic language,
formulas for reality—
Communism is a 9 letter word

235

                    used by inferior magicians with
the wrong alchemical formula for transforming earth into gold
            —funky warlocks operating on guesswork,
                    handmedown mandrake terminology
                          that never worked in 1956
        for grey-domed Dulles,
                          brooding over at State,
            that never worked for Ike who knelt to take
                the magic wafer in his mouth
                                from Dulles' hand
                      inside the church in Washington:
Communion of bum magicians
                congress of failures from Kansas & Missouri
        working with the wrong equations
        Sorcerer's Apprentices who lost control
                of the simplest broomstick in the world:
                                Language
O longhaired magician come home take care of your dumb helper
        before the radiation deluge floods your livingroom,
                          your magic errandboy's
                          just made a bad guess again
                    that's lasted a whole decade.

N B C B S U P A P I N S L I F E
        Time Mutual presents
            World's Largest Camp Comedy:
                        Magic in Vietnam—
        reality turned inside out
                changing its sex in the Mass Media
                for 30 days, TV den and bedroom farce
Flashing pictures Senate Foreign Relations Committee room
        Generals faces flashing on and off screen
                                        mouthing language
        State Secretary speaking nothing but language
        MacNamara declining to speak public language
            The President talking language,
                        Senators reinterpreting language
            General Taylor *Limited Objectives*
                                *Owls* from Pennsylvania
                    Clark's Face *Open Ended*
                            Dove's *Apocalypse*
                            Morse's hairy ears
        Stennis orating in Mississippi
                    half billion chinamen crowding into the
                                        polling booth,

Clean shaven Gen. Gavin's image
                              imagining *Enclaves*
           *Tactical Bombing* the magic formula for
        a silver haired Symington:
     Ancient Chinese apothegm:
                *Old in vain.*
        Hawks swooping thru the newspapers
              talons visible
        wings outspread in the giant updraft of hot air
                    loosing their dry screech in the skies
                                over the Capitol
Napalm and black clouds emerging in newsprint
        Flesh soft as a Kansas girl's
                ripped open by metal explosion—
        three five zero zero    on the other side of the planet
            caught in barbed wire, fire ball
            bullet shock, bayonet electricity
        bomb blast terrific in skull & belly, shrapnelled
                                    throbbing meat
While this American nation argues war:
                conflicting language, language
                        proliferating in airwaves
        filling the farmhouse ear, filling
            the City Manager's head in his oaken office
            the professor's head in his bed at midnight
            the pupil's head at the movies
                blond haired, his heart throbbing with desire
                for the girlish image bodied on the screen:
                    or smoking cigarettes
                            and watching Captain Kangaroo
                            that fabled damned of nations
                            prophecy come true—
Though the highway's straight,
        dipping downward through low hills,
        rising narrow on the far horizon
            black cows browse in caked fields
                ponds in the hollows lie frozen,
                        quietness.
In this the land that started war on China?
        This be the soil that thought Cold War for decades?
        Are these nervous naked trees & farmhouses
                            the vortex
                        of oriental anxiety molecules
     that've imagined    American Foreign Policy

and magick'd up paranoia in Peking
and curtains of living blood
surrounding far Saigon?
Are these the towns where the language emerged
from the mouths here
that makes a Hell of riots in Dominica
sustains the aging tyrany of Chiang in silent Taipeh city
Paid for the lost French war in Algeria
overthrew the Guatemalan polis in '54
maintaining United Fruit's bannana greed
another thirteen years
for the secret prestige of the Dulles family lawfirm?

Here's Marysville—
a black railroad engine in the children's park,
at rest—
and the Track Crossing
with Cotton Belt flatcars
carrying autos west from Dallas
Delaware & Hudson gondolas filled with power stuff—
a line of boxcars far east as the eye can see
carrying battle goods to cross the Rockies
into the hands of rich longshoreman loading
ships on the Pacific—
Oakland Army Terminal lights
blue illumined all night now—
Crash of couplings and the great American train
moves on carrying its cushioned load of metal doom
Union Pacific linked together with your Hoosier Line
followed by passive Wabash
rolling behind
all Erie carrying cargo in the rear,
Central Georgia's rust colored truck proclaiming
*The Right Way*, concluding
the awesome poet writ by the train
across northern Kansas,
land which gave right of way
to the massing of metal meant for explosion
in Indochina—
Passing thru Waterville,
Electronic machinery in the bus humming prophecy—
paper signs blowing in cold wind,
mid-Sunday afternoon's silence
in town

under frost-grey sky
                    that covers the horizon—
That the rest of earth is unseen,
                    an outer universe invisible,
          Unknown except thru
                              language
                              airprint
                                        magic images

     or prophecy of the secret
               heart the same
          in Waterville as Saigon one human form:
     When a woman's heart burst in Waterville
               a woman screams equal in Hanoi—
On to Wichita to prophesy! O frightful Bard!
          into the heart of the Vortex
                    where anxiety rings
                         the University with millionaire pressure,
               lonely crank telephone voices sighing in dread,
          and students waken trembling in their beds
               with dreams of a new truth warm as meat,
               little girls suspecting their elders of murder
                    committed by remote control machinery,
          boys with sexual bellies aroused
               chilled in the heart by the mailman
          with a letter from an aging white haired General
               Director of selection for service in
                                        Deathwar
               all this black language
                         writ by machine!
               O hopeless Fathers and Teachers
               in Hué        do you know
                         the same woe too?


I'm an old man now, and a lonesome man in Kansas
          but not afraid
               to speak my lonesomeness in a car,
          because not only my lonesomeness
               it's Ours, all over America,
                         O tender fellows—
               & spoken lonesomeness is Prophecy
               in the moon 100 years ago or in
                         the middle of Kansas now.
It's not the vast plains mute our mouths
               that fill at midnite with ecstatic language

when our trembling bodies hold each other
                breast to breast on a mattress—
Not the empty sky that hides
                the feeling from our faces
nor our skirts and trousers that conceal
                the bodylove emanating in a glow of beloved skin,
                white smooth abdomen down to the hair
                                between our legs,
It's not a God that bore us that forbid
                our Being, like a sunny rose
                                all red with naked joy
                between our eyes & bellies, yes
All we do is for this frightened thing
                we call Love, want and lack—
fear that we aren't the one whose body could be
                beloved of all the brides of Kansas City,
                kissed all over by every boy of Wichita—
O but how many in their solitude weep aloud like me—
On the bridge over Republican River
                almost in tears to know
                                how to speak the right language—
                on the frosty broad road
                                uphill between highway embankments
                I search for the language
                                that is also yours—
                almost all our language has been taxed by war.
Radio antennae high tension
                wires ranging from Junction City across the plains—
highway cloverleaf sunk in a vast meadow
                lanes curving past Abilene
                                to Denver filled with old
                                                heroes of love—
                                to Wichita where McClure's mind
                                burst into animal beauty
                                drunk, getting laid in a car
                                                in a neon misted street
                                                15-years ago—
                to Independence where the old man's still alive
who loosed the bomb that's slaved all human consciousness
                                and made the body universe a place of fear—
Now, speeding along the empty plain,
                no giant demon machine
                                visible on the horizon
                but tiny human trees and wooden houses at the sky's edge

I claim my birthright!
                    reborn forever as long as Man
                              in Kansas or other universe—Joy
              reborn after the vast sadness of War Gods!
A lone man talking to myself, no house in the brown vastness to hear,
              imagining the throng of Selves
                        that make this nation one body of Prophecy
                              languaged by Declaration as
                                   Happiness!
I call all Powers of imagination
         to my side in this auto to make Prophecy,
                                        all Lords
              of human kingdoms to come
Shambu Bharti Baba naked covered with ash
              Khaki Baba fat-bellied mad with the dogs
Dehorahava Baba who moans Oh how wounded, How wounded
              Citaram Onkar Das Thakur who commands
                              give up your desire
Satyananda who raises two thumbs in tranquillity
              Kali Pada Guha Roy whose yoga drops before the void
                   Shivananda who touches the breast and says OM
Srimata Krishnaji of Brindaban who says take for your guru
              William Blake the invisible father of English visions
              Sri Ramakrishna master of ecstasy eyes
                   half closed who only cries for his mother
Chaitanya arms upraised singing & dancing his own praise
              merciful Chango judging our bodies
              Durga-Ma covered with blood
                        destroyer of battlefield illusions
              million-faced Tathagata gone past suffering
Preserver Harekrishna returning in the age of pain
Sacred Heart my Christ acceptable
              Allah the Compassionate One
                        Jaweh Righteous One
                   all Knowledge-Princes of Earth-man, all
              ancient Seraphim of heavenly Desire, Devas, yogis
                   & holymen I chant to—
                        Come to my lone presence
                              into this Vortex named Kansas,
I lift my voice aloud,
         make Mantra of American language now,
                   pronounce the words beginning my own millennium,
                        I here declare the end of the War!
                   Ancient days' Illusion!—

241

Let the States tremble,
        let the Nation weep,
                let Congress legislate its own delight
                        let the President execute his own desire—
this Act done by my own voice,
                        nameless Mystery—
published to my own senses,
                        blissfully received by my own form
        approved with pleasure by my sensations
        manifestation of my very thought
        accomplished in my own imagination
                all realms within my consciousness fulfilled
        60 miles from Wichita
                        near El Dorado,
                                The Golden One,
in chill earthly mist
        houseless brown farmland plains rolling heavenward
                                        in every direction
one midwinter afternoon Sunday called the day of the Lord—
        Pure Spring Water gathered in one tower
                        where Florence is
                                set on a hill,
                        stop for tea & gas

        Cars passing their messages along country crossroads
                to populaces cement-networked on flatness,
                                giant white mist on earth
                and a Wichita Eagle-Beacon headlines
                *"Kennedy Urges Cong Get Chair in Negotiations"*
The War is gone,
        Language emerging on the motel news stand,
                                the right magic
                Formula, the language known
        in the back of the mind before, now in black print
                                daily consciousness
Eagle News Services Saigon—
        Headline Surrounded Vietcong Charge Into Fire Fight
                the suffering not yet ended
                                for others
                The last spasms of the dragon of pain
                        shoot thru the muscles
                        a crackling around the eyeballs
                        of a sensitive yellow boy by a muddy wall
Continued from page one        area

242

after the Marines killed 256 Vietcong captured 31
ten day operation Harvest Moon last December
                              Language language
U.S. Military Spokesmen
                Language language
                    Cong death toll
        has soared to 100 in First Air Cavalry
        Division's Sector of
                    Language language
            Operation White Wing near Bong Son
Some of the
        Language language
                Communist
                        Language language soldiers
charged so desperately
            they were struck with six or seven bullets before they fell
        Language Language M 60 Machine Guns
                Language language in La Drang Valley
        the terrain is rougher infested with leeches and scorpions
                The war was over several hours ago!
Oh at last again the radio opens
        blue Invitations!
            Angelic Dylan singing across the nation
                    "When all your children start to resent you
                    Won't you come see me, Queen Jane?"
        His youthful voice making glad
                        the brown endless meadows
        His tenderness penetrating aether,
            soft prayer on the airwaves,
                Language language, and sweet music too
                even unto thee,
                        hairy flatness!
            even unto thee
                    despairing Burns!


Future speeding on swift wheels
            straight to the heart of Wichita!
Now radio voices cry population hunger world
                    of unhappy people
            waiting for Man to be born
                    O man in America!
        *you certainly smell good*
                    the radio says
    passing mysterious families of winking towers

243

grouped round a quonset-hut on a hillock—
feed storage or military fear factory here?
Sensitive City, Ooh! Hamburger & Skelley's Gas
lights feed man and machine,
Kansas Electric Substation aluminum robot
signals thru thin antennae towers
above the empty football field

at Sunday dusk
to a solitary derrick that pumps oil from the unconscious
working night & day
& factory gas-flares edge a huge golf course
where tired businessmen can come and play—
Cloverleaf, Merging Traffic East Wichita turnoff
McConnel Airforce Base
nourishing the city—
Lights rising in the suburbs
Supermarket Texaco brilliance starred
over streetlamp vertebrae on Kellogg,
green jewelled traffic lights
confronting the windshield,
Centertown ganglion entered!
Crowds of autos moving with their lightshine,
signbulbs winking in the driver's eyeball—
The human nest collected, neon lit,
and sunburst signed
for business as usual, except on the Lord's Day—
Redeemer Lutheran's three crosses lit on the lawn
reminder of our sins
and Titsworth offers insurance on Hydraulic
by De Voors Guard's Mortuary for outmoded bodies
of the human vehicle
which no Titsworth of insurance will customise
for resale—
So home, traveller, past the newspaper language factory
under Union Station railroad bridge on Douglas
to the center of the Vortex, calmly returned
to Hotel Eaton—
Carry Nation began the war on Vietnam here
with an angry smashing axe
attacking Wine—
Here fifty years ago, by her violence
began a vortex of hatred that defoliated the Mekong Delta—
Proud Wichita! vain Wichita
cast the first stone!—

That murdered my mother
who died of the communist anticommunist psychosis
in the madhouse one decade long ago
complaining about wires of masscommunication in her head
and phantom political voices in the air
besmirching her girlish character.
Many another has suffered death and madness
in the Vortex from Hydraulic
to the end of 17th—enough!
The war is over now—
Except for the souls
held prisoner in Niggertown
still pining for love of your tended white bodies O children of
Wichita!

# Philip Lamantia

## AUTOMATIC WORLD

The sun has drowned
virgins are no more
there is no need for understanding
but there is so much to see

So come with me
down the boulevard
of crawling veins
Don't be afraid
blood is cheap!

A paradise song?
A dirty story?
A love sonnet?
Scream it out!
Then we'll have the human walls
tumbling down to meet our march
into the raw-meat city!

The velvet robes are strewn
across the landscape
We step upon the sidewalk
that goes up and down
up to the clouds
down to the starving people
Don't ask me what to do!

Keep on going
we'll end up somewhere fast
on the moon perhaps!

Rainbow guns are dancing
in front of the movie queens
Everyone is laughing
flying dying
never knowing when to rest
never knowing when to eat

And the fountains come falling
out of her thistle-covered breasts
and the dogs are happy
and the clowns are knifing
and the ballerinas are eating stone

O the mirror-like dirt
of freshly spilt blood
trickling down the walls
the walls that reach the stars!

O the flock of sheep
breaking their flesh open
with bones sucked
from the brothels!

O the grave of bats
sailing through shops
with the violent hands!

When will these come?
When will these go?

The sun is riding into your eye
virgins are bursting
from under my flaming palms
and we are slowly floating away

# THERE ARE MANY PATHWAYS
# TO THE GARDEN

If you are bound for the sun's empty plum
there is no need to mock the wine tongue
but if you are going to a rage of pennies
over a stevedore's wax ocean
then, remember: all long pajamas are frozen dust
unless an axe cuts my flaming grotto.

You are one for colonial lizards
and over bathhouses of your ear
skulls shall whisper
of a love for a crab's rude whip
and the rimless island of refusal shall seat itself
beside the corpse of a dog
that always beats a hurricane
in the mad run for Apollo's boxing glove.

As your fingers melt a desert
an attempt is made to marry the lily-and-fig-foot dragon
mermaids wander and play with a living cross
a child invents a sublime bucket of eyes
and I set free the dawn of your desires.

The crash of your heart
beating its way through a fever of fish
is heard in every crowd of that thirsty tomorrow
and your trip ends in the mask of my candle-lit hair.

# A CIVIL WORLD

In a moment their faces will be visible.

You shall see the women who walk in a night of offensive sunlight that cuts through their cardboard thighs.

As the street is cleaned by the presidents of the nation, I can see the bowlegged man moving over to copulate with the maniacs.

As a rose runs down an alley, a purple nugget, giving off some blood, is suspended in air.

The children who are ten feet tall are wet.

Their faces are scorched, their eyes cut by glass.

They play their games as a steeple topples, as a clown's laugh is heard in church.

Quietly the mothers are killing their sons; quietly the fathers are raping their daughters.

But the women.

The eye wanders to a garden in the middle of the street.

There are poets dipping their diamond-like heads in the luminous fountain. There are grandmothers playing with the delicate toys of the chimera. There are perfumes being spilt on the garbage. There is a drunken nun flying out of a brothel.

The women are all colors.

Their breasts open like flowers, their flesh spreads over the park like a blanket. Their hair is soaked in the blood of their lovers, those who are the mirrors of this night.

The naked lovers! All of them, fifteen years old! One can still see their hair growing! They come from the mountains, from the stars even, with their handsome eyes of stone. Ah, these somnambulistic lovers, with their bellies full of arrows!

After the street has recaptured its loneliness, a precious stone casts its light on the perambulator I am to enter. One perambulator in the center of a world. A poet—far away in the mountains—can be heard chanting like an ape. I wonder when he will stop?

# INSIDE THE JOURNEY

Quickly, I rocked between waves. Quickly, I got the god on the wing. Quickly, I picked the tarn from the twirling top. Quickly and quickly, and faster, faster: for the kill of the body's anger, for the win of the lost child, for the fall of wizards through revolving sheets of snow.

And so I walked all the streets become one street among the renegades who go unmolested, half-asleep, to the gardens of childhood—in the largess of a white love once a pink, pearl-shaped object on the horizon of their longing; a white love in a black space—no time in the land of nothing but time.

And this was my dream that lasted from some dawn to some midnight in the fallingdown room overlooking the oldest graveyard of Manhattan:

the poisonous stars:  *benign*
the rootless tree:  *nailed to the sky*
the black pit:  *enclosing ladders of white light*
the icebergs of the mind:  *floating to the tropics . . .*

For a long time I saw no other sky than the ceiling of this room where, from a chink of plaster, hung the image of paradise I embarked for like a ship to the Orient. I could hardly move my head. I could hardly say the word to ask for water. I could hardly conceive of *another* life. I threw the hex down, I swallowed the spells, I put the tumult down. If I spoke I would violate the wonder of that silence. If I moved, I would break across space like a knife cutting cheese. I knew all the constellations of infinite duration where my thoughts that flew away one day waited like brides for their bridegrooms of the infinite.

In another time, I was making blueprints for the Eternal, but the work was interrupted by some ogre who jumped out from behind a slab of magenta sky, and I was mesmerized on the spot between the poison I was wiping from my lips and the face behind the face I saw looking at me from the sky I was using as a mirror.

Anyway, I broke the spell. But another wave of invented emotions sank and another light fell on the crest of the wave: escape was a door I kept shutting all around me AND on those who were carving me, symbolically they said, for the first course at the restaurant for the initiates of the lake of love —which is to say, sperm ran high that year, breaking over the brains of those who know how to conduct themselves properly in *this* world: which is to say, life goes on gathering wool for the mothers of all the daughters whose tongues spit live lobsters and whose insatiable desire for some seasalt paradise makes thunder break in my skull: which is to say, very simply and without metaphor, that my brain was oppressing me.

—And that is not the most of it—for I took a look into the great vacuum of *this* world, in order that the journey in space of that life that puts poetry to shame, since it strained at the risk of all my senses becoming nil and hurtled me further into abysmal giddiness, would terminate at the junction where I might be able to move while in a state of suspended animation, since if I did not move in the vacuum the vacuum would move within me. And this movement of what is lusting to annihilate the sense of life (instigating panic in the mind, heart and liver) and taking its place, therefore, within life itself—would only lead to my ejection from *this* world.

It is this Vacuum that makes possible that daily hell kept going to decimate the scapegoat inhabitants of the earth, inspiring nothing but apathy and further pollution, revolving on the sexual hydra—at one pole—and fed through the swine mongering mobs at the other pole, in order to do away with the memory of what WAS or MIGHT BE—and as I opened to IT I saw its Body that is a vast machinery, in perpetual motion, for the sole consumption of a certain kind of etherealized excrement transmuted out of the bestial layers of the human condition become entirely the cretinized image of God with whom, be it added, this machine copulates perpetually . . .

# HYPODERMIC LIGHT

It's absurd I can't bring my soul to the eye of odoriferous fire

my soul whose teeth never leave their cadavers
my soul twisted on rocks of mental freeways
my soul that hates music
I would rather not see the Rose in my thoughts take on
   illusionary prerogatives
it is enough to have eaten bourgeois testicles
it is enough that the masses are all sodomites
Good Morning
the ships are in I've brought the gold to burn Moctezuma
I'm in a tipi joking with seers I'm smoking yahnah
I'm in a joint smoking marijuana with a cat who looks like
   Jesus Christ
heroin is a door always opened by white women
my first act of treason was to be born!
I'm at war with the Zodiac
my suffering comes on as a fire going out O beautiful world
   contemplation!

It's a fact my soul is smoking!

☐

That the total hatred wants to annihilate me!
it's the sickness of american pus against which I'm
   hallucinated
I'm sick of language
I want this wall I see under my eyes break up and shatter you
I'm talking all the poems after God
I want the table of visions to send me oriole opium
A state of siege

It's possible to live directly from elementals! hell stamps out
    vegetable spirits, zombies attack heaven! the marvelous put
    down by martial law, America fucked by a stick of
    marijuana
paper money larded for frying corpses!

HERE comes the Gorgon! THERE'S the outhouse!

        Come up from dead things, anus of the sun!

□

old after midnight spasm
juke box waits for junk
round about midnight music
combing bop hair
getting ready to cook
Jupiter wails!
heroins of visionary wakeup in light of Bird and The Going
    Forth By Day
the pipe's spiritual brain winters off the Nile old hypodermic
    needle under foot of Anubis
                    Mother Death
I'm at the boat of Ra Set
I'm Osiris hunting stars his black tail of the sun!
It's the end of melancholy    sad    bop    midnights.

□

They shot me full of holes at Kohlema's hut!
It's you who'll be butchered in my precise imagination
It'll be hard to withstand the reasoning of peyotl Rack

    many times my song went downstairs, people of entire hate
and I burned you in basements without tearing my face up
O people I hate the most! glass automobiles snake by to decay
    decay is living anthill
where yr automobiles lift their skirts and stiff
pricks of dead indians going in reverse
automobile graveyards where I eat fenders, bodies I crunch

mustards of engines I devour whole gallons of molding
chrome I whip cheese from cannibal hoods

O beautiful people of hate! your money fenders how creamy!
your electric eyes stinking! your geometric reconstructions
against my destructions!

## U.S.S. San Francisco

No one completes a sentence I am in hell to complete it
above the cobalt bomb magic fog crawls in the hideous park
   of addicts
I buy ectoplasmic peanut butter
roaming streets empty of opium bridges open only to the
   south
Everyone has left
my compass points to the fifth direction in space your
   typewriter eyes
The beautiful Lul in a fog of peacocks
The beautiful Lul with swans in her face
The beautiful Lul turned into a statue floating the lake
The beautiful Lul who has taken my veins tied them to the
   bark
The beautiful Lul a vapor
her breasts vapor
her fingers vapor
her breasts vapor the beautiful Lul with lips
the beautiful lips of Lul phantom of the beautiful Lul
How ugly yr typewriter eyes not like the eyes of Lul gone a
   vapor
not like the last puff of opium gone a phantom vapor
O Lul I swim from albatross shark fins in game of light
O Lul your head gone to Egypt
O Lul your head city of Indian sand
O Lul
I stamp out roses of fire
O Lul
I drown in your eyes The anchor of heroin is thrown forever!

☐

Immense blank void, melting structures, sperm steel, the last

roasted cock, geometry of inert horizontal planes, phases of
toxicomic monsters I open the door of the air!

My cock scratches the interior lint of fire, uncreated hair is
the net thru which vaginal/anal spiders feel out corners
of the universe—O cunt of bombs! true furniture for the
Creator's habitforming drugs.

An old man in a temple
shucking corn.

The Antiquities come out thru the curtain of Fuck, they have
reopened the holes of my arms
I keep chewing the leg of civilizations, at the origin of incest
morphine is equivalent to the apotheosis of cannibal
motherhood

Christ is a rocket ship

Every time I smoke a cigarette the Creator has blinked all
stars time pebbles of water in a trillion second of man's
sodomite existence my words can not lie!

It isn't a question of love it's how you find yourself out and
that, as the Master said, brings on anguish

"He who has known the world has found the body and he
who has found the body has known a corpse"

I see white alone from this horizontal plane of glass obscurity
the blackness I feed you is made to see white light

One day the quest for water was realized. I picked up arid
cactus I sucked out God and dreamt civilization. The quest
for water must go on!
            My friend keeps talking in my head of magic
herb Colombian Indians snort/shut their eyes seeing clouds
and float around like clouds
I'm looking for the seeds of the Virgin.

□

In camera of sempiternity you walk around figures molding
   dust

Amapola in white light Amapola before tribunes of furniture
   history
Amapola of Tepic in dreams of sand shore where spectral
   image of my friend John
Amapola of sempiternal Orient
black star of Amapola
white look of Amapola from a mountain of walls
Amapola commands night
seers shift in stars Amapola in clutches of white lice
escape of Amapola thru pyramids of lost light alone Amapola
   alone
flight of Corby night
Amapola in a forest of persian tapestries
Amapola the taste of spiritual sugar
                        Amapola in gardens of Araby
            Amapola born east   murdered in the west!

□


### This World's Beauty

So much for poetic prosodic bullshit
images crawl under this slice of windowpane
monkeys are caught in yr eyes
Simultaneous reality falls downstairs in a wheelchair
simultaneous reality I step on yr blue poppy head
Jeanlu is off in the forest combing sheep of hair
T is for mouth W for mandrake Ten is not a number
I fix the Vision by a snap of my cat's tail
you see world you see it not/going into the distances of the
   spirit
it is Sky, ancient heaven, microcosmos, that this poem
   breaks to

I look at smoke like a pillar of God
I go searching spirits of wood
Morgenroth fumbles the locks of dream eyes open
  Morgenroth
Morgenroth urinated on fields of marijuana eyes Morgenroth
spilled on swords of history Morgenroth I carve yr face by
  starspilled mariahs
Morgenroth who has made world upside down/tilted the
  earth again
Morgenroth shadow in the phantom's tail/maker of
  smokeballs/volcano eater!
Morgenroth is the reason reason has no reason for being
Morgenroth is soup thrown over the garden wall
Morgenroth is bombed out rotting baby chair MY
MARVELOUS KITE OF MORGENROTH!

# THE BRIDE FRONT AND BACK

*for Bruce Conner's "The BRIDE"*

Here's what you can put yr thrust into yr thrust in thrust into
thrust
into her
yuhu yoho yuhami
yugi yagi yug yug
uuugi agahama
gowhan in! put yr trust there! in yah go! yeba ya hiba ya hiba iba!

Mindless—puterin an letergo! my heap of hopskin hunk of hibi hollow
   hanging hung up hair of hails an horrible honies of higher learnings
lean on X polarial pains of pleasure SHOT BY WAX CANONS

NO MORE DIRECTIONS

TO YOU NAMELESS HIMALAYA salutations from the font of
   wisdom! may yr commanding Foot stink for Immortal noses—
                                   rhine deer!
TO YOU NAMELESS HIMALAYA I cringe in funicular aberrations
   of yr feline fenders
YOU NAMELESS HIMALAYA the name in smoke ice light
fog
   I'VE WAITED A MILLION YEARS FOR!
you sink named nameless unamable forever nameless NAMED
   HIMALAYA
you sink I walk under yr sex fountain THRU THE HIMALAYAN VEIL

Coming up to get going to cut thru to make it out to further future
       penetrations
           to swim out towards infinity

these are just words

BUT SHE IS SOLID AIR FOR SHE IS MOVED BY SALAMANDER
   MAKING MACHINES BUT SHE IS SPOTLESS
SHE IS ROCK OF SICK AGES
FOR I AM SICK TO HAVE HER FURLINED OR BEACHED
       IN FOAM A SOLID SEA HALLUCINATION—

WHAT SECRET DRUGS in her womb?
what watches out of her toenails tied to atomic submarine breasts?
Who's torn her open in dark turkish skyscraper ATLANTEAN PRIESTS
      SUNK HER IN BELL AT BELLY OF THE SEA
          The Christians have slaughtered themselves.

# THE MERMAIDS HAVE COME TO THE DESERT

The mermaids have come to the desert
They are setting up a boudoir next to the camel
who lies at their feet of roses

A wall of alabaster is drawn over their heads
by four rainbow men
whose naked figures give off a light
that slowly wriggles upon the sands

I am touched by the marvelous
as the mermaids' nimble fingers go through my hair
that has come down forever from my head
to cover my body:
a savage fruit of lunacy

Behold, the boudoir is flying away
and I am holding onto the leg of the lovely one
called beneath the sea
BIANCA
She is turning
with the charm of a bird
into two giant lips
as I drink from the goblet of suicide

She is the angelic doll turned black
She is the child of broken elevators
She is the curtain of holes you never want to throw away
She is the first woman and the first man
and I am lost to have her

I am looking for the region
where the smoke of your hair is thick

where you are again climbing over the white wall
where your eardrums play music
to the cat that crawls in my eyes
I am recalling memories of you BIANCA

I am looking beyond the hour and the day
to find you BIANCA

# Gail Dusenbery

## I CARRIED WITH ME POEMS

I carried with me poems, poems which spewed out of everything; I saw
   poems hanging from the clotheslines, hanging from the streetlamps:
   I saw poems glowing in the bushes, pushing out of the earth as
   tulips do;
I felt poems breathe in the dark March night like ghosts which squared
   and wheeled through the air;
I felt poems brushing the tops of chimneys, brushing by in the dark; I
   felt poems being born in the city, Venuses breaking through a
   shattered sea of mirrors;
   I felt all the poets of the city straining,
   isolated poets, knowing none of the others, straining;
I felt that some gazed into the March night, looking, and finding;
and others were running down the steep streets, seeking, and seeking to
embrace;
and others stood in empty bookstores turning over pages of fellow poets
  whom
   they loved but didn't know;
and some pondered over coffee growing cold, in harshly lit cafeterias, and
   gazed at the reflections of the eaters in the wall-to-wall mirrors;
some dwelt on what it was to grow old;
some dwelled on love;
some had gone out of time;
some, going out of time, looked back into time, and started;

I felt all of these lives and existences, all with poems at their center;
I knew none of these poets;
but I felt these intimations augured well, for me, and for poetry;
and my steps grew big, giant steps, I bounded down Parker Street,
a tall, taciturn, fast-walking poets' accomplice.

# THE MURDER POEM

The murder glowed from the center of the dark woods. It was dark red and muscular, beating, like a heart. In the center of the dark woods.

The Spanish actress in her hood and cloak stood at the edge of the wood. Her lips were red, her eyes were brown, and she had a joking handshake.

The White Ranger coursed the periphery of the cosmos, eternally separated from that which lay at its heart, by a constantly fluctuating barricade which crossed completely round the cosmos, never still, made of cellophane and stones, in constant motion, always between the White Ranger and the dark red glowing heart of the cosmos.

The White Ranger had been thrown off as the moon once was thrown off from the world; and now he circled about it, in absolute relation to it, a far-swinging radial course over which he galloped night and day, his white face always turned toward the wood.

Far on a northern island, perhaps one of the Hebrides, on a moonlit stony shore, a tall man with silvery hair chanted mystic incantations in a cave looking out to the sea. He wore a black cloak with a dark blue lining. He had long, old, white hands and long beautiful old fingers. He made signs; blessings; and chanted to himself and to the sea and to the moonlight gleaming on the stony beach.

The murder gleaming dark red at the heart of the woods. No one had committed it. It had committed itself. The Spanish actress in a red hood stood guardian to the wood. The northern Master of Secrets who saw all blessed and unblessed encompassed the murder within his knowing.

The White Ranger rode furiously in guilt, questioning himself. Had he meant to kill?

Turquoise and oranges shone from the cape of the Spanish actress. Her smile was long and somber. She occasionally beat her stick on the forest floor, with a dull rapping noise, against the earth.

And the Master of Secrets slid his hands together in a prayer or incantation.

Beads of sweat and anguish grew on the white face of the galloping Ranger. A giant fish grabbing his brain at the base of his skull was forcing him off his course. He felt the huge flounder guiding him from behind. His calves and thighs sunk into his Horse's sides, but then, horse and rider were slowly forced off the circle—charging, rearing, galloping, careering toward outermost black, with the giant fish propelling them from behind.

The teeth of the Spanish actress gleamed in a smile. She beat the wood with her stick.

The eyes of the Dhyanibuddha Master of Secrets twinkled, although his face was long and somber.

With a noiseless choking curse the White Ranger slid forward toward the blackness his horse underneath him a scream emanating from Ranger and Horse a bellowing blinding NAY of rider and horse indistinguishable. Together they charged into outermost black crashing and falling forward, always further and forward. NAY! NAY! bellowing horse and rider.

They both now rode astride a giant fish, a monstrous dark fish, who flew with them, forward, toward, what came on toward them, black, NAY! shrieking, rearing, pulling back but still forward toward release?

Turquoises shone on the dull orange scales of the flounder who was huger than the moon. Fish shone in the sky, turquoise and smoky orange, and the Spanish actress beat her stick, and the murder flared and flamed in the center of the wood.

Frightened and bound, the White Ranger was dragged before the court-cave. The Master of Secrets sat, with a tall pointed cap, fearfully embroidered, its silhouette nodding by the fire. Behind the court came the sloshing of the ocean against the stones. Very near. Very wet.

The White Ranger stood, eyeing the Master with a long askance glance, not believing what he saw or where he was. Hurt, bound, confused, still he stood half-sideways to them, total defiance and hatred of them apparent in his narrowed sideways doubting stare.

No women were there. The waves lapped at the stones. Beneath his embroidered cap, the face of the ancient Master of Secrets was indistinguishable from that of the bound, raging captive, the White Ranger. Feature for feature, the two faces were one.

Fire flickered. The White Ranger's face flickered, with hatred. And the magician's hand crackled, snapping out with length of arm and wand, toward the White Ranger, who despite his defiance, involuntarily drew back. The snap of the wand cracked open the cave and sea. The White Ranger grew taller and taller, his wand pinpointing the White Ranger. The White Ranger's shoulders grew like mountains and down the length of his wand he sighted the tiny microscopic figure of the tiny pinpointing White Ranger.

The murder gleamed and flared in the wood.

It gleamed and flared and danced in pinpoints along the length of the wand and emitted a brilliant snapping crackling.

The White Ranger sighted the White Ranger along the length of the murder. It lay between them the length of the wand, whirling, dark red, flaring in brilliant charges, vibrating in brilliant colorless waves down the length of the wand.

The wand stretched through the center of the wood, its fulcrum was the murder, and it poised on the murder, delicately, a magnetic needle trembling toward true north.

The two White Rangers hurried into their riding clothes and flung their legs, quick with anxiety, over their horses. Saluting with one accord, they bent low down the route of the trembling wand.

Fishes sang in the sky. The Spanish actress flung back her hood. She was young and beautiful. Dark. Freed. Maroon notes resounded from her throat and from the vaults of heaven over her.

VII

# Kenneth Rexroth

*From* THE HEART'S GARDEN, THE GARDEN'S HEART

I

Young rice plants are just being
Transplanted. Tea bushes are
Low and compact. Eggplants are
Still under their little tents.
K'oto meadows, samisen
Lakes, mountain drums; water flutes
Falling all night in moonlight.
Migrating birds twitter on
The roofs. Azaleas bloom.
Summer opens. A man of
Sixty years, still wandering
Through wooded hills, gathering
Mushrooms, bracken fiddle necks
And bamboo shoots, listening
Deep in his mind to music
Lost far off in space and time.
The valley's soul is deathless.
It is called the dark woman.
The dark woman is the gate
To the root of heaven and earth.
If you draw her out like floss
She is inexhaustible.
She is possessed without effort.
It was a green jacket, a green
Jacket with a yellow lining.

When will the heartbreak stop?
It was a green jacket, a green
Jacket with a yellow skirt.
When will the heartbreak go?
The evergreen pines grow more
Green as Spring draws to an end.
Yellow rice blades in blue water.


III

Gathering early morning
Mushrooms the music of the
Waterfall washes my ears.
Jumbled rocks clog the clear stream
But the trout love the whirlpools
And riffles. K'ao P'an Tsai Kien.
Two thousand years ago that was
A synonym for happiness—
"Find a hut by a mountain stream."
Hard as stone, water glitters
Like a diamond, and makes a huge
Mountain towering into
The clouds, and carves out canyons
Ten thousand feet deep, and caps
The poles. The same water is
An invisible vapor
Which materializes
When it comes near the mountain.
Here, where bones and mud piled up
And turned to stone and made this
Mountain, the sea once stretched from
Horizon to horizon.
Deep under the shallow sea,
And in the monk's rosary
Amber remembers the pine.
Millions of pearls in the mist
Of the waterfall added
Together make a rainbow.
Deep in the heart one pearl glows

With ten million rainbows.
Weary of the twin seas of
Being and Not Being, I
Long for the mountain of bliss
Untouched by the changing tides.
Deep in the mountain wilderness
Where nobody ever comes,
Only once in a while something
Like the sound of a far off voice,
The low rays of the sun slip
Through the dark forest and gleam
In pools on the shadowy moss.
Wild flowers and grass grow on
The ancient ceremonial
Stairs. The sun sinks between the
Forested mountains. The swallows
Who nested once in the painted
Eaves of the palaces of
The young prince are flying
This evening between the homes
Of woodcutters and quarrymen.
More ancient by far than the stairs
Are the cyclopean walls
Of immense dry laid stones covered
With moss and ferns. If you approach
Quietly and imitate their
Voices, you can converse all day
With the tree frogs who live there.
Peach petals float on the stream
Past the rubbish of the village.
Twilight gathers in the mountain
Village. Peach petals scatter
On the stream at the boom of
The evening bell. All past and
Future sounds can be heard in
A temple bell. The mountain
Goes on being a mountain,
And the sea, a sea, but life
Is frail as a petal in

A world like an insect's shell.
I sit in the hot spring and
Wash my body, spotless from
Its creation, in radiant
Waters, virgin and electric
From the earth womb, pillowed on
Water, a pebble in my mouth.
Tired of the twin peaks of plus
And minus, I float in the
Unruffled sea.

## VI

The Eve of Ch'ing Ming—Clear Bright,
A quail's breast sky and smoky hills,
The great bronze gong booms in the
Russet sunset. Late tonight
It will rain. Tomorrow will
Be clear and cool once more. One more
Clear bright day in this floating life.
The slopes of Mt. Hiei arc veiled
In haze for the last day of Spring.
Spring mist turns to Summer haze
And hides the distant mountains,
But the first evening breeze
Brings the scent of their flowers.
I say a few words and the haze
Lifts from Mt. Hiei and trees
And temples and climbing people
Stand out as sharp as glass.
Three red pigeons on the sunbaked
Gravel, murmuring like the
Far off voices of people
I loved once. The turtles sleep
On the surface of the moat.
If belief and anxiety,
Covetousness and grasping,
Be banished from experience
Of any object whatever,

Only its essence remains,
Only its ultimate being.
He who lives without grasping
Lives always in experience
Of the immediate as the
Ultimate. The solution
Of the problem of knowing
And being is ethical.
Epistemology is moral.
The rutting cock pigeons fill
Their craws with cob from the wall.
Each has his territory,
Where, already this season,
He has dug a hole as big
As a tea cup. They defend
The holes against intrusion
Like they quarrel over the hens.
The knot tied without a rope
Cannot be untied. The seven
Bridges of Koenigsberg cannot
Be crossed but you can always
Go for a swim in the river.
The lower leaves of the trees
Tangle the sunset in dusk.
Awe perfumes the warm twilight.
St. John of the Cross said it,
The desire for vision is
The sin of gluttony.
The bush warbler sings in the
Ancient white pine by the temple
Of the Buddha of Healing.


VII

Tea drinking, garden viewing,
The voices of Japanese
Women are like happy birds.
A calico cat rolls in
The sun on the silky moss.

At the end of the branches
The youngest maple leaves are
As red as they will be again
This autumn when they are old.
Another cat, brown as a mink.
Most Japanese don't like cats.
The monks at this temple are
Eccentrics. However in
The daytime their cats wear bells.
Birds are nesting in the maples.
The women are admiring
The iris and waterlilies.
Beyond the wall—Nishikigi—
The click of the looms—
In all this quarter they are
Weaving obis.
       "All day I
Work in the click of the looms.
At night I go out and play
Packinko amidst the clinks
Of a hundred pinball machines."
The goddess of mercy has
A hundred arms. The steel balls
Fall from heaven to hell
Bouncing through the wickets
Of circumstance. On the field
Of Law? On the field of chance.
Where Krishna drove, Arjuna fought.
All over Japan pinballs fall
Like the myriad gonads of the
Human race through history.
The clicks of the looms, the clinks
Of the wickets are the random
Ticking of organic time.
Shizu, shizu, shizu, yo—
Bobbins whisper through the threads,
Endlessly repeating, "If
Only I could somehow make
Yesterday today."

Curite ducentes subtegmina curite fusi.
Two black swallow tailed butterflies
Hover over the two cats.
They are too old and wise to mind.
A cicada cries in the heat
Of late afternoon and then
A telephone bell answers him.
Is this right? Should Buddhist monks
Have telephones? Who hears
The world cry out in pain?
A young man with immense teeth
And stiff hair is working himself
Into a lather explaining
The contemplative mysteries
Of the garden to five
Remarkably beautiful
Young women. He sees neither
Garden nor girls. He sounds like
A cheer leader. A baby
Breaks away from its mother,
The lady who sells tickets,
And runs across the limitless sea
Of raked gravel, just where
The film box was yesterday.
Life is unruly in the
Zendo. What is the secret,
The reward of right contemplation?
The revelation that it is all
Gravel and moss and rocks and clipped
Shrubbery. That it doesn't
Symbolize anything at all.
The birds are quite aware
Of its meaning. They ignore
Monastery walls and are
Furiously mating everywhere
In the hot perfumed sunlight.
The secret of the moss garden
Is sprinkling it just enough,
Depending on the weather,

And sweeping it twice a day
So lightly the leaves are removed,
And the moss is stimulated.
Except for the ancient masterpiece
That hangs in the kakemono
The best calligraphy in this
Monastery is a white strip
Of plain typing paper, on it
In straightforward clerk's hand,
"These examples of cloud writing
By our saintly Zen Master
Are for sale for fifteen thousand yen each."
I am startled to discover
The papilio Indra
Has gone as the day grew cool
And the smaller black butterfly
I had thought was still him
Is one of the rarest that flies,
Found only in Kyoto.
Like the owl of Minerva
He is still flying as the sunset
Makes long patches of
Ruddy gold on moss and lichened
Maple trunks and the gongs
Ring for evening prayers
All about us, temple calling
To temple, and the doves in
The eaves murmur sleepily,
And the swallows fly one last
Circuit and the bats come out
Under the half moon. I walk
Slowly away through the outer
Garden as the sounds of night
Both of city and forest
Grow around me. Outside the
Monastery workmen have
Been repairing the wall and
Have left three neat piles of rubbish,
Red earth, white gravel, yellow

Wet clay and straw. A little
Further along is a neat
Stack of cobbles. The ground is
Carefully swept between the
Four mounds and around a pine tree
And a stump cut off at ground
Level. The strokes of the broom
Make interlocked spirals in the dust.
On the other side of the wall
Is the famous garden, a long
Rectangle of white raked gravel
Separated from another
Equal rectangle of moss
With two standing rocks, a spreading
Pine and some azalea bushes.
The bushes echo the shapes
Of the vast distant mountains.
The sea is placid. The forest
Drowses in the sunset. Far
Away the Himalayas
Guard the world from all trouble.
The hands move from gesture to
Gesture. "Peace to the earth."
"I protect you from evil."
"I am the source of power."
"I turn the orbits of the planets."
"The mind rests in the clear void."

# Gary Snyder

## MID-AUGUST AT SOURDOUGH MOUNTAIN LOOKOUT

> Down valley a smoke haze
> Three days heat, after five days rain
> Pitch glows on the fir-cones
> Across rocks and meadows
> Swarms of new flies.
>
> I cannot remember things I once read
> A few friends, but they are in cities.
> Drinking cold snow-water from a tin cup
> Looking down for miles
> Through high still air.

# WATER

Pressure of sun on the rockslide
Whirled me in dizzy hop-and-step descent,
Pool of pebbles buzzed in a Juniper shadow,
Tiny tongue of a this-year rattlesnake flicked,
I leaped, laughing for little boulder-color coil—
Pounded by heat raced down the slabs to the creek
Deep tumbling under arching walls and stuck
Whole head and shoulders in the water:
Stretched full on cobble—ears roaring
Eyes open aching from the cold and faced a trout.

# RIPRAP

Lay down these words
Before your mind like rocks.
          placed solid, by hands
In choice of place, set
Before the body of the mind
          in space and time:
Solidity of bark, leaf, or wall
          riprap of things:
Cobble of milky way,
          straying planets,
These poems, people,
          lost ponies with
Dragging saddles—
          and rocky sure-foot trails.
The worlds like an endless
          four-dimensional
Game of *Go*.
          ants and pebbles
In the thin loam, each rock a word
          a creek-washed stone
Granite:  ingrained
          with torment of fire and weight
Crystal and sediment linked hot
          all change, in thoughts,
As well as things.

# CARTAGENA

Rain and thunder beat down and flooded the streets—
We danced with Indian girls in a bar,
       water half-way to our knees,
The youngest one slipped down her dress and danced
       bare to the waist,
The big negro deckhand made out with his girl on his lap
       in a chair her dress over her eyes
Coca-cola and rum, and rainwater all over the floor.
In the glittering light I got drunk and reeled through
       the rooms,
And cried, "Cartagena! swamp of unholy loves!"
And wept for the Indian whores who were younger than me,
       and I was eighteen,
And splashed after the crew down the streets wearing
       sandals bought at a stall
And got back to the ship, dawn came,
       we were far out at sea.

COLOMBIA 1948—ARABIA 1958

*From* MYTHS & TEXTS

## Part 3  Burning

    I   SECOND SHAMAN SONG

Squat in swamp shadows.
         mosquitoes sting;
             high light in cedar above.
Crouched in a dry vain frame
        —thirst for cold snow
        —green slime of bone marrow
Seawater fills each eye

Quivering in nerve and muscle
Hung in the pelvic cradle
Bones propped against roots
A blind flicker of nerve

Still hand moves out alone
Flowering and leafing
             turning to quartz
Streaked rock     congestion of karma
The long body of the swamp.
A mud-streaked thigh.

Dying carp biting air
         in the damp grass,
River recedes. No matter.

Limp fish sleep in the weeds
The sun dries me as I dance

## II

One moves continually with the consciousness
Of that other, totally alien, non-human:
Humming inside like a taut drum,
Carefully avoiding any direct thought of it,
Attentive to the real-world flesh and stone.

Intricate layers of emptiness
This only world, juggling forms
                    a hand, a breast, two clasped
Human tenderness scuttles
Down dry endless cycles
Forms within forms falling
                              clinging
Loosely, what's gone away?
                    —love

In Spring the Avocado sheds dead leaves
Soft rattling through the Cherry greens
Bird at this moment
All these books
        wearing a thin sweater
        & no brassiere
        in failing light
One glance, miles below
Bones & flesh knit in the rock
    "have no regret—
chip chip
        (sparrows)
& not a word about the void
To which one hand diddling
Cling

## IX

Night here,          a covert
All spun, webs in one
                how without grabbing hold it?

—Get into the bird-cage
             without starting them singing.

"Forming the New Society
             Within the shell of the Old"
The motto in the Wobbly Hall
Some old Finns and Swedes playing cards
Fourth and Yesler in Seattle.
O you modest, retiring, virtuous young ladies
             pick the watercress, pluck the yarrow
"Kwan kwan" goes the crane in the field,
             I'll meet you tomorrow;
A million workers dressed in black and buried,
We make love in leafy shade.

Bodhidharma sailing the Yangtze on a reed
Lenin in a sealed train through Germany
Hsüan Tsang, crossing the Pamirs
Joseph, Crazy Horse, living the last free
        starving high-country winter of their tribes.
Surrender into freedom, revolt into slavery—
Confucius no better—
             (with Lao-tzu to keep him in check)
"Walking about the countryside
             all one fall
To a heart's content beating on stumps."

X AMITABHA'S VOW

"If, after obtaining Buddhahood, anyone in my land
    gets tossed in jail on a vagrancy rap, may I
    not attain highest perfect enlightenment.

    wild geese in the orchard
    frost on the new grass

"If, after obtaining Buddhahood, anyone in my land
    loses a finger coupling boxcars, may I
    not attain highest perfect enlightenment.

mare's eye flutters
jerked by the lead-rope
stone-bright shoes flick back
ankles trembling: down steep rock

"If, after obtaining Buddhahood, anyone in my land
can't get a ride hitch-hiking all directions, may I
not attain highest perfect enlightenment.

wet rocks buzzing
rain and thunder southwest
hair, beard, tingle
wind whips bare legs
we should go back
we don't

XIII

Spikes of new smell driven up nostrils
Expanding & deepening, ear-muscles
Straining and grasping the sounds
Mouth filled with bright fluid coldness
Tongue crushed by the weight of its flavours
        —the Nootka sold out for lemon drops
(What's this talk about not understanding!
        you're just a person who refuses to see.)
Poetry a riprap on the slick rock of metaphysics
"Put a Spanish halter on that whore of a mare
& I'll lead the bitch up any trail"

(how gentle! He should have whipped her first)

the wind turns.
a cold rain blows over the shale
we sleep in the belly of a cloud.
(you think sex art and travel are enough?
        you're a skinful of cowdung)

South of the Yellow River the Emperor Wu

Set the army horses free in the mountain pastures,
Set the Buffalo free on the Plain of the Peach Grove.
Chariots and armor were smeared with blood
        and put away. They locked up
        the Arrows bag.
Smell of crushed spruce and burned snag-wood.
        remains of men,
Bone-chopped foul remains, thick stew
Food for crows—
        (blind, deaf, and dumb!
        shall we give him another chance?)
At Nyahaim-kuvara
Night has gone
Traveling to my land
        —that's a Mohave night
Our night too, you think brotherhood
Humanity & good intentions will stop it?
As long as you hesitate, no place to go.

Bluejay, out at the world's end
        perched, looked, & dashed
Through the crashing: his head is squashed.
        symplegades, the *mumonkwan,*
It's all vagina dentata
        (Jump!)
"Leap through an Eagle's snapping beak"

Actacon saw Dhyana in the Spring.

        it was nothing special,
      misty rain on Mt. Baker,
         Neah Bay at low tide.

XVII   *the text*

Sourdough mountain called a fire in:
Up Thunder Creek, high on a ridge.
Hiked eighteen hours, finally found
A snag and a hundred feet around on fire:

All afternoon and into night
Digging the fire line
Falling the burning snag
It fanned sparks down like shooting stars
Over the dry words, starting spot-fires
Flaring in wind up Skagit valley
From the Sound.
Toward morning it rained.
We slept in mud and ashes,
Woke at dawn, the fire was out,
The sky was clear, we saw
The last glimmer of the morning star.


*the myth*

Fire up Thunder Creek and the mountain—
                    troy's burning;
The cloud mutters
The mountains are your mind.
The woods bristle there,
Dogs barking and children shrieking
Rise from below.

Rain falls for centuries
Soaking the loose rocks in space
Sweet rain, the fire's out
The black snag glistens in the rain
& the last wisp of smoke floats up
Into the absolute cold
Into the spiral whorls of fire
The storms of the Milky Way
"Buddha incense in an empty world"
Black pit cold and light-year
Flame tongue of the dragon
Licks the sun

The sun is but a morning star

CRATER MT. L.O. 1952-MARIN-AN 1956

# James Wright

## TO A DEFEATED SAVIOUR

Do you forget the shifting hole
Where the slow swimmer fell aground,
And floundered for your fishing pole
Above the snarl of string and sound?
You never seem to turn your face
Directly toward the river side,
Or up the bridge, or anyplace
Near where the skinny swimmer died.

You stand all day and look at girls,
Or climb a tree, or change a tire;
But I have seen the colored swirls
Of water flow to livid fire
Across your sleeping nose and jaws,
Transfiguring both the bone and skin
To muddy banks and sliding shoals
You and the drowned kid tumble in.

You see his face, upturning, float
And bob across your wavering bed;
His wailing fingers call your boat,
His voice throws up the ruddy silt,
The bleary vision prays for light
In sky behind your frozen hands;
But sinking in the dark all night

You charm the shore with bloomless wands.
The circling tow, the shadowy pool
Shift underneath us everywhere.
You would have raised him, flesh and soul,
Had you been strong enough to dare;
You would have lifted him to breathe,
Believing your good hands would keep
His body clear of your own death:
This dream, this drowning in your sleep.

## SAINT JUDAS

When I went out to kill myself, I caught
A pack of hoodlums beating up a man.
Running to spare his suffering, I forgot
My name, my number, how my day began,
How soldiers milled around the garden stone
And sang amusing songs; how all that day
Their javelins measured crowds; how I alone
Bargained the proper coins, and slipped away.

Banished from heaven, I found this victim beaten,
Stripped, kneed, and left to cry. Dropping my rope
Aside, I ran, ignored the uniforms:
Then I remembered bread my flesh had eaten,
The kiss that ate my flesh. Flayed without hope,
I held the man for nothing in my arms.

# A BLESSING

Just off the highway to Rochester, Minnesota,
Twilight bounds softly forth on the grass.
And the eyes of those two Indian ponies
Darken with kindness.
They have come gladly out of the willows
To welcome my friend and me.
We step over the barbed wire into the pasture
Where they have been grazing all day, alone.
They ripple tensely, they can hardly contain their
    happiness
That we have come.
They bow shyly as wet swans. They love each other.
There is no loneliness like theirs.
At home once more,
They begin munching the young tufts of spring in the
    darkness.
I would like to hold the slenderer one in my arms,
For she has walked over to me
And nuzzled my left hand.
She is black and white,
Her mane falls wild on her forehead,
And the light breeze moves me to caress her long ear
That is delicate as the skin over a girl's wrist.
Suddenly I realize
That if I stepped out of my body I would break
Into blossom.

# ARRIVING IN THE COUNTRY AGAIN

The white house is silent.
My friends can't hear me yet.
The flicker who lives in the bare tree at the
field's edge
Pecks once and is still for a long time.
I stand still in the late afternoon.
My face is turned away from the sun.
A horse grazes in my long shadow.

# MARY BLY

I sit here, doing nothing, alone, worn out by long winter.
I feel the light breath of the newborn child.
Her face is smooth as the side of an apricot,
Eyes quick as her blond mother's hands.
She has full, soft, red hair, and as she lies quiet
In her tall mother's arms, her delicate hands
Weave back and forth.
I feel the seasons changing beneath me,
Under the floor.
She is braiding the waters of air into the plaited manes
Of happy colts.
They canter, without making a sound, along the shores
Of melting snow.

# TWO HANGOVERS

I slouch in bed.
Beyond the streaked trees of my window,
All groves are bare.
Locusts and poplars change to unmarried women
Sorting slate from anthracite
Between railroad ties:
The yellow-bearded winter of the depression
Is still alive somewhere, an old man
Counting his collection of bottle caps
In a tarpaper shack under the cold trees
Of my grave.

I still feel half drunk,
And all those old women beyond my window
Are hunching toward the graveyard.

Drunk, mumbling Hungarian,
The sun staggers in,
And his big stupid face pitches
Into the stove.
For two hours I have been dreaming
Of green butterflies searching for diamonds
In coal seams;
And children chasing each other for a game
Through the hills of fresh graves.
But the sun has come home drunk from the sea,
And a sparrow outside
Sings of the Hanna Coal Co. and the dead moon.
The filaments of cold light bulbs tremble
In music like delicate birds.
Ah, turn it off.

In a pine tree,
A few yards away from my window sill,
A brilliant blue jay is springing up and down, up and down,
On a branch.
I laugh, as I see him abandon himself
To entire delight, for he knows as well as I do
That the branch will not break.

# THE MINNEAPOLIS POEM

## I

I wonder how many old men last winter
Hungry and frightened by namelessness prowled
The Mississippi shore
Lashed blind by the wind, dreaming
Of suicide in the river.
The police remove their cadavers by daybreak
And turn them in somewhere.
Where?
How does the city keep lists of its fathers
Who have no names?
By Nicollet Island I gaze down at the dark water
So beautifully slow.
And I wish my brothers good luck
And a warm grave.

## II

The Chippewa young men
Stab one another shrieking
Jesus Christ.
Split-lipped homosexuals limp in terror of assault.
High school backfields search under benches
Near the Post Office. Their faces are the rich
Raw bacon without eyes.
The Walker Art Center crowd stare
At the Guthrie Theater.

## III

Tall Negro girls from Chicago
Listen to light songs.

They know when the supposed patron
Is a plainclothesman.
A cop's palm
Is a roach dangling down the scorched fangs
Of a light bulb.
The soul of a cop's eyes
Is an eternity of Sunday daybreak in the suburbs
Of Juárez, Mexico.

IV

The legless beggars are gone, carried away
By white birds.
The Artificial Limbs Exchange is gutted
And sown with lime.
The whalebone crutches and hand-me-down trusses
Huddle together dreaming in a desolation
Of dry groins.
I think of poor men astonished to waken
Exposed in broad daylight by the blade
Of a strange plough.

V

All over the walls of comb cells
Automobiles perfumed and blindered
Consent with a mutter of high good humor
To take their two naps a day.
Without sound windows glide back
Into dusk.
The sockets of a thousand blind bee graves tier upon tier
Tower not quite toppling.
There are men in this city who labor dawn after dawn
To sell me my death.

VI

But I could not bear
To allow my poor brother my body to die
In Minneapolis.

The old man Walt Whitman our countryman
Is now in America our country
Dead.
But he was not buried in Minneapolis
At least.
And no more may I be
Please God.

VII

I want to be lifted up
By some great white bird unknown to the police,
And soar for a thousand miles and be carefully hidden
Modest and golden as one last corn grain,
Stored with the secrets of the wheat and the mysterious lives
Of the unnamed poor.

# David Wagoner

## DIARY

At Monday dawn, I climbed into my skin
And went to see the money. There were the shills:
I conned them—oh, the coins fell out of their mouths,
And paint peeled from the walls like dollar bills.
Below their money-belts, I did them in.

All day Tuesday, grand in my underwear,
I shopped for the world, bought basements and airplanes,
Bargained for corners and pedestrians
And, when I'd marketed the elms away,
Swiped from the water, stole down to the stones.

Suddenly Wednesday offered me my shirt,
Trousers, and shoes. I put them on to dream
Of the one-way stairway and the skittering cloud,
Of the dangerous, footsore crossing at the heart
Where trees, rivers, and stones reach for the dead.

And the next day meant the encircling overcoat
Wherein I sweltered, woolly as a ram:
From butt to swivel, I hoofed it on the loam,
Exacting tribute from the flock in the grass.
My look passed through the werewolf to the lamb.

Friday shied backwards, pulling off my clothes:
The overcoat fell open like a throat;

Shirt-tail and shoe went spidery as a thought,
And covetous drawers whipped knee-deep in a knot.
My skin in a spiral tapered into gold.

And it was naked Saturday for love
Again: the graft grew milky at a kiss.
I lay on the week with money, lust, and vapor,
Megalomania, fear, the tearing-off,
And love in a coil. On Sunday, I wrote this.

# GOING TO PIECES

*Pull yourself together, pal.*
—ADVICE FROM A STRANGER

Those marionette-show skeletons can do it
Suddenly, after their skulls have been
Alone in the rafters, after their wishbones
Have fluttered in the wings, leaving the feet onstage
To hoof it solo: they pull themselves together,
Bring everything back and thread it on their spines.

But looking around and seeing other people
Coming apart at parties, breaking up
And catching their own laughter in both hands,
Or crossing the lawn and throwing up their spirits
Like voice-balloons in funnies, touching noses
In bedroom mirrors, one after another,
I figure something can be said for it:
Maybe some people break in better halves
Or some of the parts are greater than the whole.

Pal, take a look around: a heap of coats
Discarded in one spot like empty skins;
Under the tables enough shoes and gloves.
Enough loose hair, saliva, and fingernails
To conjure bodies off a hundred souls.
Now I'll tell *you* one: the palolo worms,
One night a year at the bottom of the sea,
Back halfway out of the burrows where they spend
Long lives; their tails turn luminous, twist free,
And all by themselves swim up to the surface,
Joining with millions of other detached tails;
The sea in a writhing mass lies white for miles

Under a gibbous moon; the bright halves die
And float away like scraps after a party,
But leave behind their larvae, set for life.

Meanwhile, the old ones, steady in their holes,
Can go about their business, fanning food
Into their sleek, uninterrupted gullets.
Think of them there, pal, chewing the ocean,
Staying alive by going to pieces.

# STAYING ALIVE

Staying alive in the woods is a matter of calming down
At first and deciding whether to wait for rescue,
Trusting to others,
Or simply to start walking and walking in one direction
Till you come out—or something happens to stop you.
By far the safer choice
Is to settle down where you are, and try to make a living
Off the land, camping near water, away from shadows.
Eat no white berries;
Spit out all bitterness. Shooting at anything
Means hiking further and further every day
To hunt survivors;
It may be best to learn what you have to learn without a gun,
Not killing but watching birds and animals go
In and out of shelter
At will. Following their example, build for a whole season:
Facing across the wind in your lean-to,
You may feel wilder,
But nothing, not even you, will have to stay in hiding.
If you have no matches, a stick and a fire-bow
Will keep you warmer,
Or the crystal of your watch, filled with water, held up to the
    sun
Will do the same in time. In case of snow
Drifting toward winter,
Don't try to stay awake through the night, afraid of freezing—
The bottom of your mind knows all about zero;
It will turn you over
And shake you till you waken. If you have trouble sleeping
Even in the best of weather, jumping to follow
With eyes strained to their corners
The unidentifiable noises of the night and feeling

Bears and packs of wolves nuzzling your elbow,
Remember the trappers
Who treated them indifferently and were left alone.
If you hurt yourself, no one will comfort you
Or take your temperature,
So stumbling, wading, and climbing are as dangerous as
     flying.
But if you decide, at last, you must break through
In spite of all danger,
Think of yourself by time and not by distance, counting
Wherever you're going by how long it takes you;
No other measure
Will bring you safe to nightfall. Follow no streams: they run
Under the ground or fall into wilder country.
Remember the stars
And moss when your mind runs into circles. If it should rain
Or the fog should roll the horizon in around you,
Hold still for hours
Or days if you must, or weeks, for seeing is believing
In the wilderness. And if you find a pathway,
Wheel-rut, or fence-wire,
Retrace it left or right; someone knew where he was going
Once upon a time, and you can follow
Hopefully, somewhere,
Just in case. There may even come, on some uncanny evening,
A time when you're warm and dry, well fed, not thirsty,
Uninjured, without fear,
When nothing, either good or bad, is happening.
This is called staying alive. It's temporary.
What occurs after
Is doubtful. You must always be ready for something to
     come bursting
Through the far edge of a clearing, running toward you,
Grinning from ear to ear
And hoarse with welcome. Or something crossing and
     hovering
Overhead, as light as air, like a break in the sky,
Wondering what you are.
Here you are face to face with the problem of recognition.

Having no time to make smoke, too much to say,
You should have a mirror
With a tiny hole in the back for better aiming, for reflecting
Whatever disaster you can think of, to show
The way you suffer.
These body signals have universal meaning: If you are lying
Flat on your back with arms outstretched behind you,
You say you require
Emergency treatment; if you are standing erect and holding
Arms horizontal, you mean you are not ready;
If you hold them over
Your head, you want to be picked up. Three of anything
Is a sign of distress. Afterward, if you see
No ropes, no ladders,
No maps or messages falling, no searchlights or trails blazing,
Then, chances are, you should be prepared to burrow
Deep for a deep winter.

# James Dickey

## THE LIFEGUARD

In a stable of boats I lie still,
From all sleeping children hidden.
The leap of a fish from its shadow
Makes the whole lake instantly tremble.
With my foot on the water, I feel
The moon outside

Take on the utmost of its power.
I rise and go out through the boats.
I set my broad sole upon silver,
On the skin of the sky, on the moonlight,
Stepping outward from earth onto water
In quest of the miracle

This village of children believed
That I could perform as I dived
For one who had sunk from my sight.
I saw his cropped haircut go under.
I leapt, and my steep body flashed
Once, in the sun.

Dark drew all the light from my eyes.
Like a man who explores his death
By the pull of his slow-moving shoulders,
I hung head down in the cold,

Wide-eyed, contained, and alone
Among the weeds,

And my fingertips turned into stone
From clutching immovable blackness.
Time after time I leapt upward
Exploding in breath, and fell back
From the change in the children's faces
At my defeat.

Beneath them I swam to the boathouse
With only my life in my arms
To wait for the lake to shine back
At the risen moon with such power
That my steps on the light of the ripples
Might be sustained.

Beneath me is nothing but brightness
Like the ghost of a snowfield in summer.
As I move toward the center of the lake,
Which is also the center of the moon,
I am thinking of how I may be
The savior of one

Who has already died in my care.
The dark trees fade from around me.
The moon's dust hovers together.
I call softly out, and the child's
Voice answers through blinding water.
Patiently, slowly,

He rises, dilating to break
The surface of stone with his forehead.
He is one I do not remember
Having ever seen in his life.
The ground I stand on is trembling
Upon his smile.

I wash the black mud from my hands.

On a light given off by the grave
I kneel in the quick of the moon
At the heart of a distant forest
And hold in my arms a child
Of water, water, water.

# THE HOSPITAL WINDOW

I have just come down from my father.
Higher and higher he lies
Above me in a blue light
Shed by a tinted window.
I drop through six white floors
And then step out onto pavement.

Still feeling my father ascend,
I start to cross the firm street,
My shoulder blades shining with all
The glass the huge building can raise.
Now I must turn round and face it,
And know his one pane from the others.

Each window possesses the sun
As though it burned there on a wick.
I wave, like a man catching fire.
All the deep-dyed windowpanes flash,
And, behind them, all the white rooms
They turn to the color of Heaven.

Ceremoniously, gravely, and weakly,
Dozens of pale hands are waving
Back, from inside their flames.
Yet one pure pane among these
Is the bright, erased blankness of nothing.
I know that my father is there,

In the shape of his death still living.
The traffic increases around me

Like a madness called down on my head.
The horns blast at me like shotguns,
And drivers lean out, driven crazy—
But now my propped-up father

Lifts his arm out of stillness at last.
The light from the window strikes me
And I turn as blue as a soul,
As the moment when I was born.
I am not afraid for my father—
Look! He is grinning; he is not

Afraid for my life, either,
As the wild engines stand at my knees
Shredding their gears and roaring,
And I hold each car in its place
For miles, inciting its horn
To blow down the walls of the world

That the dying may float without fear
In the bold blue gaze of my father.
Slowly I move to the sidewalk
With my pin-tingling hand half dead
At the end of my bloodless arm.
I carry it off in amazement,

High, still higher, still waving,
My recognized face fully mortal,
Yet not; not at all, in the pale,
Drained, otherworldly, stricken,
Created hue of stained glass.
I have just come down from my father.

# THE LEAP

The only thing I have of Jane MacNaughton
Is one instant of a dancing-class dance.
She was the fastest runner in the seventh grade,
My scrapbook says, even when boys were beginning
To be as big as the girls,
But I do not have her running in my mind,
Though Frances Lane is there, Agnes Fraser,
Fat Betty Lou Black in the boys-against-girls
Relays we ran at recess: she must have run

Like the other girls, with her skirts tucked up
So they would be like bloomers,
But I cannot tell; that part of her is gone.
What I do have is when she came,
With the hem of her skirt where it should be
For a young lady, into the annual dance
Of the dancing class we all hated, and with a light
Grave leap, jumped up and touched the end
Of one of the paper-ring decorations

To see if she could reach it. She could,
And reached me now as well, hanging in my mind
From a brown chain of brittle paper, thin
And muscular, wide-mouthed, eager to prove
Whatever it proves when you leap
In a new dress, a new womanhood, among the boys
Whom you easily left in the dust
Of the passionless playground. If I said I saw
In the paper where Jane MacNaughton Hill,

Mother of four, leapt to her death from a window
Of a downtown hotel, and that her body crushed-in

The top of a parked taxi, and that I held
Without trembling a picture of her lying cradled
In that papery steel as though lying in the grass,
One shoe idly off, arms folded across her breast,
I would not believe myself. I would say
The convenient thing, that it was a bad dream
Of maturity, to see that eternal process

Most obsessively wrong with the world
Come out of her light, earth-spurning feet
Grown heavy: would say that in the dusty heels
Of the playground some boy who did not depend
On speed of foot, caught and betrayed her.
Jane, stay where you are in my first mind:
It was odd in that school, at that dance.
I and the other slow-footed yokels sat in corners
Cutting rings out of drawing paper

Before you leapt in your new dress
And touched the end of something I began,
Above the couples struggling on the floor,
New men and women clutching at each other
And prancing foolishly as bears: hold on
To that ring I made for you, Jane—
My feet are nailed to the ground
By dust I swallowed thirty years ago—
While I examine my hands.

# Margaret Atwood

## A PLACE: FRAGMENTS

I

Here on the rim, cringing
under the cracked whip of winter
we live
in houses of ice,
but not because we want to:
in order to survive
we make what we can and have to
with what we have.

II

Old woman I visited once
out of my way
in a little-visited province:

she had a neat
house, a clean parlour
though obsolete and poor:

a cushion with a fringe;
glass animals arranged
across the mantlepiece (a swan, a horse,
a bull); a mirror;
a teacup sent from Scotland;
several heraldic spoons;

a lamp; and in the center
of the table, a paperweight:
hollow glass globe
filled with water, and
a house, a man, a snowstorm.

The room was as
dustless as possible
and free of spiders.

I

stood in the door-
way, at the fulcrum where

this trivial but
stringent inner order
held its delicate balance
with the random scattering or
  clogged merging of
things: ditch by the road; dried
reeds in the wind; flat
wet bush, grey sky
sweeping away outside.

III

The cities are only outposts.

Watch that man
walking on cement as though on snowshoes:
senses the road
a muskeg, loose mat of roots and brown
vegetable decay
or crust of ice that
easily might break and
slush or water under
suck him down

The land flows like a
sluggish current.
The mountains eddy slowly towards the sea.

IV

The people who come here also
flow: their bodies becoming
nebulous, diffused, quietly
spreading out into the air across
these interstellar sidewalks

V

This is what it must be
like in outer space
where the stars are pasted flat
against the total
black of the expanding
eye, fly-
specks of burning dust

VI

There is no center;
the centers
travel with us unseen
like our shadows
on a day when there is no sun.

We must move back:
there are too many foregrounds.

Now, clutter of twigs
across our eyes, tatter
of birds at the eye's edge; the straggle
of dead treetrunks; patch
of lichen
and in love, tangle

of limbs and fingers, the texture
of pores and lines on the skin.

VII

An other sense tugs at us:
we have lost something,
some key to these things
which must be writings
and are locked against us
or perhaps (like a potential
mine, unknown vein
of metal in the rock)
something not lost or hidden
but just not found yet

that informs, holds together
this confusion, this largeness
and dissolving:

not above or behind
or within it, but one
with it: an

identity:
something too huge and simple
for us to see.

# A. R. Ammons

**DUNES**

Taking root in windy sand
        is not an easy
way
to go about
        finding a place to stay.

A ditchbank or wood's edge
        has firmer ground.

In a loose world though
        something can be started—
a root touch water,
        a tip break sand—

Mounds from that can rise
        on held mounds,
a gesture of building, keeping,
        a trapping
into shape.

Firm ground is not available ground.

# CORSONS INLET

I went for a walk over the dunes again this morning
to the sea,
then turned right along
    the surf

               rounded a naked headland
               and returned

    along the inlet shore:

it was muggy sunny, the wind from the sea steady and high,
crisp in the running sand,
    some breakthroughs of sun
  but after a bit

continuous overcast:

the walk liberating, I was released from forms,
from the perpendiculars,
    straight lines, blocks, boxes, binds
of thought
into the hues, shadings, rises, flowing bends and blends
       of sight:

               I allow myself eddies of meaning:
yield to a direction of significance
running
like a stream through the geography of my work:
    you can find
in my sayings
            swerves of action
            like the inlet's cutting edge:

      there are dunes of motion,

organizations of grass, white sandy paths of remembrance
in the overall wandering of mirroring mind:

but Overall is beyond me: is the sum of these events
I cannot draw, the ledger I cannot keep, the accounting
beyond the account:

in nature there are few sharp lines: there are areas of
primrose
        more or less dispersed;
disorderly orders of bayberry; between the rows
of dunes,
irregular swamps of reeds.
though not reeds alone, but grass, bayberry, yarrow, all . . .
predominantly reeds:

I have reached no conclusions, have erected no boundaries,
shutting out and shutting in, separating inside
        from outside: I have
        drawn no lines:
        as

manifold events of sand
change the dune's shape that will not be the same shape
tomorrow,

so I am willing to go along, to accept
the becoming
thought, to stake off no beginnings or ends, establish
        no walls:

by transitions the land falls from grassy dunes to creek
to undercreek: but there are no lines, though
        change in that transition is clear
        as any sharpness: but "sharpness" spread out,
allowed to occur over a wider range
than mental lines can keep:

the moon was full last night: today, low tide was low:
black shoals of mussels exposed to the risk
of air

and, earlier, of sun,
waved in and out with the waterline, waterline inexact,
caught always in the event of change:
    a young mottled gull stood free on the shoals
      and ate
to vomiting: another gull, squawking possession, cracked a crab,
picked out the entrails, swallowed the soft-shelled legs, a ruddy
turnstone running in to snatch leftover bits:

risk is full: every living thing in
siege: the demand is life, to keep life: the small
white blacklegged egret, how beautiful, quietly stalks and spears
       the shallows, darts to shore
              to stab—what? I couldn't
    see against the black mudflats—a frightened
    fiddler crab?


       the news to my left over the dunes and
reeds and bayberry clumps was
      fall: thousands of tree swallows
      gathering for flight:
      an order held
      in constant change: a congregation
rich with entropy: nevertheless, separable, noticeable
      as one event,
        not chaos: preparations for
flight from winter,
cheet, cheet, cheet, cheet, wings rifling the green clumps,
beaks
at the bayberries:
    a perception full of wind, flight, curve,
    sound:
    the possibility of rule as the sum of rulelessness:
the "field" of action
with moving, incalculable center:
in the smaller view, order tight with shape:
blue tiny flowers on a leafless weed: carapace of crab:
snailshell:
      pulsations of order
      in the bellies of minnows: orders swallowed,

broken down, transferred through membranes
to strengthen larger orders: but in the large view, no
lines or changeless shapes: the working in and out, together
          and against, of millions of events: this,
                    so that I make
                    no form of
                    formlessness:

orders as summaries, as outcomes of actions override
or in some way result, not predictably (seeing me gain
the top of a dune,
the swallows
could take flight—some other fields of bayberry
          could enter fall
          berryless) and there is serenity:

                    no arranged terror: no forcing of image, plan,
or thought:
no propaganda, no humbling of reality to precept:

terror pervades but is not arranged, all possibilities
of escape open: no route shut, except in
          the sudden loss of all routes:

          I see narrow orders, limited tightness, but will
not run to that easy victory:
          still around the looser, wider forces work:
          I will try
          to fasten into order enlarging grasps of disorder, widening
scope, but enjoying the freedom that
Scope eludes my grasp, that there is no finality of vision,
that I have perceived nothing completely,
          that tomorrow a new walk is a new walk.

# VIII

# David Ignatow

## GET THE GASWORKS

Get the gasworks into a poem,
and you've got the smoke and smokestacks,
the mottled red and yellow tenements,
and grimy kids who curse with the pungency
of the odor of gas. You've got America, boy.

Sketch in the river and barges,
all dirty and slimy.
How do the seagulls stay so white?
And always cawing like little mad geniuses?
You've got the kind of living
that makes the kind of thinking we do:
gaswork smokestack whistle tooting wisecracks.
They don't come because we like it that way,
but because we find it outside our window each morning,
in soot on the furniture,
and trucks carrying coal for gas,
the kid hot after the ball under the wheel.
He gets it over the belly, all right.
He dies there.

So the kids keep tossing the ball around
after the funeral.
So the cops keep chasing them,
so the mamas keep hollering,
and papa flings his newspaper outward,
in disgust with discipline.

## THE DREAM

Someone approaches to say his life is ruined
and to fall down at your feet
and pound his head upon the sidewalk.
Blood spreads in a puddle.
And you, in a weak voice, plead
with those nearby for help;
your life takes on his desperation.
He keeps pounding his head.
It is you who are fated;
and you fall down beside him.
It is then you are awakened,
the body gone, the blood washed from the ground,
the stores lit up with their goods.


## MOVING PICTURE

When two take gas
by mutual consent
and the cops come in
when the doors are broken down
and the doctor pays respect
by closing the books
and the neighbors stand about
sniffing and afraid
and the papers run a brief
under a whiskey ad
and the news is read
eating ice cream or a fruit

and the paper is used
to wrap peelings
and the garbage man
dumps the barrel
into the truck
and the paper flares
in the furnace and sinks back
charred and is scooped up
for mud flats and pressed down
by steam rollers for hard ground
and a house on it
for two to enter.

## STATEMENT FOR THE TIME

On Sunday, day of rest, I stroll the park,
visiting the lake and the ducks in it.
I look at the hills in the distance in another state.
I sit and rest.
I go home, and go to work
I go to war with my ambition against my mind.

The larger wars are for the masses,
and the smaller ones are for you and me,
but they have the same value,
and the same result.

Are we at peace when we are at rest?
Are we not resting in order to dream?
We could not dream while we fought.
We fought all our dreams out of us.
We asked for peace so that we could understand again.
But after peace we shall go back to fight,
with a high purpose and a stubborn will.
We shall burn down the cities,
and build them up again.
We shall burn them down again,
and be damned for it.
But we shall build them up.
Each time for a stubborn ideal, and a good cause.

# TO WHAT AM I RESIGNED

To what am I resigned?
To earth and trees, to rock and water:
to all that I must live with;
to friends, myself, relatives and enemies,
and people envious of me.
They need not be, while we are together.

I am resigned to being,
without any importance attached to it:
without escape from it, and without consequence,
such as I could imagine,
but I am manifestation, and not mover.

I am resigned to being the hundred millionth person,
or near that figure produced by earth,
who praises nature and life like an impartial witness,
while the heart ticks off its time.

I am resigned to doing as I have been given to do,
then, along with my contemporaries, books and nations,
ideas and societies disappear.

But I resign into the wealth of being,
out of which I come; and out of being,
as part of it, count my immortality,
and importance.

# HOW COME?

I'm in New York covered by a layer of soap foam.
The air is dense from the top of skyscrapers
to the sidewalk in every street, avenue
and alley, as far as Babylon on the East,
Dobbs Ferry on the North, Coney Island
on the South and stretching far over
the Atlantic Ocean. I wade
through, breathing by pushing
foam aside. The going is slow,
with just a clearing ahead
by swinging my arms. Others are groping
from all sides, too. We keep moving.
Everything else has happened here
and we've survived: snow storms,
traffic tieups, train breakdowns, bursting
water mains; and now I am writing
with a lump of charcoal stuck between my toes,
switching it from one foot to the other—
this monkey trick learned visiting
with my children at the zoo of a Sunday.
But soap foam filling the air,
the bitter, fatty smell of it . . . How come?
My portable says it extends to San Francisco!
Listen to this, and down to the Mexican border
and as far north as Canada. All the prairies,
the Rocky Mountains, the Great Lakes, Chicago,
the Pacific Coast. No advertising stunt
could do this. The soap has welled out of the ground
says the portable suddenly. The scientists report
the soil saturated. And now what?

We'll have to start climbing for air,
a crowd forming around the Empire State Building
says the portable. God help the enemy
who will die of soap foam.

## SIMULTANEOUSLY

Simultaneously, five thousand miles apart,
two telephone poles, shaking and roaring
and hissing gas, rose from their emplacements
straight up, leveled off and headed
for each other's land, alerted radar
and ground defense, passed each other
in midair, escorted by worried planes,
and plunged into each other's place,
steaming and silent and standing straight,
sprouting leaves.

## A SEMBLANCE

Over your mother's grave
speak a prayer of bafflement,
grasp the hand of the rabbi,
nearest to steady you.
He recites the prayer
for you to follow unsteadily
its meaning. You pray
to the air.

## RITUAL ONE

As I enter the theatre the play is going on.
I hear the father say to the son on stage,
You've taken the motor apart.
The son replies, The roof is leaking.
The father retorts, The tire is flat.
Tiptoeing down the aisle, I find my seat,
edge my way in across a dozen kneecaps
as I tremble for my sanity.
I have heard doomed voices calling on god the electrode.
Sure enough, as I start to sit
a scream rises from beneath me.
It is one of the players.
If I come down, I'll break his neck,
caught between the seat and the backrest.
Now the audience and the players on stage,
their heads turned towards me, are waiting
for the sound of the break. Must I?
Those in my aisle nod slowly, reading my mind,
their eyes fixed on me, and I understand
that each has done the same.
Must I kill this man as the price of my admission
to this play? His screams continue loud and long.
I am at a loss as to what to do,
I panic, I freeze.

My training has been to eat the flesh of pig.
I might even have been able to slit a throat.
As a child I witnessed the dead chickens
over a barrel of sawdust absorbing their blood.
I then brought them in a bag to my father
who sold them across his counter. Liking him,
I learned to like people and enjoy their company too,

which of course brought me to this play.
But how angry I become.
Now everybody is shouting at me to sit down,
sit down or I'll be thrown out.
The father and son have stepped off stage
and come striding down the aisle side by side.
They reach me, grab me by the shoulder
and force me down. I scream, I scream,
as if to cover the sound of the neck breaking.

All through the play I scream
and am invited on stage to take a bow.
I lose my senses and kick the actors in the teeth.
There is more laughter
and the actors acknowledge my performance with a bow.
How should I understand this?
Is it to say that if I machine-gun the theatre
from left to right they will respond with applause
that would only gradually diminish with each death?
I wonder then whether logically I should kill myself
too out of admiration. A question indeed,
as I return to my seat and observe a new act
of children playfully aiming their kicks
at each other's groins.

# SELF-EMPLOYED

(*For Harvey Shapiro*)

I stand and listen, head bowed,
to my inner complaint.
Persons passing by think
I am searching for a lost coin.
You're fired, I yell inside
after an especially bad episode.
I'm letting you go without notice
or terminal pay. You just lost
another chance to make good.
But then I watch myself standing at the exit,
depressed and about to leave,
and wave myself back in wearily,
for who else could I get in my place
to do the job in dark, airless conditions?

# THE VENDING MACHINE

I look at a vending machine filled
with candies and say to it,
Disgorge yourself, one for me
and all the rest for the others.
But the machine remains stolid
and silent. It needs a nickel
to make it work, and I remain
stolid and silent.

# AND THAT NIGHT

A photo is taken of the family
enjoying the sunshine
and that night someone sneaks up
from behind in your flat
as you sit reading the papers
and clobbers you. You never
find out why or who, you just
lean back and die.
The sunshine is gone too,
the photograph gets into the news.
You bring up a family in three small rooms,
this crazy man comes along
to finish it off.

# BROODING

The sadness of our lives.
We will never be good enough to each other,
to our parents and friends.
We go along like old sailing ships,
loaded with food and drink for a long voyage,
self-sufficient, without any outside contact
with the world.
                    The truth faces me
all the time. We are in a world
in which nobody listens to anybody,
in which we do as we please
until we are stopped by others.
We live our whole lives as in a husk,
which keeps us separate from any influence.
While those who reflect the influence
of others are either idiots, or people
who never gained consciousness.

# THE RIGHTFUL ONE

I heard my son burst out of his room
and shout, He is here, dad. He is here.
I understood and I managed to stand up,
melting within, and walk the hall
between our rooms to meet Him
whom I had neglected in my thoughts;
but not my son who was ill
and had searched for Him.
He had come. I saw Him standing,
his hair long, face exhausted, eyes sad
and knowing, and I bent my knee,
terrified at the reality,
but he restrained me with a hand
and said, I am a sufferer like yourself.
I have come to let you know.
And I arose, my heart swelling, and said,
I have failed and bitterness is in me.
And he replied, And forgiveness too.
Bless your son. And I blessed him
and his face brightened. And the Rightful One
was gone and left a power to feel free.

# Harvey Shapiro

## NATIONAL COLD STORAGE COMPANY

The National Cold Storage Company contains
More things than you can dream of.
Hard by the Brooklyn Bridge it stands
In a litter of freight cars,
Tugs to one side; the other, the traffic
Of the Long Island Expressway.
I myself have dropped into it in seven years
Midnight tossings, plans for escape, the shakes.
Add this to the national total—
Grant's tomb, the Civil War, Arlington,
The young President dead.
Above the warehouse and beneath the stars
The poets creep on the harp of the Bridge.
But see,
They fall into the National Cold Storage Company
One by one. The wind off the river is too cold,
Or the times too rough, or the Bridge
Is not a harp at all. Or maybe
A monstrous birth inside the warehouse
Must be fed by everything—ships, poems,
Stars, all the years of our lives.

# EPITAPH

To make nothing out of nothing
Was all my study.
I had a wife to help me.
Though I came out bloody,
I made nothing out of nothing.

## PAST TIME

I believe we came together
Out of ignorance not love,
Both being shy and hunted in the city.
In the hot summer, touching each other,
Amazed at how love could come
Like a waterfall, with frightening force
And bruising sleep. Waking at noon,
Touching each other for direction,
Out of ignorance not love.

# CAPTAIN

"Old solitary whiff-beard,"
As another poet has sung you,
I pass you twice a day
Corner of Fulton and Cranberry—
Palms up, pushing the spirit—
On my way toward work or wife,
To the subway or returning.
And you were after?
"A passage to India,"
Mottoes the bronze plaque
On the brick of the Spanish eatery
Where your leaves were first collected.
Though I remember
"Come lovely and soothing death"
Where I wound it into my skull—
A depressed kid of twelve—
As tight as the mockingbird's shuttle,
I never take up your book.
Serenely arriving, arriving,
You coast to each young poet.
Your day, delicate death,
And Century!

# FOR WCW

Now they are trying to make you
The genital thug, leader
Of the new black shirts—
Masculinity over all!
I remember you after the stroke
(Which stroke? I don't remember which stroke.)
Afraid to be left by Flossie
In a hotel lobby, crying out
To her not to leave you
For a minute. Cracked open
And nothing but womanish milk
In the hole. Only a year
Before that we were banging
On the door for a girl to open,
To both of us. Cracked,
Broken. Fear
Slaughtering the brightness
Of your face, stroke and
Counter-stroke, repeated and
Repeated, for anyone to see.
And now, grandmotherly,
You stare from the cover
Of your selected poems—
The only face you could compose
In the end. As if having
Written of love better than any poet
Of our time, you stepped over
To that side for peace.
What valleys, William, to retrace
In memory after the masculine mountains,
What long and splendid valleys.

# Alan Dugan

## COOLED HEELS LAMENT AGAINST FRIVOLITY, THE MASK OF DESPAIR

Dugan's deathward, darling: you
in your unseeable beauty, oh
fictitious, legal person, need
be only formally concerned,
but there is someone too much here,
perspiring in your waiting room.
Because I did not listen when you said,
"Don't call us: we'll call you,"
your credulous receptionist
believes I am a phoney fairy jew
capitalist-communist spy
for Antichrist, a deviated mal-
adjusted lobbyist for the Whiskey Trust,
or else accepts me as I am: a fool.
So while I sit here fouling song,
wasting my substance on the air,
the universe is elsewhere, out
the window in the sky. You,
in your inner office, Muse,
smoking a given, good cigar
and swapping dated stories with
star-salesmen of the soul,
refuse to hear my novel pitch
while I sit out here getting old.

## LETTER TO DONALD FALL

I walked a hangover like my death down
the stairs from the shop and opened the door
to a spring snow sticking only to the tops
of air-conditioners and convertibles, and thought
of my friend Donald Fall in San Francisco.
Toothless in spring!, old friend, I count
my other blessings after friendship
unencumbered by communion: I have:
a money-making job, time off it, a wife
I still love sometimes unapproachably
hammering on picture frames, my own
city that I wake to, that the snow
has come to noiselessly at night, it's there
by morning, swallowing the sounds of spring
and traffic, and my new false teeth,
shining and raw in the technician's lab
like Grails, saying, "We are the resurrection
and the life: tear out the green stumps
of your aching and put plastic on instead:
immortality is in science and machines."
I, as an aging phoney, stale, woozy, and corrupt
from unattempted dreams and bad health habits,
am comforted: the skunk cabbage generates its
frost-thawing fart-gas in New Jersey and the first
crocuses appear in Rockefeller Center's Channel Gardens:
Fall, it is not so bad at Dugan's Edge.

# WALL, CAVE, AND PILLAR STATEMENTS, AFTER ASÔKA

In order to perfect all readers
the statements should be carved
on rock walls, on cave walls,
and on the sides of pillars so
the charm of their instruction can
affect the mountain climbers near
the cliffs, the plainsmen near
the pillars, and the city people near
the caves they go to on vacations.

The statements should, and in a fair
script, spell out the right text and gloss
of the Philosopher's jocular remark. Text
"Honesty is the best policy." Gloss:
"He means not 'best' but 'policy,'
(this is the joke of it) whereas in fact
    Honesty is Honesty, Best
    is Best, and Policy is Policy,
    the three terms being not
    related, but here loosely allied.
What is more important is that 'is'
is, but the rock-like truth of the text
resides in the 'the.' The 'the' is The.
    By this means the amusing sage
    has raised or caused to be raised
    the triple standard in stone:
the single is too simple for life,
the double is mere degrading hypocrisy,
but the third combines the first two
in a possible way, and contributes
something unsayable of its own:

this is the pit, nut, seed or stone
of the fruit when the fruit has been
digested: It is good to do good for the wrong
        reason, better to do good for the good
        reason, and best of all to do good
        good: i.e.: when the doer and doee
        and whatever passes between them
        are beyond all words like 'grace'
        or 'anagogic insight,' or definitions like
        'particular instance of a hoped-at-law,'
        and which the rocks alone can convey.
This is the real reason for the rock walls,
the cave walls and pillars, and not the base
desires for permanence and display
that the teacher's conceit suggests."

        That is the end of the statements, but,
        in order to go on a way after the end
        so as to make up for having begun
        after the beginning, and thus to come around
        to it in order to include the whole thing,
add: "In some places the poignant slogan,
'Morality is a bad joke like everything else'
may be written or not, granted that space
exists for the vulgar remarks, the dates,
initials and hearts of lovers, and all
other graffiti of the prisoners of this world."

# TRIPTYCH

*Scoundrels, Scoundrels*

## ADAM SMITH     KARL MARX     JESUS CHRIST

Wheat is probably a better food than oats,

But if we are to demand that the rate of profit, say 14.876934. . , should be exactly equal in every business and every year, down to the hundredth decimal place, on pain of degradation to a fiction, we should be grossly misunderstanding the nature of the rate of profit and economic laws in general —none of them has any reality except as

34. Think not that I am come to send peace on earth. I am not come to send peace, but a sword.

but not than potatoes.

approximation, tendency, average, but not in *immediate* reality.

35. For I am come to set a man at variance against his father, and the daughter against her mother and the daughter-in-law against her mother-in-law.

Potatoes, however, are perishable.

This is partly due to the fact that their action is thwarted by the simultaneous action of other laws, but also in part to their own nature as

concepts.

# NOON'S WORLD

The day is full of people, Sun,
walking around the staring noon
of paid endeavor: it is a shock
to someone who has slept apart
all morning in a shaded room
to come out into traffic. I
am hopelessly in arrears. I try
to catch up on the action, eat
a lunch for breakfast and pretend:
What have I missed except life?

# Galway Kinnell

## ANOTHER NIGHT IN THE RUINS

I

In the evening
haze darkening on the hills,
purple
of the eternal, a last bird
crosses over, *'flop flop,'*
adoring
only the instant.

II

Nine years ago,
in a plane that rumbled all night
above the Atlantic,
I could see, lit up
by lightning bolts jumping out of it,
a thunderhead formed like the face
of my brother, looking nostalgically down
on blue,
lightning-flashed moments of the Atlantic.

III

He used to tell me,
"What good is the day?

On some hill of despair
the bonfire
you kindle can light the great sky—
though it's true, of course, to make it burn
you have to throw yourself in . . ."


IV

Wind tears itself hollow
in the eaves of my ruins, ghost-flute
of snowdrifts
that build out there in the dark:
upside-down
ravines into which night sweeps
our torn wings, our ink-spattered feathers.


V

I listen.
I hear nothing. Only
the cow, the cow
of nothingness, mooing
down the bones.


VI

Is that a
rooster? He
thrashes in the snow
for a grain. Finds
it. Rips
it into
flames. Flaps. Crows.
Flames
bursting out of his brow.


VII

How many nights must it take
one such as me to learn

that we aren't, after all, made
from that bird which flies out of its ashes,
that for a man
as he goes up in flames, his one work
is
to open himself, to *be*
the flames?

# SPINDRIFT

## I

On this tree thrown up
From the sea, its tangle of roots
Letting the wind go through, I sit
Looking down the beach: old
Horseshoe crabs, broken skates,
Sand dollars, sea horses, as though
Only primeval creatures get destroyed,
At chunks of sea-mud still quivering,
At the light as it glints off the water
And the billion facets of the sand,
At the soft, mystical shine the wind
Blows over the dunes as they creep.

## II

Sit down
By the clanking shore
Of this bitter, beloved sea,

Pluck sacred
Shells from the icy surf,
Fans of gold light, sunbursts,

Lift one to the sun
As a sign you accept to go,
As bid, to the shrine of the dead,

And as it blazes
See the lost life within
Alive again in the fate-shine.

III

This little bleached root
Drifted from some foreign shore,
Brittle, cold, practically weightless,

If anything is dead, it is,
This castout worn
To the lost grip it always essentially was.

If it has lost hold
It at least keeps the wild
Shape of what it held,

And it remains the hand
Of that gravel, one of the earth's
Wandering icons of "to have."


IV

I sit listening
To the surf as it falls,
The power and inexhaustible freshness of the sea,
The suck and inner boom
As a wave tears free and crashes back
In overlapping thunders going away down the beach.

It is the most we know of time,
And it is our undermusic of eternity.


V

I think of how I
Sat by a dying woman,
Her shell of a hand,
Wet and cold in both of mine,
Light, nearly out, existing as smoke,
I sat in the glow of her wan, absorbed smile.

VI

Under the high wind
That moans in the grass
And whistles through crabs' claws
I sit holding this little lamp,
This icy fan of the sun.

Across gull tracks
And wind ripples in the sand
The wind seethes. My footprints
Slogging for the absolute
Already begin vanishing.

VII

What does he really love,
That old man,
His wrinkled eyes
Tortured by smoke,
Walking in the ungodly
Rasp and cackle of old flesh?

The swan dips her head
And peers at the mystic
In-life of the sea,
The gull drifts up
And eddies towards heaven,
The breeze in his arms . . .

Nobody likes to die
But an old man
Can know
A kind of gratefulness
Towards time that kills him,
Everything he loved was made of it.

In the end
What is he but the scallop shell
Shining with time like any pilgrim?

# THE AVENUE BEARING THE INITIAL OF CHRIST INTO THE NEW WORLD

*Was diese kleine Gasse doch für ein Reich an*
*sich war . . .*                                       *for Gail*


I

pcheek pcheek pcheek pcheek pcheek
They cry. The motherbirds thieve the air
To appease them. A tug on the East River
Blasts the bass-note of its passage, lifted
From the infra-bass of the sea. A broom
Swishes over the sidewalk like feet through leaves.
Valerio's pushcart Ice Coal Kerosene
Moves    clack
          clack
            clack
On a broken wheelrim. Ringing in its chains
The New Star Laundry horse comes down the street
Like a roofleak whucking in a pail.
At the redlight, where a horn blares,
The Golden Harvest Bakery brakes on its gears,
Squeaks, and seethes in place. A propane-
gassed bus makes its way with big, airy sighs.

Across the street a woman throws open
Her window,
She sets, terribly softly,
Two potted plants on the windowledge
      tic         tic
And bangs shut her window.
A man leaves a doorway tic toc tic toc tic toc tic hurrah
   toc splat on Avenue C tic etc and turns the corner.

Banking the same corner
A pigeon coasts 5th Street in shadows,
Looks for altitude, surmounts the rims of buildings,
And turns white.

The babybirds pipe down. It is day.


II

In sunlight on the Avenue
The Jew rocks along in a black fur shtraimel,
Black robe, black knickers, black knee-stockings,
Black shoes. His beard like a sod-bottom
Hides the place where he wears no tie.
A dozen children troop after him, barbels flying,
In skullcaps. They are Reuben, Simeon, Levi, Judah, Issachar,
    Zebulun, Benjamin, Dan, Naphtali, Gad, Asher.
With the help of the Lord they will one day become
Courtiers, thugs, rulers, rabbis, asses, adders, wrestlers,
    bakers, poets, cartpushers, infantrymen.

The old man is sad-faced. He is near burial
And one son is missing. The women who bore him sons
And are past bearing, mourn for the son
And for the father, wondering if the man will go down
Into the grave of a son mourning, or if at the last
The son will put his hands on the eyes of his father.

The old man wades towards his last hour.
On 5th Street, between Avenues A and B,
In sunshine, in his private cloud, Bunko Certified Embalmer,
Cigar in his mouth, nose to the wind, leans
At the doorway of Bunko's Funeral Home & Parlour,
Glancing west towards the Ukrainians, eastward idly
Where the Jew rocks towards his last hour.

Sons, grandsons at his heel, the old man
Confronts the sun. He does not feel its rays
Through his beard, he does not understand

Fruits and vegetables live by the sun.
Like his children he is sallow-faced, he sees
A blinding signal in the sky, he smiles.

Bury me not Bunko damned Catholic I pray you in Egypt.


III

From the Station House
Under demolishment on Houston
To the Power Station on 14th,
Jews, Negroes, Puerto Ricans
Walk in the spring sunlight.

The Downtown Talmud Torah
Blosztein's Cutrate Bakery
Areceba Panataria Hispano
Peanuts Dried Fruit Nuts & Canned Goods
Productos Tropicales
Appetizing Herring Candies Nuts
Nathan Kugler Chicken Store Fresh Killed Daily
Little Rose Restaurant
Rubinstein the Hatter Mens Boys Hats Caps Furnishings
J. Herrmann Dealer in All Kinds of Bottles
Natural Bloom Cigars
Blony Bubblegum
Mueren las Cucarachas Super Potente Garantizada de Matar
                                                      las
        Cucarachas mas Resistentes
Wenig מצבות
G. Schnee Stairbuilder
Everyouth la Original Loción Eterna Juventud Satisfacción
                                                      Dinero
        Devuelto
Happy Days Bar & Grill

Through dust-stained windows over storefronts
Curtains drawn aside, onto the Avenue
Thronged with Puerto Ricans, Negroes, Jews,

Baby carriages stuffed with groceries and babies,
The old women peer, blessed damozels
Sitting up there young forever in the cockroached rooms,
Eating fresh-killed chicken, productos tropicales,
Appetizing herring, canned goods, nuts;
They puff out smoke from Natural Bloom cigars
And one day they puff like Blony Bubblegum.
Across the square skies with faces in them
Pigeons skid, crashing into the brick.
From a rooftop a boy fishes at the sky,
Around him a flock of pigeons fountains,
Blown down and swirling up again, seeking the sky.
From a skyview of the city they must seem
A whirlwind on the desert seeking itself;
Here they break from the rims of the buildings
Without rank in the blue military cemetery sky.
A red kite wriggles like a tadpole
Into the sky beyond them, crosses
The sun, lays bare its own crossed skeleton.

To fly from this place—to roll
On some bubbly blacktop in the summer,
To run under the rain of pigeon plumes, to be
Tarred, and feathered with birdshit, Icarus,

In Kugler's glass headdown dangling by yellow legs.


IV

First Sun Day of the year. Tonight,
When the sun will have turned from the earth,
She will appear outside Hy's Luncheonette,
The crone who sells the *News* and the *Mirror*,
The oldest living thing on Avenue C,
Outdating much of its brick and mortar.
If you ask for the *News* she gives you the *Mirror*
And squints long at the nickel in her hand
Despising it, perhaps, for being a nickel,
And stuffs it in her apron pocket

And sucks her lips. Rain or stars, every night
She is there, squatting on the orange crate,
Issuing out only in darkness, like the cucarachas
And strange nightmares in the chambers overhead.
She can't tell one newspaper from another,
She has forgotten how Nain her dead husband looked,
She has forgotten her children's whereabouts
Or how many there were, or what the *News*
And *Mirror* tell about that we buy them with nickels.
She is sure only of the look of a nickel
And that there is a Lord in the sky overhead.
She dwells in a flesh that is of the Lord
And drifts out, therefore, only in darkness
Like the streetlamp outside the Luncheonette
Or the lights in the secret chamber
In the firmament, where Yahweh himself dwells.
Like Magdelene in the Battistero of Saint John
On the carved-up continent, in the land of sun,
She lives shadowed, under a feeble bulb
That lights her face, her crab's hands, her small bulk on the
                                                        crate.
She is Pulchería mother of murderers and madmen,
She is also Alyona whose neck was a chicken leg.

Mother was it the insufferable wind?
She sucks her lips a little further into the mousehole.
She stares among the stars, and among the streetlamps.

The mystery is hers.

v

That violent song of the twilight!
Now, in the silence, will the motherbirds
Be dead, and the infantbirds
That were in the dawn merely transparent
Unfinished things, nothing but bellies,
Will they have been shoved out
And in the course of a morning, casually,
On scrawny wings, have taken up the life?

In the pushcart market, on Sunday,
A crate of lemons discharges light like a battery.
Icicle-shaped carrots that through black soil
Wove away lie like flames in the sun.
Onions with their skirts ripped seek sunlight
On green skins. The sun beats
On beets dirty as boulders in cowfields,
On turnips pinched and gibbons
From budging rocks, on embery sweets,
Peanut-shaped Idahos, short-pebble Long Islands and Maines,
On horseradishes still growing weeds on the flat ends,
Cabbages lying about like sea-green brains
The skulls have been shucked from,
On tomatoes, undented plum-tomatoes, alligator-skinned
Cucumbers, that float pickled
In the wooden tubs of green skim milk—

Sky-flowers, dirt-flowers, underdirt-flowers,
Those that climbed for the sun in their lives
And those that wormed away—equally uprooted,
Maimed, lopped, shucked, and misaimed.

In the market in Damascus a goat
Came to a stall where twelve goatheads
Were lined up for sale. It sniffed them
One by one. Finally thirteen goats started
Smiling in their faintly sardonic way.

A crone buys a pickle from a crone,
It is wrapped in the *Mirror*,
At home she will open the wrapping, stained,
And stare and stare and stare at it.
And the cucumbers, and the melons,
And the leeks, and the onions, and the garlic.

## VII

Already the Avenue troughs the light of day.
Southwards, towards Houston and Pitt,

Where Avenue C begins, the eastern ranges
Of the wiped-out lives—punks, lushes,
Panhandlers, pushers, rumsoaks, everyone
Who took it easy when he should have been out failing at
   something—
The pots-and-pans man pushes his cart,
Through the intersection of the light, at 3rd,
Where sunset smashes on the aluminum of it,
On the bottoms, curves, handles, metal panes,
Mirrors: of the bead-curtained cave under the falls
In Freedom, Seekonk Woods leafing the light out,
Halfway to Kingston where a road branches out suddenly,
Between Pamplonne and Les Salins two meeting paths
Over a sea the green of churchsteeple copper.
Of all places on earth inhabited by men
Why is it we find ourselves on this Avenue
Where the dusk gets worse,
And the mirrorman pushing his heaped mirrors
Into the shadows between 3rd and 2nd,
Pushes away a mess of old pots and pans?

The ancient Negro sits as usual
Outside the Happy Days Bar & Grill. He wears
Dark glasses. Every once in a while, abruptly,
He starts to sing, chanting in a hoarse, nearly breaking
Voice—
               ooooooooooooo      jawwwwwww
                     v                  w
                  u                    w
                   h                    w
                  u                    w
                  h                 din
And becomes silent
    Stares into the polaroid Wilderness
Gross-Rosen, Maidanek, Flössenberg, Ravensbruck, Stutthof,
                                            Riga,
Bergen-Belsen, Mauthausen, Birkenau, Treblinka, Natzweiler,
Dachau, Buchenwald, Auschwitz—
                                Villages,
Pasture-bordered hamlets on the far side of the river.

VIII

The promise was broken too freely
To them and to their fathers, for them to care.
They survive like cedars on a cliff, roots
Hooked in any crevice they can find.
They walk Avenue C in shadows
Neither conciliating its Baalim
Nor whoring after landscapes of the senses,
Tarig bab el Amoud being in the blood
Fumigated by Puerto Rican cooking.

Among women girthed like cedar trees
Other, slenderer ones appear:
One yellow haired, in August,
Under shooting stars on the lake, who
Believed in promises which broke themselves—
In a German flower garden in the Bronx
The wedding of a child and a child, one flesh
Divided in the Adirondack spring—
One who found in the desert city of the West
The first happiness, and fled therefore—
And by a southern sea, in the pines, one loved
Until the mist rose blue in the trees
Around the spiderwebs that kept on shining,
Each day of the shortening summer.

And as rubbish burns
And the pushcarts are loaded
With fruit and vegetables and empty crates
And clank away on iron wheels over cobblestones,
And merchants infold their stores
And the carp ride motionlessly sleeplessly
In the dark tank in the fishmarket,
The figures withdraw into chambers overhead—
In the city of the mind, chambers built
Of care and necessity, where, hands lifted to the blinds,
They glimpse in mirrors backed with the blackness of the
                                                    world
Awkward, cherished rooms containing the familiar selves.

Children set fires in ashbarrels,
Cats prowl the fires, scraps of fishes burn.

A child lay in the flames.
It was not the plan. Abraham
Stood in terror at the duplicity.
Isaac whom he loved lay in the flames.
The Lord turned away washing
His hands without soap and water
Like a common housefly.

The children laugh.
Isaac means *he laughs*.
Maybe the last instant,
The dying itself, *is* easier,
Easier anyway than the hike
From Pitt the blind gut
To the East River of Fishes,
Maybe it is as the poet said,
And the soul turns to thee
O vast and well-veiled Death
And the body gratefully nestles close to thee—

I think of Isaac reading Whitman in Chicago,
The week before he died, coming across
Such a passage and muttering, Oi!
What shit! And smiling, but not for you—I mean,

For *thee*, Sane and Sacred Death!

X

It was Gold's junkhouse, the one the clacking
Carts that little men pad after in harnesses
Picking up bedbugged mattresses, springs
The stubbornness has been loved out of,
Chairs felled by fat, lampshades lights have burned through,
Linoleum the geometry has been scuffed from,

Carriages a single woman's work has brought to wreck,
Would come to in the dusk and unload before,
That the whole neighborhood came out to see
Burning in the night, flames opening out like
Eyelashes from the windows, men firing the tears in,
Searchlights coming on like streams of water, smashing
On the brick, the water blooming up the wall
Like pale trees, reaching into the darkness beyond.

Nobody mourned, nobody stood around in pajamas
And a borrowed coat steaming his nose in coffee.
It was only Gold's junkhouse.
                                    But this evening
The neighborhood comes out again, everything
That may abide the fire was made to go through the fire
And it was made clean: a few twisted springs,
Charred mattresses (crawling still, naturally),
Perambulator skeletons, bicycles tied in knots—
In a great black pile at the junkhouse door,
Smelling of burnt rubber and hair. Rustwater
Hangs in icicles over the windows and door,
Like frozen piss aimed at trespassers,
Combed by wind, set overnight. Carriages we were babies in,
Springs that used to resist love, that gave in
And were thrown out like whores—the black
Irreducible heap, mausoleum of what we were—
It is cold suddenly, we feel chilled,
Nobody knows for sure what is left of him.


XI

The fishmarket closed, the fishes gone into flesh.
The smelts draped on each other, fat with roe,
The marble cod hacked into chunks on the counter,
Butterfishes mouths still open, still trying to eat,
Porgies with receding jaws hinged apart
In a grimace of dejection, as if like cows
They had died under the sledgehammer, perches
In grass-green armor, spotted squeteagues

In the melting ice meek-faced and croaking no more,
Except in the plip plop plip plip in the bucket,
Mud-eating mullets buried in crushed ice,
Tilefishes with scales like chickenfat,
Spanish mackerels, buttercups on the flanks,
Pot-bellied pikes, two-tone flounders
After the long contortion of pushing both eyes
To the brown side that they might look up,
Brown side down, like a mass laying-on of hands,
Or the oath-taking of any army.

The only things alive are the carp
That drift in the black tank in the rear,
Kept living for the usual reason, that they have not died,
And perhaps because the last meal was garbage and they
                              might begin stinking
On dying, before the customer was halfway home.
They nudge each other, to be netted,
The sweet flesh to be lifted thrashing in the air,
To be slugged, and then to keep on living
While they are opened on the counter.
Fishes do not die exactly, it is more
That they go out of themselves, the visible part
Remains the same, there is little pallor,
Only the cataracted eyes which have not shut ever
Must look through the mist which crazed Homer.

These are the vegetables of the deep,
The Sheol-flowers of darkness, swimmers
Of denser darknesses where the sun's rays bend for the last
                              time
And in the sky there burns this shifty jellyfish
That degenerates and flashes and re-forms.

Motes in the eye land is the lid of,
They are plucked out of the green skim milk of the eye.

Fishes are nailed on the wood,
The big Jew stands like Christ, nailing them to the wood,

He scrapes the knife up the grain, the scales fly,
He unnails them, reverses them, nails them again,
Scrapes and the scales fly. He lops off the heads,
Shakes out the guts as if they did not belong in the first place,
And they are flesh for the first time in their lives.

Dear Frau ——————:
    Your husband, ——————, died in the Camp Hos-
pital on ——————. May I express my sincere sympathy
on your bereavement. —————— was admitted to the
Hospital on —————— with severe symptoms of exhaustion, complaining of difficulties in breathing and pains
in the chest. Despite competent medication and devoted medical attention, it proved impossible, unfortunately, to keep the
patient alive. The deceased voiced no final requests.
                    Camp Commandant, ——————

On 5th Street Bunko Certified Embalmer Catholic
Leans in his doorway drawing on a Natural Bloom Cigar.
He looks up the street. Even the Puerto Ricans are Jews
And the Chinese Laundry closes on Saturday.


XII

Next door, outside the pink-fronted Bodega Hispano—

(A crying: you imagine
Some baby in its crib, wailing
As if it could foresee everything.
The crying subsides: you imagine
A mother or father clasping
The damned creature in their arms.
It breaks out again,
This time in a hair-raising shriek—ah,
The alleycat, in a pleasant guise,
In the darkness outside, in the alley,
Wauling, shrieking slowly in its blood.

Another, loftier shrieking

Drowns it out. It begins always
On the high note, over a clang of bells:
Hook & Ladder 11 with an explosion of mufflers
Crab-walking out of 5th Street,
Accelerating up the Avenue, siren
Sliding on the rounded distances
Returning fainter and fainter,
Like a bee looping away from where you lie in the grass.

The searchlights catch him at the topfloor window,
Trying to move, nailed in place by the shine.
The bells of Saint Brigid's
On Tompkins Square
Toll for someone who has died—
J'oïs la cloche de Serbonne,
Qui tousjours à neuf heures sonne
Le Salut que l'Ange prédit . . .

Expecting the visitation
You lie back on your bed,
The sounds outside
Must be outside. Here
Are only the dead spirituals
Turning back into prayers—
You rise on an elbow
To make sure they come from outside,
You hear nothing, you lay down
Your head on the pillow
Like a pick-up arm—
    swing low
          swing low
               sweet
    lowsweet—)
—Carols of the Caribbean, plinkings of guitars.


XIII

The garbage disposal truck
Like a huge hunched animal

*371*

That sucks in garbage in the place
Where other animals evacuate it
Whines, as the cylinder in the rear
Threshes up the trash and garbage,
Where two men in rubber suits
(It must be raining outside)
Heap it in. The groaning motor
Rises in a whine as it grinds in
The garbage, and between-times
Groans. It whines and groans again.
All about it as it moves down
5th Street is the clatter of trashcans,
The crashes of them as the sanitary engineers
Bounce them on the sidewalk.
If it is raining outside
You can only tell by looking
In puddles, under the lifted streetlamps.

It would be the spring rain.


XIV

Behind the Power Station on 14th, the held breath
Of light, as God is a held breath, withheld,
Spreads the East River, into which fishes leak:
The brown sink or dissolve,
The white float out in shoals and armadas,
Even the gulls pass them up, pale
Bloated socks of riverwater and rotted seed,
That swirl on the tide, punched back
To the Hell Gate narrows, and on the ebb
Steam seaward, seeding the sea.

On the Avenue, through air tinted crimson
By neon over the bars, the rain is falling.
You stood once on Houston, among panhandlers and winos
Who weave the eastern ranges, learning to be free,
To not care, to be knocked flat and to get up clear-headed
Spitting the curses out. "Now be nice,"

The proprietor threatens; "Be nice," he cajoles.
"Fuck you," the bum shouts as he is hoisted again,
"God fuck your mother." (In the empty doorway,
Hunched on the empty crate, the crone gives no sign.)

That night a wildcat cab whined crosstown on 7th.
You knew even the traffic lights were made by God,
The red splashes growing dimmer the farther away
You looked, and away up at 14th, a few green stars;
And without sequence, and nearly all at once,
The red lights blinked into green,
And just before there was one complete Avenue of green,
The little green stars in the distance blinked.

It is night, and raining. You look down
Towards Houston in the rain, the living streets,
Where instants of transcendence
Drift in oceans of loathing and fear, like lanternfishes,
Or phosphorous flashings in the sea, or the feverish light
Skin is said to give off when the swimmer drowns at night.

From the blind gut Pitt to the East River of Fishes
The Avenue cobbles a swath through the discolored air,
A roadway of refuse from the teeming shores and ghettos
And the Caribbean Paradise, into the new ghetto and new
paradise,
This God-forsaken Avenue bearing the initial of Christ
Through the haste and carelessness of the ages,
The sea standing in heaps, which keeps on collapsing,
Where the drowned suffer a C-change,
And remain the common poor.

Since Providence, for the realization of some unknown
purpose, has
seen fit to leave this dangerous people on the face of the
earth, and

did not destroy it . . .

Listen! the swish of the blood,
The sirens down the bloodpaths of the night,
Bone tapping on the bone, nerve-nets
Singing under the breath of sleep—
We scattered over the lonely seaways,
Over the lonely deserts did we run,
In dark lanes and alleys we did hide ourselves . . .

The heart beats without windows in its night,
The lungs put out the light of the world as they
Heave and collapse, the brain turns and rattles
In its own black axlegrease—

                    In the nightime
Of the blood they are laughing and saying,
Our little lane, what a kingdom it was!

                    oi weih, oi weih

IX

# Kenneth Koch

*From* **WHEN THE SUN TRIES TO GO ON**

Lucky the moaning caretaker, favorite the sea
And numb to dirt, exhaustion, face, each, flax,
Cologne, pitiful comic strips commingling gold
Fracas Endymion dimples with clocklike rhubarb
The cuckooclock shouts, mad cuckooclock
Bartender silence-creation "fills." There are.
Homily of shops "mock," dear house of yoyos!
Horse "nay," a differing comet of yoyos'
Balanced deserving cheese "giants" cuckooclock
O matadors! defying and "oh," levels of sweetness'
Cheese. Blah. They are Harry, Susan, Lynn
Blotter. "Major" Blotter, with film of "Gordon"
Cuckooclocks, the passageway to Easter. Motto:
"Cosine the defeated hips." O pazzling dizzling author
Of "Chow Face, a Nincompoop for Dogs"! "Murray,
Lyle, and Jean" Cuckooclocks. O Madagascar
Mazda wintry tights. Sascha films
"Ellen's Back," "Eileen's Bock," "the"s, "so"s.
O sartorial "tree"-camps of demanding yoyos'
Faces of "von Mirror" 's. Hobby. Natal. House.
"Wotan, leaf are my cuckooclock. Show me, that imp
Cheese! He are forgotten satch bell of a glue bell,
Listener-bell." Train sigh in the "Andy" bell show-off,
Too "Yorick" "Bill." Ding dong ding dong there is the bell!

Stove! you cursing troopers of Egypt
Black. "heart"-egret, result "scowl-balcony"

Midnight, "What" bottles of, looms!
Intelligent valentines, "spent" 's, and "cap" 's!
Hoe'd youth, not beside. Mineral's little
"Agnes the lea, O terrible Hoo 'Kays' of frost's
My general'll coming down. So match, is
'Pet'-gown, whacking, miss, and four 'got
Ladles.' Danish." What short script "Ha Bessarabia
Ha Bessarabia." Taster of Northern Lights,
The cheerful disuse of Safety matches, the period
Of "Oh I hate the murdered street-cars"
Stove! the blanched pyramid, sounds nice, bee,
Kom Tom, hoodoo, banana class, array, likes who,
Plaza. Carolina of useful fêtes O lovely soup the
Carved, gentleman, lonely, of raided springtime
Dance, cocoa-pain! Billionaire loading-guns, is
Bending myopia for glass steaks. Monster vealchops
And mint cuckoo consomme, glass bananas, glass
Oysters and peace-less bicycles, running
To, fats! the train, a glass arch-remover, Ben
Loth, light-rays, O shoes! 'Rather than kill
Be killed'-store of wavy nickels. Shore! see their
Little hands," the month of coat-Lambeth spare sea monsters!

"A copy of 'Chews' has ripped my cheers a pack"
"The somnolence of Genji" "Hopeful" "Engine-ski-mo
Modern" "German pea hospital" "O cloud binge"
"Country notice mother, 'll take the city
In marriage" "Baked snow" "Empirin tablets
There is a closet of every beneath" "Youthful
Marzipan" "Chow frigidaire" Now, be uncommon
There is a package of
Red, white, and blue RATS! charging. Houseboat!
Film star! "The eating I mentioned to you
Last Thursday was totally unlimited by
Mediterranean comic billboards wordings'
Sailboats of misdirection, as if soap
"Mocks" the tea-tablets' December wrongdoing's
Bear." He was more British than an icebox. Out
The rats ripped him. Shovel. A pier

Of sudden "Flo" gladness. The minted peach-fly
Sounds, "O badger of repeated adzes,
Long-time, few, hat, het, boat, sand,
Lockers, knee, mistress of Aix, umpire with three shouts,
O blue tapeworm, sonnet of powerful indifference, nest
Of hallways of birthday sheep, soror, tie
On pretty benches lay my ore coaty head
Wind the banjo 'mock-hooped.' Andy dust 'Freemason.' "

Earthworks of genuine Pierre! Molly. Champac's. Egypt.
Esteban Vicente. Melodies'. Cow. Advance is chewing gum.
Saith Bill de Kooning, "I turned my yoyo into a gun,
Bang bank! Half of the war close pinstripes.
Timothy Tomato, Romulus Gun." "The magic of his
Cousse-cousse masterpiece," saith Pierre, "is apple blossoms'
Merchant marine gun." Ouch. The world is Ashbery
Tonight. "I am flooding you with catacombs,"
Saith Larry Rivers (more of him later on).
There is also some fools laying on their stomachs.
O show! merchant marine of Venice!
At lilac wears a beetle on its chest!
These modern masters chew up moths. How many drawers
Are in your chest? Moon Mullins' Moon Mullins
Put his feet in my Cincinnati apple blossoms. Many
Dry cigarettes have fallen into work's colors. The shop
Of geniuses has closed. Jane Freilicher
Might walk through this air like a French lilac,
Her maiden name is Niederhoffer, she tends the stove.
"O shouting shop, my basement's apple blossoms!"
There is a tiny drawer more hot than elbows,
Season. Number, favor, say. Old winter oh
Winter. The park is full of water veins and
Surly council members, or sad Creons. Sway, unsound
    airplanes!

## AUS EINER KINDHEIT

Is the basketball coach a homosexual lemon manufacturer?
   It is suspected by O'Ryan in his submarine.
When I was a child we always cried to be driven for a ride in
   that submarine. Daddy would say Yes!
Mommy would say No! The maid read *Anna Karenina* and
   told us secrets. Some suspected her of a liaison with
   O'Ryan. Nothing but squirrels
Seemed to be her interest, at the windows, except on holidays,
   like Easter and Thanksgiving, when
She would leave the basement and rave among the leaves,
   shouting, I am the Spirit of Softball! Come to me!
Daddy would always leave town. And a chorus of spiders
Would hang from my bedroom wall. Mommy had a hat made
   out of pasty hooks. She gave a party to limburger cheese.
We all were afraid that O'Ryan would come!
He came, he came! as the fall wind comes, waving and razing
   and swirling the leaves
With his bags, his moustache, his cigar, his golfball, his
   pencils, his April compasses, and over his whole
Body we children saw signs of life beneath the water! Oh!
Will he dance the hornpipe? we wondered, Will he smoke a
   cigar underneath eleven inches of ocean? Will he beat the
   pavement
Outside our door with his light feet, for being so firm? Is he a
   lemon Memnon?
O'Ryan O'Ryan O'Ryan! The maid came up from the
   basement, we were all astonished. And she said, "Is it
   Thanksgiving? Christmas? I felt
A force within me stir." And then she saw O'Ryan! The
   basketball coach followed her up from the cellar. He and
   O'Ryan fight!
No one is homosexual then! happily I swim through the
   bathtubs with my scarlet-haired sister

Z. ("O women I love you!" O'Ryan cried.) And we parked
  under water. Then, looking out the window,
We saw the snow had begun to fall, upon the green grass,
  and both shyly entered the new world of our bleached
  underwear. Rome! Rome!
Was our maid entertaining that limburger cheese, or my
  mother? has the passageway fallen asleep? and can one's
  actions for six years be called "improper"?
I hope not. I hope the sea. I hope cigars will be smoked. I
  hope it from New York to California. From Tallahassee to
  St. Paul.
I hope the orange punching bag will be socked, and that
  you'll be satisfied, sweet friend. I hope international
  matrimony, lambent skies, and "Ship, ahoy!"
For we're due to be dawned on, I guess.

## FRESH AIR

I

At the Poem Society a black-haired man stands up to say
"You make me sick with all your talk about restraint and
  mature talent!
Haven't you ever looked out the window at a painting by
  Matisse,
Or did you always stay in hotels where there were too many
  spiders crawling on your visages?
Did you ever glance inside a bottle of sparkling pop,
Or see a citizen split in two by the lightning?
I am afraid you have never smiled at the hibernation
Of bear cubs except that you saw in it some deep relation
To human suffering and wishes, oh what a bunch of
  crackpots!"
The black-haired man sits down, and the others shoot arrows
  at him.
A blond man stands up and says,
"He is right! Why should we be organized to defend the
  kingdom
Of dullness? There are so many slimy people connected with
  poetry,
Too, and people who know nothing about it!
I am not recommending that poets like each other and
  organize to fight them,
But simply that lightning should strike them."
Then the assembled mediocrities shot arrows at the
  blond-haired man.
The chairman stood up on the platform, oh he was physically
  ugly!
He was small-limbed and -boned and thought he was quite
  seductive,

But he was bald with certain hideous black hairs,
And his voice had the sound of water leaving a vaseline
  bathtub,
And he said, "The subject for this evening's discussion is
  poetry
On the subject of love between swans." And everyone threw
  candy hearts
At the disgusting man, and they stuck to his bib and tucker,
And he danced up and down on the platform in terrific glee
And recited the poetry of his little friends—but the blond
  man stuck his head
Out of a cloud and recited poems about the east and thunder,
And the black-haired man moved through the stratosphere
  chanting
Poems of the relationships between terrific prehistoric
  charcoal whales,
And the slimy man with candy hearts sticking all over him
Wilted away like a cigarette paper on which the bumblebees
  have urinated,
And all the professors left the room to go back to their duty,
And all that were left in the room were five or six poets
And together they sang the new poem of the twentieth century
Which, though influenced by Mallarmé, Shelley, Byron, and
  Whitman,
Plus a million other poets, is still entirely original
And is so exciting that it cannot be here repeated.
You must go to the Poem Society and wait for it to happen.
Once you have heard this poem you will not love any other,
Once you have dreamed this dream you will be inconsolable,
Once you have loved this dream you will be as one dead,
Once you have visited the passages of this time's great art!


II

"Oh to be seventeen years old
Once again," sang the red-haired man, "and not know that
  poetry
Is ruled with the sceptre of the dumb, the deaf, and the
  creepy!"

383

And the shouting persons battered his immortal body with
  stones
And threw his primitive comedy into the sea
From which it sang forth poems irrevocably blue.


Who are the great poets of our time, and what are their
  names?
Yeats of the baleful influence, Auden of the baleful influence,
  Eliot of the baleful influence
(Is Eliot a great poet? no one knows), Hardy, Stevens,
  Williams (is Hardy of our time?),
Hopkins (is Hopkins of our time?), Rilke (is Rilke of our
  time?), Lorca (is Lorca of our time?), who is still of our
  time?
Mallarmé, Valéry, Apollinaire, Eluard, Reverdy, French poets
  are still of our time,
Pasternak and Mayakovsky, is Jouve of our time?


Where are young poets in America, they are trembling in
  publishing houses and universities,
Above all they are trembling in universities, they are bathing
  the library steps with their spit,
They are gargling out innocuous (to whom?) poems about
  maple trees and their children,
Sometimes they brave a subject like the Villa d'Este or a
  lighthouse in Rhode Island,
Oh what worms they are! they wish to perfect their form.

Yet could not these young men, put in another profession,
Succeed admirably, say at sailing a ship? I do not doubt it,
  Sir, and I wish we could try them.
(A plane flies over the ship holding a bomb but perhaps it will
  not drop the bomb,
The young poets from the universities are staring anxiously
  at the skies,
Oh they are remembering their days on the campus when they
  looked up to watch birds excrete,
They are remembering the days they spent making their
  elegant poems.)

Is there no voice to cry out from the wind and say what it is
    like to be the wind,
To be roughed up by the trees and to bring music from the
    scattered houses
And the stones, and to be in such intimate relationship with
    the sea
That you cannot understand it? Is there no one who feels
    like a pair of pants?


III

Summer in the trees! "It is time to strangle several bad
    poets."
The yellow hobbyhorse rocks to and fro, and from the
    chimney
Drops the Strangler! The white and pink roses are slightly
    agitated by the struggle,
But afterwards beside the dead "poet" they cuddle up
    comfortingly against their vase. They are safer now, no one
    will compare them to the sea.

Here on the railroad train, one more time, is the Strangler.
He is going to get that one there, who is on his way to a
    poetry reading.
Agh! Biff! A body falls to the moving floor.

In the football stadium I also see him,
He leaps through the frosty air at the maker of comparisons
Between football and life and silently, silently strangles him!

Here is the Strangler dressed in a cowboy suit
Leaping from his horse to annihilate the students of myth!

The Strangler's ear is alert for the names of Orpheus,
Cuchulain, Gawain, and Odysseus,
And for poems addressed to Jane Austen, F. Scott Fitzgerald,
To Ezra Pound, and to personages no longer living
Even in anyone's thoughts—O Strangler the Strangler!

385

He lies on his back in the waves of the Pacific Ocean.


IV

Supposing that one walks out into the air
On a fresh spring day and has the misfortune
To encounter an article on modern poetry
In *New World Writing,* or has the misfortune
To see some examples of some of the poetry
Written by the men with their eyes on the myth
And the Missus and the midterms, in the *Hudson Review,*
Or, if one is abroad, in *Botteghe Oscure,*
Or indeed in *Encounter,* what is one to do
With the rest of one's day that lies blasted to ruins
All bluely about one, what is one to do?
O surely one cannot complain to the President,
Nor even to the deans of Columbia College,
Nor to T. S. Eliot, nor to Ezra Pound,
And supposing one writes to the Princess Caetani,
"Your poets are awful!" what good would it do?
And supposing one goes to the *Hudson Review*
With a package of matches and sets fire to the building?
One ends up in prison with trial subscriptions
To the *Partisan, Sewanee,* and *Kenyon Review!*


V

Sun out! perhaps there is a reason for the lack of poetry
In these ill-contented souls, perhaps they need air!

Blue air, fresh air, come in, I welcome you, you are an art
    student,
Take off your cap and gown and sit down on the chair.
Together we shall paint the poets—but no, air! perhaps you
    should go to them, quickly,
Give them a little inspiration, they need it, perhaps they are
    out of breath,
Give them a little inhuman company before they freeze the
    English language to death!

(And rust their typewriters a little, be sea air! be noxious! kill
   them, if you must, but stop their poetry!
I remember I saw you dancing on the surf on the Côte d'Azur,
And I stopped, taking my hat off, but you did not remember
   me,
Then afterwards you came to my room bearing a handful of
   orange flowers
And we were together all through the summer night!)

That we might go away together, it is so beautiful on the sea,
   there are a few white clouds in the sky!

But no, air! you must go . . . Ah, stay!

But she has departed and . . . Ugh! what poisonous fumes and
   clouds! what a suffocating atmosphere!
Cough! whose are these hideous faces I see, what is this rigor
Infecting the mind? where are the green Azores,
Fond memories of childhood, and the pleasant orange
   trolleys,
A girl's face, red-white, and her breasts and calves, blue eyes,
   brown eyes, green eyes, fahrenheit
Temperatures, dandelions, and trains, O blue?!
Wind, wind, what is happening? Wind! I can't see any bird
   but the gull, and I feel it should symbolize . . .
Oh, pardon me, there's a swan, one two three swans, a great
   white swan, hahaha how pretty they are! Smack!
Oh! stop! help! yes, I see—disrespect of my superiors—
   forgive me, dear Zeus, nice Zeus, parabolic bird, O feathered
   excellence! white!
There is Achilles too, and there's Ulysses, I've always wanted
   to see them, hahaha!
And there is Helen of Troy, I suppose she is Zeus too, she's so
   terribly pretty—hello, Zeus, my you are beautiful, Bang!
One more mistake and I get thrown out of the Modern Poetry
   Association, help! Why aren't there any adjectives around?
Oh there are, there's practically nothing else—look, here's
   *grey, utter, agonized, total, phenomenal, gracile, invidious,
   sundered,* and *fused,*

*Elegant, absolute, pyramidal,* and . . . Scream! but what can I
describe with these words? States!

States symbolized and divided by two, complex states, magic
states, states of consciousness governed by an aroused
sincerity, cockadoodle doo!

Another bird! is it morning? Help! where am I? am I in the
barnyard? oink oink, scratch, moo! Splash!

My first lesson. "Look around you. What do you think and
feel?" *Uhhh* . . . "Quickly!" *This Connecticut landscape
would have pleased Vermeer.* Wham! A-Plus.
"Congratulations!" I am promoted.

OOOhhhhh I wish I were dead, what a headache! My second
lesson: "Rewrite your first lesson line six hundred times.
Try to make it into a magnetic field." I can do it too. But my
poor line! What a nightmare! Here comes a tremendous
horse,

Trojan, I presume. No, it's my third lesson. "Look, look!
Watch him, see what he's doing? That's what we want you
to do. Of course it won't be the same as his at first, but
. . ." I demur. Is there no other way to fertilize minds?

Bang! I give in . . . Already I see my name in two or three
anthologies, a serving girl comes into the barn bringing me
the anthologies,

She is very pretty and I smile at her a little sadly, perhaps it
is my last smile! Perhaps she will hit me! But no, she smiles
in return, and she takes my hand.

My hand, my hand! what is this strange thing I feel in my
hand, on my arm, on my chest, my face—can it be . . . ? it
is! AIR!

Air, air, you've come back! Did you have any success? "What
do you think." I don't know, air. You are so strong, air.

And she breaks my chains of straw, and we walk down the
road, behind us the hideous fumes!

Soon we reach the seaside, she is a young art student who
places her head on my shoulder,

I kiss her warm red lips, and here is the Strangler, reading
the *Kenyon Review!* Good luck to you, Strangler!

Goodbye, Helen! goodbye, fumes! goodbye, abstracted
dried-up boys! goodbye, dead trees! goodbye, skunks!

Goodbye, manure! goodbye, critical manicure! goodbye, you
  big fat men standing on the east coast as well as the west
  giving poems the test! farewell, Valéry's stern dictum!
Until tomorrow, then, scum floating on the surface of poetry!
  goodbye for a moment, refuse that happens to land in
  poetry's boundaries! adieu, stale eggs teaching imbeciles
  poetry to bolster up your egos! adios, boring anomalies of
  these same stale eggs!
Ah, but the scum is deep! Come, let me help you! and soon
  we pass into the clear blue water. Oh GOODBYE, castrati
  of poetry! farewell, stale pale skunky pentameters (the
  only honest English meter, gloop gloop!) until tomorrow,
  horrors! oh, farewell!

Hello, sea! good morning, sea! hello, clarity and excitement,
  you great expanse of green—

O green, beneath which all of them shall drown!

# THE ARTIST

Ah, well, I abandon you, cherrywood smokestack,
Near the entrance to this old green park! . . .

□

Cherrywood avalanche, my statue of you
Is still standing in Toledo, Ohio.
O places, summer, boredom, the static of an acrobatic blue!

And I made an amazing zinc airliner
It is standing to this day in the Minneapolis zoo . . .

Old times are not so long ago, plaster-of-paris haircut!

□

I often think *Play* was my best work.
It is an open field with a few boards in it.

Children are allowed to come and play in *Play*
By permission of the Cleveland Museum.
I look up at the white clouds, I wonder what I shall do, and
    smile.

Perhaps somebody will grow up having been influenced by
    *Play*,
I think—but what good will that do?
Meanwhile I am interested in steel cigarettes . . .

□

The orders are coming in thick and fast for steel cigarettes,
    steel cigars.
The Indianapolis Museum has requested six dozen packages.

*390*

I wonder if I'd still have the courage to do a thing like *Play?*

I think I may go to Cleveland . . .

□

Well, here I am! Pardon me, can you tell me how to get to the
 Cleveland Museum's monumental area, *Play?*

"Mister, that was torn down a long time ago. You ought to go
 and see the new thing they have now—*Gun.*"
What? *Play* torn down?
"Yes, Mister, and I loved to climb in it too, when I was a kid!"
 And he shakes his head
Sadly . . . But I am thrilled beyond expectation!
He liked my work!
And I guess there must be others like that man in Cleveland
 too . . .

So you see, *Play* has really had its effect!
Now I am on the outskirts of town
And . . . here it is! But it has changed! There are some blue
 merds lying in the field
And it's not marked *Play* anymore—and here's a calf!
I'm so happy, I can't tell why!
Was this how I originally imagined *Play*, but lacked the
 courage?

It would be hard now, though, to sell it to another museum.
I wonder if the man I met's children will come and play in it?
How does one's audience survive?

□

Pittsburgh, May 16th. I have abandoned the steel cigarettes.
 I am working on *Bee.*
*Bee* will be a sixty-yards-long covering for the elevator shaft
 opening in the foundry sub-basement
Near my home. So far it's white sailcloth with streams of
 golden paint evenly spaced out

391

With a small blue pond at one end, and around it orange and
   green flowers. My experience in Cleveland affected me so
That my throat aches whenever I am not working at full
   speed. I have never been so happy and inspired and
*Play* seems to me now like a juvenile experience!

□

June 8th. *Bee* is still not finished. I have introduced a huge
   number of red balloons into it. How will it work?
Yesterday X. said, "Are you still working on *Bee?* What's
   happened to your interest in steel cigarettes?"
Y. said, "He hasn't been doing any work at all on them since
   he went to Cleveland." A shrewd guess! But how much can
   they possibly know?

□

November 19th. Disaster! *Bee* was almost completed, and now
   the immense central piece of sailcloth has torn. Impossible
   to repair it!

December 4th. I've gone back to work on *Bee!* I suddenly
   thought (after weeks of despair!), "I can place the balloons
   over the tear in the canvas!" So that is what I am doing.
   All promises to be well!

December 6th. The foreman of the foundry wants to look at
   my work. It seems that he too is an "artist"—does sketches
   and watercolors and such . . . What will he think of *Bee?*

□

Cherrywood! I had left you far from my home
And the foreman came to look at *Bee*
And the zinc airliner flew into *Play!*

The pink balloons aren't heavy, but the yellow ones break.
The foreman says, "It's the greatest thing I ever saw!"
Cleveland heard too and wants me to come back and
   reinaugurate *Play*

I dream of going to Cleveland but never will
*Bee* has obsessed my mind.

□

March 14th. A cold spring day. It is snowing. *Bee* is
    completed.

□

O *Bee* I think you are my best work
In the blue snow-filled air
I feel my heart break

I lie down in the snow
They come from the foundry and take *Bee* away
Oh what can I create now, Earth,

Green Earth on which everything blossoms anew?
"A bathroom floor cardboard trolley line
The shape and size of a lemon seed with on the inside
A passenger the size of a pomegranate seed
Who is an invalid and has to lean on the cardboard side
Of the lemon-seed-sized trolley line so that he won't fall off
    the train."

□

□

I just found these notes written many years ago.
How seriously I always take myself! Let it be a lesson to me.
To bring things up to date: I have just finished *Campaign*,
    which is a tremendous piece of charcoal.
Its shape is difficult to describe; but it is extremely large and
    would reach to the sixth floor of the Empire State Building.
    I have been very successful in the past fourteen or fifteen
    years.

□

*Summer Night*, shall I never succeed in finishing you? Oh you are the absolute end of all my creation! The ethereal beauty of that practically infinite number of white stone slabs stretching into the blue secrecy of ink! O stabs in my heart!

. . . .Why not a work *Stabs in My Heart?* But *Summer Night?*

January. . . . A troubled sleep. Can I make two things at once? What way is there to be sure that the impulse to work on *Stabs in My Heart* is serious? It seems occasioned only by my problem about finishing *Summer Night* . . . ?

□

The *Magician of Cincinnati* is now ready for human use. They are twenty-five tremendous stone staircases, each over six hundred feet high, which will be placed in the Ohio River between Cincinnati and Louisville, Kentucky. All the boats coming down the Ohio River will presumably be smashed up against the immense statues, which are the most recent work of the creator of *Flowers, Bee, Play, Again* and *Human Use.* Five thousand citizens are thronged on the banks of the Ohio waiting to see the installation of the work, and the crowd is expected to be more than fifteen times its present number before morning. There will be a game of water baseball in the early afternoon, before the beginning of the ceremonies, between the Cincinnati Redlegs and the Pittsburgh Pirates. The *Magician of Cincinnati,* incidentally, is said to be absolutely impregnable to destruction of any kind, and will therefore presumably always be a feature of this part of the Ohio. . . .

□

May 16th. With what an intense joy I watched the installation of the *Magician of Cincinnati* today, in the Ohio River, where it belongs, and which is so much a part of my original scheme. . . .

May 17th. I feel suddenly freed from life—not so much as if my work were going to change, but as though I had at last seen what I had so long been prevented (perhaps I prevented myself!) from seeing: that there is too much for me to do. Somehow this enables me to relax, to breathe easily. . . .

□

There's the *Magician of Cincinnati*
In the distance
Here I am in the green trees of Pennsylvania

How strange I felt when they had installed
The *Magician!* . . . Now a bluebird trills, I am busy making my
  polished stones
For *Dresser*.

The stream the stone the birds the reddish-pink Pennsylvania
  hills
All go to make up *Dresser*
Why am I camping out?
I am waiting for the thousands of tons of embalming fluid
That have to come and with which I can make these hills.

□

GREATEST ARTISTIC EVENT HINTED BY GOVERNOR
Reading, June 4. Greatest artistic event was hinted today by
  governor. Animals converge on meadow where artist
  working.

CONVERGE ON MEADOW WHERE WORKING

ARTIST HINTED, SAME MAN

. . . the *Magician of Cincinnati*

THREE YEARS

October 14th. I want these hills to be striated! How naive the
  *Magician of Cincinnati* was! Though it makes me happy to

think of it. . . . Here, I am plunged into such real earth! Striate, hills! What is this deer's head of green stone? I can't fabricate anything less than what I think should girdle the earth. . . .

PHOTOGRAPH

PHOTOGRAPH

PHOTOGRAPH

Artist who created the *Magician of Cincinnati;* Now at work in Pennsylvania; The Project—*Dresser*—So Far.

□

Ah! . . .

□

TONS

SILICON, GRASS AND DEER-HEAD RANGE
Philadelphia. Your voice as well as mine will be appreciated to express the appreciation of *Dresser,* which makes of Pennsylvania the silicon, grass and stone deer-head center of the world. . . . Artist says he may change his mind about the central bridges. Fountains to give forth real tar-water. Mountain lake in center. Real chalk cliffs. Also cliffs of clay. Deep declivities nearby. "Wanted forest atmosphere, yet to be open." Gas . . .

□

PHOTOGRAPH

SKETCH

DEDICATION CEREMONY

GOES SWIMMING IN OWN STREAM

SHAKING HANDS WITH GOVERNOR

COLOR PICTURE

THE HEAD OF THE ARTIST

THE ARTIST'S HAND

STACK OF ACTUAL BILLS NEEDED TO PAY FOR
  PROJECT

Story of *Dresser*

PENNSYLVANIA'S PRIDE: *DRESSER*

Creator of *Dresser*

☐

STILL SMILING AT FORGE
Beverly, South Dakota, April 18. Still smiling at forge, artist
of *Dresser* says, "No, of course I haven't forgotten *Dresser*.
Though how quickly the years have gone by since I have been
doing *Too*!" We glanced up at the sky and saw a large white
bird, somewhat similar to an immense seagull, which was as
if fixed above our heads. Its eyes were blue sapphires, and its
wings were formed by an ingenious arrangement of whitened
daffodil-blossom parts. Its body seemed mainly charcoal, on
the whole, with a good deal of sand mixed in. As we watched
it, the creature actually seemed to move. . . .

August 4th . . . Three four five, and it's finished! I can see it in
  Beverly . . .

☐

BEVERLY HONORS ARTIST. CALLED "FOUNDING
  FATHER"

Beverly, South Dakota, August 14 . . .

MISSISSIPPI CLAIMS BIRTHPLACE

HONORS BIRTHPLACE

BIRTHPLACE HONORS HELD

☐

INDIANS AND SAVANTS MEET TO PRAISE *WEST WIND*

*PAT* HONORED

*PAT* AND *WEST WIND* HONORED

☐

June 3rd. It doesn't seem possible—the Pacific Ocean! I have
  ordered sixteen million tons of blue paint. Waiting
  anxiously for it to arrive. How would grass be as a
  substitute? cement?

☐

# A POEM OF THE FORTY-EIGHT STATES

I

O Kentucky! my parents were driving
Near blue grass when you became
For me the real contents of a glass
Of water also the first nozzle of a horse
The bakery truck floating down the street
The young baboon woman walking without a brace
Over a fiord

The electric chair steamed lightly, then touched
Me. I drove, upward,
Into the hills of Montana. My pony!
Here you are coming along with your master!
Yet I am your master! You're wearing my sweater.
O pony, my pony!

As in a dream I was waiting to be seventh
To smile at my brothers in the happy state of Idaho
Each and every one of them condemned to the electric chair!
What have we done? Is it a crime
To shoe horses? Beside a lemon-yellow stream
There seemed to be compact bassoons,
And I was happy and a crackerjack.

My stovepipe hat! Perhaps you think I am Uncle Sam?
No, I am the State of Pennsylvania . . .
O hills! I remember writing to a city
So as to be contented with my name
Returning in the mails near the mark "Pennsylvania!"
"Somewhere over that hill is Georgia."
What romance there was for me in the words the old man
    said!

I wanted to go, but was afraid to wander very far.
Then he said, "I will take you in my wagon of hay."
And so we rode together into the Peach State.
I will never forget that day, not so long as I live,
I will never forget the first impressions I had in Georgia!


II

In Zanesville, Ohio, they put a pennant up,
And in Waco, Texas, men stamped in the streets,
And the soldiers were coughing on the streetcar in
    Minneapolis, Minnesota.
In Minocqua, Wisconsin, the girls kissed each other and
    laughed,
The poison was working in Monroe, Illinois,
And in Stephanie, New Hampshire, burning fragments were
    thrown up.

It was the day of the States, and from Topeka, Kansas,
To Lumberville, New York, trees were being struck
Down so they could put the platforms up. However I lay
    struck
By sunlight on the beach at Waikiki, Hawaii . . .
Why can't Hawaii be one of the United States?
Nothing is being celebrated here; yet the beaches are covered
    with sun . . .

Florida, Vermont, Alabama, Mississippi!
I guess that I will go back to the United States.
Dear friend, let's pack our bags and climb upon the steamer!
Do not forget the birds you have bought in the jolly land of
    France,
They are red white orange yellow green and pink and they sing
    so sweetly,
They will make music to us upon the tedious ocean voyage.


III

Tedious! How could I have said such a thing?
O sea, you are more beautiful than any state!

You are fuller and bluer and more perfect than the most
   perfect action.
What is a perfect action?
In the streets of Kokomo a cheer goes up,
And the head of the lion is cursed by a thousand vicissitudes.

Indiana! it is so beautiful to have tar in it!
How wonderful it is to be back on a trollycar, ding dong ding!
I think I will wander into the barbershop and get my hair cut!
Just hear the slice of the scissors, look at the comb!
Now to be once more out in the streets of Indiana
With my hair much shorter, with my neck smelling of talcum
   powder!
O lucky streetcar wires to be able to look at me, and through
   whom I can see the sun!

I did not know there was so much sun in North Dakota!
But the old man who is telling me about it nods his head and
   says yes.
I believe him because my skin is peeling. Now I see people
   going to the voting booth.
The voting wagon is red and wooden, it stands on wheels
   where it is anchored to the curb.
I had no idea there were so many old men and old women in
   North Dakota.
But the old man who is explaining things to me says that each
   is above voting age.


IV

I cannot remember what all I saw
In northern Florida, all the duck we shot.

You have asked me to recall Illinois,
But all I have is a handful of wrinkles.

Perhaps you would like me to speak of California.
But I hope not, for now I am very close to death.

The children all came down to see the whale in Arkansas,
I remember that its huge body lay attached to the side of the
river.

V

O Mississippi joys!
I reckon I am about as big and dead as a whale!
I am slowly sinking down into the green ooze
Of the Everglades, that I feared so much when I was a child!
I have become about as flat as the dust on a baseball diamond
And as empty and clear as the sky when it is just-blue
And you are three, and you stand on the rim of the zone of
one of the United States
And think about the forty-seven others; then in the evening
Air you hear the sound of baseball players, and the splash of
canoes!
You yourself would like to play baseball and travel, but you
are too young;
However you look up into the clear flat blue of the evening
sky
And vow that you will one day be a traveler like myself,
And wander to all the ends of the earth until you are
completely exhausted,
And then return to Texas or Indiana, whatever state you
happen to be from.
And have your death celebrated by a lavish funeral
Conducted by starlight, with numerous boys and girls
reading my poems aloud!

VI

O Charleston! why do you always put me in the mood for
kidding?
I am not dead yet, who do you make me say I am?
But I think I am growing older, my shoes are falling off,
I think it must be that my feet are getting thinner and that
I am ready to die.
Here comes my pony from Montana, he is a mere skull and
crossbones,

And here is the old man who told me about North Dakota, he
   is a little baby,
And here is Illinois, and here is Indiana, I guess they are my
   favorite states,
I guess I am dying now in Charleston, South Carolina.
O Charleston, why do you always do this . . . Gasp! Goodbye!

## VII

In Illinois the trees are growing up
Where he planted them; for he has died.
But I am the one who originally intended to read
You the fast movements. Now we will hear the Brandenburg
Concertos. Now we will go up in an
Airplane. Steady . . . The poet of America, Walt Whitman, is
   dead.
But many other poets have died that are reborn
In their works. He also shall be reborn,
Walt Whitman shall be reborn.

## VIII

I did not understand what you meant by the Hudson Tunnel,
But now I understand, New Jersey, I like it fine,
I like the stifling black smoke and the jagged heave-ho of the
   trains,
I like the sunlight too at the end of the tunnel, like my rebirth
   in the poems of Kenneth Koch,
I like the way the rosy sunlight streams down upon the silver
   tracks,
I like the way the travelers awake from their dreams and
   step upon the hard paving stone of the station,
But I reckon what I should like best would be to see Indiana
   again,
Or Texas or Arkansas, or Alabama, the "Cotton State,"
Or Big Rose Pebble Island off the coast of Maine
Where I used to have so much fun during the summer,
   cooking and kidding and having myself a good time,
I like Pennsylvania too, we could have a lot of fun there,
You and I will go there when Kenneth is dead.

# John Ashbery

## EUROPE

1 To employ her
  construction ball
  Morning fed on the
  light blue wood
  of the mouth
                    cannot understand
  feels deeply)

2 A wave of nausea—

3 a few berries

4 the unseen claw
  Babe asked today
  The background of poles roped over
  into star jolted them

5 filthy or into backward drenched flung heaviness
  lemons asleep pattern crying

6 The mouth of elephant—
  embroidery over where
  ill page sees.

7 What might have
        children singing

the horses
        the seven
breaths under tree, fog
clasped—absolute, unthinking
menace to our way of life.
uh unearth more cloth
This could have been done—
This could not be done


8 In the falling twilight of the wintry afternoon all looked
dull and cheerless. The car stood outside with Ronald Pryor
and Collins attending to some slight engine trouble—the fast,
open car which Ronnie sometimes used to such advantage. It
was covered with mud, after the long run from Suffolk, for
they had started from Harbury long before daylight, and,
until an hour ago, had been moving swiftly up the Great
North Road, by way of Stamford, Grantham and Doncaster
to York. There they had turned away to Ripon, where, for
an hour, they had eaten and rested. In a basket the waiter had
placed some cold food with some bread and a bottle of wine,
and this had been duly transferred to the car.
All was now ready for the continuance of the journey.


9 The decision in his life
   soul elsewhere
   the gray hills
   out there on the road darkness
   covering lieutenant
        there is a cure


10 He had mistaken his book for garbage


11 The editor realized
      its gradual abandonment
      a kind of block where other men come down
      spoiling the view
      wept blood
      on the first page and following snow
      gosh flowers upset ritual

a mass of black doves
over the scooter, snow outlining the tub
flowers until dawn

12 that surgeon must operate
I had come across
to the railway from the Great North
Road, which I had followed up to London.

13 the human waste cannibals designed the master
and his life
robot you underground sorrow to the end
can unlack horsemen. Storm seems berries—
until the truth can be explained
Nothing can exist. Rain
blossomed in the highlands—a
secret to annul grass sticks—razor today engraved sobs.
The lion's skin—ears, to travel.

14 Before the waste
went up
Before she had worked
The sunlight in the square—
apples, oranges, the compass
tears of joy—over rotten stone flesh
is dyspepsia uncorked—that's
leaf of the story
mitigated

15 Absolve me from the hatred I never
she—all are wounded against
Zeppelin—wounded carrying dying
three colors over land
thistles again closed around voice.
She is dying—
automatically—
wanting to see you again, but the stone
must be rebuilt. Time stepped

16 before I started
  I was forced to          flying
  she said
  higher and higher on
  next tree, am as wire
  when canvas the must spread
              to new junk

17 I moved up
              glove
        the field

18 I must say I
  suddenly
  she left the room, oval tear tonelessly fell.

19 Life pursued down these cliffs.
  the omened birds
  intrusion; skated, at night
  clear waves of weather
  fur you bring genius
  over hell's curiosity
  the librarian shabbily books on
  You cannot illusion; the dust.
  abstract vermin the garden worn smiles

20 That something desperate was to be attempted
     was,
  however, quite plain.

21 Night hunger
  of berry . . . stick

22 "Beautiful morning for a flip miss," remarked the
mechanic in brown overalls. "Are you going up alone."

23 "Then I'll take the bombs out," he said, and at once
removed the six powerful bombs from the rack, the projectiles
intended for the destruction of zeppelins.

24 The tables gleamed—soft lighting
        covered the place.
    There was a certain pleasure in all this for him.
    The twelve girls wept. She willed him
    loveliest diamond of the tree; the old lawyer kept
        his mule there.
    They had gone. The weather was very pure that
        night like
    leaves of paper placed on the black—the opal
    crescent still dangled on the little chain—
    a pleasant memory of a kiss, completely
    given to recollection. Only
    faded water remained. The last memory left.

25 She was dying but had time for him—
    brick. Men were carrying the very heavy things—
        dark purple, like flowers.
    Bowl lighted up the scare just right

26 water
            thinking
                a

27        A notice:

28        wishing you were a
        the bottle really before the washed
                handed over to her:
                    hundreds
    light over her
        hanging her
    you can remember

29 Have you encouraged judge
        inked commentary
    approaching obvious battle
    summer night less ecstatic
        train over scream . . . mountain
            into woods

30 sweetheart . . .      the stamp
     ballooning you
   vision I thought you
   forget, encouraging your vital organs.
   Telegraph. The rifle—a page folded over.
   More upset, wholly meaningless, the willing sheath
   glide into fall . . . mercury to passing
   the war you said won—milling around the picket
      fence, and noise of the engine from the sky
   and flowers—here is a bunch
   the war won out of cameos.
   And somehow the perfect warrior is fallen.

31 They wore red
   the three children dragged into next year
   sad . . . gold under the feet.
   sadly more music is divine to them.

32 The snow stopped falling
   on the head of the stranger.
   In a moment the house would be dark

33 mirrors—insane

34 dying for they do not
   the hole no crow can
   and finally the day of thirst
   in the air.
   whistles carbon dioxide. Cold
   pavement grew. The powerful machine
   The tractor, around edge
   the listless children. Good night
   staining the naughty air
   with marvelous rings. You are going there.
   Weeps. The wreath not decorating.
   The kids pile over the ample funeral hill.
   had arrived from London
                          o'clock
      baited tragically

This time the others grew.
The others waited
by the darkening pool—"a world of silence"
you can't understand their terror
means more to these people waste
the runt crying in the pile of colored
snapshots offal in the wind
that's the way we do it terror
the hand of the large person falls
to the desk. The people all leave.
the industries begin
moment       puts on the silencer
You crab into the night

35 The sheiks protest use of
   aims. In the past
   coal has protected their
   O long, watchful hour.
   the engines had been humming
   stones of March in the gray woods
   still, the rods, could not they take long
   More anthems until dust
   flocks disguised machine. The stone
   the valentine couldn't save. . . . Hooks

36 he ran the machine swiftly across the frosty grass.
   Soon he rose, and skimming the trees, soon
   soared away into the darkness.

37 From where Beryl sat she saw the glow
   of the little electric bulb set over the instruments
      shining into
   her lover's strong clean-shaven face, and, by the
      compass, gathered that
   they had decribed a half-circle, and, though
   still rising rapidly, were now heading eastward in
   the direction of the sea.

38 The roar of the engine, of course,

rendered speech impossible,
while the mist was very chilly, causing her to draw
    her brown woollen comforter around her legs.
There was no sign of light anywhere below
—all was a bright black void.

39  The few children
Seeds under the glare
The formal tragedy of it all
Mystery for man—engines humming
Parachutes opening. The newspaper being read
Beside the great gas turbine
The judge calls his assistant over
And together they try to piece together the secret
    message contained in today's paper.

40  The police
Had been forgotten
Scarlet, blue and canary
Heads tossing on the page
        grunting to the coatroom
there was another ocean, ballads and legends, the
    children returning to the past—head

41  She was saying into the distance
        It was a sad day
the riders drinking in the car
haze of trees behind
                            dummy woods
    plans and sketches
    soda, glasses, ice
    bumped off
"with these strange symbols."

42  the club had bought aperture

43  Their hidden storage (to you, murder)
    but what testimony buried under colored sorrow—the
nerve

children called upon
assassination this racket.


44 He ran the ferret
backing him hard nest
      The chil—
One day the children particularly surrounded
he had read about him.


45 Like a long room
Monsignor
    pushed away it
studio artificially small
  pine rounds


46 The last time she crossed close to Berck,
beyond Paris-Plage, she passed over Folke-
stone, and then over to Cape Grisnez
alone into the night


47 Or he hides bodies
stone night,
pleasant city, gray
    hides
perfect dictionary for you
valentine not wanted storm under the
snow backed rubbers
The city hides, desolate
rocks snow tile hides
over the door marked "The Literature
beginning veins hide the mind
robot—" —capped by all. release.


48 Then she studied her map, took her bearings
and, drawing on her ample gauntlet gloves
         (for it had become chilly)
she followed a straight line of railway leading
  through Suffolk and Norfolk

49 I'm on my way to Hull
         grinned the girl

50 It was in German. The aviator and his
     observer climbed out of the seats and stood
     with Mr. Aylesworth, chatting and laughing.

51 They are written upon English paper, and English
         penny stamps are upon them . . .
     they can be put into any post-box. . . . They
     mostly contain instructions to our good friends
         in Great Britain.

52 The rose
                         dirt
         dirt you

     pay
     The buildings
     is tree

Undecided
         protest
                 This planet.

53 The vegetable wagon had not been placed yet
     Scotchmen with their plaids—all the colorful
     Photography, horror of all
     That has died
     The hundred year old stones—deceived
     by the mind of these things—the stairs
     climbing up out of dark hollyhocks
     old, dirt, smell of the most terrifying thing in the
     world.

54 "He is probably one of the gang."

55            mood seems the sort
              to brag
              end

56           songs like
              You came back to me
              you were wrong about the gravestone
    that nettles hide quietly
The sun is not ours.

57 Precise mechanisms
Love us.

He came over the hill
He held me in his arms—it was marvelous

But the map of Europe
shrinks around naked couples

Even as you lick the stamp
A brown dog lies down beside you and dies

In the city an eleven year old girl with pig tails
Tied with a yellow ribbon takes the trolley

All of this ends somewhere—the book is replaced
  on the shelf
By an unseen hand

We are not more loved than now
The newspaper is ruining your eyes.

58 The professor—a large "S"
           One kitten escaped
                Take plane
or death by hanging
And naturally it is all over again, beginning to get tired you
  realize

59 The real thing the matter
      with him you see studio end
    of day masked
you didn't see him—he went

escape is over on the lighted steps
"My blood went into this"
Misunderstandings arise cathedral
twenty years later catching sight of him
his baggy trousers the porch daylight
playing tennis before we realize the final dream is
    razed
Today, of course.

60 Wing
            Bostonian
and his comments
thirty-three years old the day
    of his third birthday the legs
Lenin De Gaulle three days later
    also comparing simple

61 reflecting trout

62 All of us fear the secret
guarded too carefully
    An assortment

63 she ran along the grass for a short distance
couple of beers
eats   being corpse tables

64 ice   dirt
five minutes
get your money back
    the hole screamed
two persons
                two cut flowers

65 nothing is better than
glowing coals
The perfect animal
    during the summer, sleep of brine and ice

66  She followed a straight line leading
    due north through Suffolk and Norfolk

67  over the last few years
    there is one terrifying
wild
              the error of sleep
                    love

68  The straight line out of sight
    of beads
    decades cheapest
    the more post card
        "genius"

69  because it is
    That is to say

70              Her last dollar

71  They must hold against
    The fire rain
    or when sometime it seems
    upward, hands down
        against
    pilloried
        sell quickly took her bearings
    did not appear entirely
    upper hand of her
    a height of five thousand feet

72  The village (using the new headache system) were
        cut
    With the stops running
    A French or Swiss
    had hit bottom and gotten back up
    wild margins are possible
    The gold a "call"
    options his life . . . flea

73 A least
   four days
   A surprise
   mothers
   suppose
   Is not a "images"
   to "arrange"
   He is a descendant, for example
   The Swiss bank—a village.

74 Man come for one is humanity
   the lowest pickpocket helps

75 Like the public,
   reactions
   from Crystal Palace

76 A roar
   "sweetness and light"
   pickpocket—stem
   and more scandalous . . . well, forgotten
   The snow is around storm
   He laughed lightly at cliff
   and used that term

77 "Perhaps you've heard of her. She's a great flying
      woman."

   "Oh yes," replied the stranger. "I've seen things
      about
   her in the papers. Does she fly much?"

78 applauding itself—wiser
      more gun   I come from the district
   four times carrying a small,
         oval
   the movie was also
         in the entire crystal

79 to stroll down Main Street
   the dignified and paternal image
   telegraph—magnificent
                     dump
porch
          flowers    store
      weed local relatives
                  whine

80 multitude headquarters shout there
   Because there are no
   because the majority is toxic
   An exquisite sense—like pretzels.
   He was sent to the state senate
   wage conceal his disapproval
   The  arguments  situation  lawyers  worthlessness  sullen
      cafeterias

81 barcarolle

82 The silencer. "Is he not . . ."

83 Soon after noon, carrying a narrow,

84    about her

85 ghost of stone—massive
      hangs halfway
polishing
      whose winding
Strong, sad half-city
   gardens
                     from the bridge of
   stair
                  broom
      recent       past    symbolized
   hair  banana
   does not evoke a concrete image
   the splendid

86 nourished on the
   railings of bare stone—

87 Your side
   is majestic—the dry wind
   timeless stones. a deep sigh
   dragged up with a piercing scream
   the clean, crisp air
   aging on the villas
   little openings for her bath
   façades of the the—all alike, the hard rain
   "the dignity of this fortress."

88 the invaders
                    so bad just now
       go up and see the shabby traveler
                        ordered a pint
   At half-past two, the visitor, taking
    his bag, set out on a tour of the
       village.           An endeavor
                          remained
       rolls on them
              at night

89 This car has some private
   more than one cottage the chintzes were bright its
   brass candlestick forgotten
   twenty-five cents.
   could offer was a feeble

90 I have a perfect memory and
   the sky seems to pass
   a couple of them like a huge bowl
   and encircle the earth

91 flanked by his lieutenants—lemon—
   his chief outside
   "if I am wrong
      a fine sieve

telephones I do not
strong nature who wrote of him while starving himself

92  to be dying, he gets them into magazines
and some of them mangy and rabid
hardly seemed necessary.

I was horrified. I felt sorry for him.
No branch without . . .
down to the lakes the ornamental
bronze—isn't it the fear that

Hand in hand like fire
and in your souls

93  A searchlight sweeping
picked up "The Hornet"
Hardly had he undressed when he
heard again that low swish of
"The Hornet" on her return from scouting circuit of
   the Thames estuary
solidifying disguises

who died in an automobile accident
had developed a
then, imperceptibly

94  The snow had begun to fall on Paris
It is barely noon

95  Between the legs of her
Cobwebs  the lip  reads  chewing
and taste seem uncertain;
powerless creating images
shut up and leave me . . . Hush! This
two men who have
   most profoundly
      the islanders

96 Mr. Bean remained indoors
   at the small boats
   of our defences, our intentions

97 out upon the lawn after a few months in the village
      big
   "Like some of my friends
   Otherwise we'll chop off his head

98 This was the third thing
   another giant

99 dark wool, summer
   and winter

100 gun metal—her right foot in both hands
                   things

101 the doctor, comb
                Sinn Fein

102            dress

103 streaming sweeping the surface
   long-handled twig-brooms
                starving
   wall   great   trees

104 blaze
                                                aviators
            out
                                            dastardly

105 We must be a little more wary in
      future, dear

106 she was trying to make sense of
   what was quick laugh
   hotel—cheap for them
   caverns the bed
      box of cereal

Ere long a flare was lit
I don't understand wreckage

107 blue smoke?            The steel bolts
   It was as though     having been replaced
     She had          by a painting of
the river             one of wood!
  above the water     Ronnie, thoughtfully
                      of the silencer
        plot to kill both of us, dear
pet
       oh
  it that she was there

108    the bridge crosses
              dragon ships
  canal lock
     was effect
        There are but two seasons
  the map of Paris
    through the center of the sheet
      character
 sewers empty into under the
  literally choked the river with
    bodies
      "on the coast, I think . . ."
    passing over

109 Magnificent trees—the old
   chateau—he said he was
 going home for their needs
    only the other—
       exchanged another meaning
     here lately
     the inn-keeper's
110 Dry, the bush
  settling       Everybody
  knows him
       close to the Thwaite

passing close to where
   The bookshop
      were crouched in conceal—
up a steep, narrow path
   to the summit of Black Hill
      recognized him
lavatory—dogging
            his footsteps
               out to sea


111 Half an hour later
    Ronald recognized him.
    They suddenly saw a beam of intense, white light,
    A miniature searchlight of great brilliance,
    —pierce the darkness, skyward.


    They now recognized to be a acetylene,
    a cylinder mounted
    upon a light tripod of aluminum
    with a bright reflector behind the gas-jet,
    that the light began to "wink,"
       three times in quick succession
    the Morse letter "S."


    Slowly the beam turned from north to south,
    making the Morse "S." upon the clouds,
    time after time.


    Suddenly the light was shut off—for five minutes by
       Ronald's watch no flicker was shown
    Then suddenly, once again, the series of S's was repeated
    in a semi-circle from north to south
    and back again.


    Another five minutes passed in darkness.


    Once more the light opened out and commenced
    to signal the Morse flashes and flares,

"N.F.", "N.F."
followed by a long beam of
light skyward, slowly sweeping in a circle
                              the breath

# THESE LACUSTRINE CITIES

These lacustrine cities grew out of loathing
Into something forgetful, although angry with history.
They are the product of an idea: that man is horrible,
   for instance.
Though this is only one example.

They emerged until a tower
Controlled the sky, and with artifice dipped back
Into the past for swans and tapering branches,
Burning, until all that hate was transformed into useless love.

Then you are left with an idea of yourself
And the feeling of ascending emptiness of the afternoon
Which must be charged to the embarrassment of others
Who fly by you like beacons.

The night is a sentinel.
Much of your time has been occupied by creative games
Until now, but we have all-inclusive plans for you.
We had thought, for instance, of sending you to the middle
   of the desert.

To a violent sea, or of having the closeness of the others be air
To you, pressing you back into a startled dream
As sea-breezes greet a child's face.
But the past is already here, and you are nursing some private
   project.

The worst is not over, yet I know
You will be happy here. Because of the logic
Of your situation, which is something no climate can
   outsmart.
Tender and insouciant by turns, you see.

You have built a mountain of something,
Thoughtfully pouring all your energy into this single
    monument,
Whose wind is desire starching a petal,
Whose disappointment broke into a rainbow of tears.

# Ted Berrigan

## BEAN SPASMS

*to George Schneeman*

New York's lovely weather

           hurts my forehead

           in praise of thee

               the? white dead

               whose eyes know:

        what are they

of the tiny cloud my brain:

The City's tough red buttons:

            O Mars, red, angry planet, candy

               bar, with sky on top,

       "why, it's young Leander hurrying to his death"

    what?   what time is it in New York      in these here alps

    City of lovely tender hate

           and beauty making beautiful

              old rhymes?

   I ran away from you

when you needed something strong

     then I leand against the toilet bowl (ack)

     Malcolm X

         I love my brain

    it all mine now is

    saved not knowing

      that &

      that (happily)

      being that:

     "wee kill our selves to propagate our kinde"

                John Donne

   yes, that's true

        the hair on yr nuts & my

big blood-filled cock are a part in that too

PART 2

Mister Robert Dylan doesn't feel well today
That's bad
This picture doesn't show that
It's not bad, too

it's very ritzy in fact

here I stand I can't stand
to be thing
I don't use                                   atop
                                   the empire state
                                   building
                                   & so sauntered out the door
That reminds me of the time
I wrote that long piece about a gangster name of "Jr."
O Harry James! had eyes to wander but lacked tongue to praise
                         so later peed under his art
            paused only to lay a sneeze
                                   on Jack Dempsey
                                   asleep with his favorite Horse

That reminds me of I buzz
            on & off Miro pop
                  in & out a Castro convertible
            minute by minute            GENEROSITY!

Yes now that the seasons totter in their walk
      I do a lot of wondering about Life      in praise of ladies dead of
& Time plaza(s), Bryant Park by the Public            eye of brow
Library, Smith Bros. black boxes, Times
                                   Square
                        Pirogi, Houses
                              with long skinny rivers thru them
                        they lead the weary away
                              off!   hey!
                                   I'm no sailor
                                   off a ship
                                        at sea      I'M HERE
                                   & "The living is easy"
It's "HIGH TIME"
                        & I'm in shapes
                        of shadow, they
                        certainly can warm, can't they?

428

Have you ever seen one?                              NO!
                         of those long skinny Rivers
                         O well hung, in New York City?
                    NO!   in fact
                         I'm the Wonderer
& as yr train goes by              forgive me, Rene!   'just oncet'
    I woke up in Heaven
                         He woke, and wondered more; how many angels
    on this train huh?         snore
                         for there she lay
              on sheets that mock lust      done that 7 times
                                   been caught
                              and brought back
                         to a peach nobody.
                    To Continue:
                    Ron Padgett & Ted Berrigan
                         hates yr brain
                              my dear
                              amidst the many other little buzzes
                    & like, Today, as Ron Padgett might say
                              is
                    "A tub of vodka"
                                   "in the morning"
         she might reply
and it keeps it up
         past icy poles
                    where angels beg fr doom then zip
                         ping in-and-out, joining the army
              wondering about Life
              by the Public Library of
                         Life
                                   No Greater Thrill!
                    (I wonder)
Now that the earth is changing I wonder what time it's getting to be
    sitting on this New York Times Square
that actually very ritzy, Lauren      it's made of yellow wood or
                         I don't know something      maybe
              This man was my              its been fluffed up
                    friend
                    He had a sense for the
                         vast                doesn't he?
                    Awake my Angel! give thyself
                         to the lovely hours      Don't cheat
         The victory is not always to the sweet.
                    I mean that.
Now the picture is pretty good here
Though it once got demerits from the lunatic Arthur Cravan

429

He wasn't feeling good that day
Maybe because he had nothing on
                              paint-wise I mean
          PART 3
                    I wrote that
                    about what is
              this empty room   without a heart
                    in three parts
                    a white flower
                  came home wet & drunk      2 pepsis
                  and smashed my fish thru her window
                                    in the nude
        As the hand zips you see
              Old Masters, you can see
              well hung in New York      they grow fast here
                  Conflicting, yet  purposeful
                      yet with outcry vain!
                    4.
              Praising, that's it!
you string a sonnet around yr fat gut
    and falling on your knees
                        you invent the shoe
                        for a horse. It brings you luck
                  while sleeping
                        "You have it seems a workshop nature"
                        "Good Lord!"
                              Some folks is wood
                        Ron Padgett wd say
                            amidst many other little buzzes
                    past the neon on & off
                    night & day       STEAK SANDWICH
              Have you ever tried one, Anne?           SURE!
      "I wonder what time 'its'?
          as I sit on this new Doctor
NO   I only look at buildings they're in
as you and he, I mean he & you & I buzz past
                        in yellow ties      I call that gold
          THE HOTEL BUCKINGHAM
          (facade) is black, and taller than last time
is looming over lunch    naked    high time    poem  & I, equal in
                                    perfection & desire
          is looming    both eyes    over coffee-cup (white) nature
                and man:    both hell on poetry.
                    Art is art and life is
                        "A monograph on Infidelity"
                    Oh. Forgive me stench of sandwich
                    O pneumonia in American Poetry

                                                    *430*

Do we have time?         well look at Burroughs
    7 times been caught and brought back to Mars
          & eaten.
"Art is art & Life
is home," Fairfield Porter said that
          turning himself in
              The night arrives again in red
some go on     even in Colorado         on the run
          the forests shook
      meaning:
           coffee    the cheerfulness of this poor
                  fellow is terrible, hidden in
                  the fringes of the eyelids
          blue mysteries' (I'M THE SKY)
     The sky is bleeding now
            onto 57th Street
        of the 20th Century &
              HORN & HARDART'S
Right Here. That's Part 5.
    I'm not some sailor off a ship at sea
I'm the wanderer              (age 4)
          & now everyone is dead
   sinking bewildered of hand, of foot, of lip
  nude, thinking
laughter burnished brighter than hate

                  goodbye.
     André Breton said that
              what a shit!
He's gone!
      up bubbles all his amorous breath
     & Monograph on Infidelity entitled
              The Living Dream
I never again played
          I dreamt that December 27th, 1965
     all in the blazon of sweet beauty's breast

      I mean   "a rose"    Do you understand that?
                  Do you?
The rock&roll songs of this earth
commingling absolute joy AND
  incontrovertible joy of intelligence
               certainly can warm
               cant they?   YES!
       and they do.
    Keeping eternal whisperings around.
         (Mr. Macadams writes in
         the nude: no that's not

(we want to take the underground
   revolution to Harvard!

       and yet this girl has
        so much grace
           I wonder!
      Were all their praises simply prophecies
    of this
          the time!    NO GREATER THRILL
                my friends

me that: then zips in &
out of the boring taxis, re-
fusing to join the army
asleep "on the springs"
of red GENEROSITY

But I quickly forget them, those other times, for what are they
  but parts in the silver lining of the tiny cloud my brain
drifting up into smoke the city's tough blue top:

      I think a picture always
      leads you gently to someone else
   Don't you? like when you ask to leave the room
        and go to the moon.

# David Shapiro

## THE CONTRIBUTION

A dollar for Whitman, you are all stumbling.
Well in a field of malacostraca the child picks up
The claw which is still limber and open and king.
The child examines the claw for Abyssinian crap
But only lobster pimples pink the claw and the top
Is swollen like a popular mouth that's about to sing.

Furiously at the hedges the claw starts bouncing.
Then Cleopatra strides in with a check for Charmian,
Her famous maid, and almost faints meeting the striking
And voyaging claw, whose attraction will soon be gone
Like the purple member of a child nearly eaten
Thrown into the vestibule of a vagina in the ring.

# FIRST LOVE

I imagine you dressed up as a gowned Hasid
A blackbearded girl—a girl I might have married
A stick we take to bed and call John in bed
Later a white-breasted Protestant girl to be buried.
Who are you and what cruelty in what theater
Do you still play cello and strip for friends
Atlantic City fingers warmed by the electric-heater
Sun—a decadent image everybody understands.

And you smile by the chorus of a Psalm of David
Your smile twirls in the air just before I cry
"Your team is my team" and you change the bid
On your body to a strangulating price I cannot buy.
Slowly walking in Boston with a music note
Your composition stabs me like a bat.


# JANUARY

I want you
This morning
winter rocking
my ear: there is no
promise for it,
but simultaneous
and soft voices
deprive, deprive
No stain
is on the streetlight

between falling things
and the hands only
wave dusty loaves
as the heart in
her cone of cold
waves the winter witch
on all the boys
making them wake and twitch
I want you
your hair and the puzzling
things your body
removes   Is it winter
The school is
Thirty girls are running
laughing to watch
the teacher strain
I cannot listen anymore
because I want you
because there is no name
that morning recreates
except yours
because my feeling
surrounds me
I want you

## ODE

Permit me to take this sleeping man
And I will help him on his way.

Even with Be and Ice, my head
Bowed down as if I were sleepy.

If I could describe how Frank's
Eyes fell asleep, on hearing of Frank,

Like a painter working from a model
I could show how I went to sleep!

In my ramblings I closed my eyes
And transmuted thought into a product.

Moving in a trance with a keen face
I fell, and what happened to me

She knows who did this: She took my head
And held it down until I swallowed.

A girl walked by and said: I am Julia,
Open your eyes and see who I am.

When I heard this invitation,
She and my sleep went away together.

I have something of New York in me,
Lying against cement to bring it back.

There was almost no time between one "when"
And the other, I mean the "when" of waiting

And the "when" of seeing a woman in bed.
Thus, in presenting sleep

The poem must leap over the cut-offs.
You see clearly in a revolution,

Look down and notice how you have slept.

## ELEGY TO SPORTS

Orestes pointed out what was despotic
    In youth and stingy hunger.
From his golden injuries he got
    What he wanted from you.

The key used to dial was at last in place,
    The house asbestos.
And he dressed up like a piece of human candy
    With great hustling.

Last stop! Your clothes fill up the trunk
    With a pitiful hand.
The seer in old age follows the raindrops,
    Touring an inhuman scene.

The Swiss have no wars, though they lose combats,
    The English are hemmed in by waves,
Those who drink the rivers Po, Tagus, and Danube
    Are found on the river bottom.

And so the vaulter, who rebounds into gravel
    Dragging his pole behind,
Like gasoline sets the hurdles on fire
    Jumping and jumping again.

The pianist whistles during the accompaniment;
    Mrs. closes her eyes;
She retires from us, seeing you dislike her
    And her rowboat collection.

Now you are happy, and you are more than happy,
    You swan of Lancaster.

Don't complain about the dull apartment life
    A thousand times a day.

The gnome brought suit against the cedarwood,
    And Libya owes money to a tree.
Your father has received the gems amber and garnet
    For a year's work on his bed.

You beat your hand, you jump out of line,
    And you say among yourselves:
"This is what Italy and Greece dumped on us
    In a thousand poems."

So you give away your violin, the other his trumpet;
    The girl gives you away.
And the women, the pedestrians, and the detective
    Desert the champ.

# John Hollander

## PHILOMEL *

I

*Tape*
(Eeeeeeeeeeeeeee)

*Philomel*

Eeeeeeeeeeeeeeeeeeeeeee!
Feeeeeeeeeeeeeeeeeeeee!
Feeeeeeeeeeeeeeeeeeeeel!
I feel—
Feel a million trees
And the heat of trees

Not true trees—

Feel a million tears

Not true tears—
Not true trees—

Is it Tereus I feel?

Not Tereus; not a True
    Tereus—

Feel a million filaments;
Fear the tearing, the feeling
Trees, that are full of
    felony—

Trees tear,
And I bear
Families of tears—

* Text for a musical composition of title (1963), for soprano and electron-
ically synthesized accompaniment, by Milton Babbitt.

443

I feel a million Philomels—

Trees filled with mellowing
Feminine fame—

I feel trees in my hair
And on the ground, vines,
Honeymelons fouling
My knees and feet
Soundlessly in my
Flight through the forest;
I founder in quiet.

Here I find only
Famine of melody,
Miles of felted silence
Unwinding behind me,
Lost, lost in the wooded
  night.

Pillowing melody,
Honey unheard—

My hooded voice, lost.

Lost, as my first
Unhoneyed tongue;
Forced, as my last
Unfeathered defense;
Fast-tangled in lust
Of these woods so dense.

Emptied, unfeeling and
  unfilled
By trees here where no birds
  have trilled—

Feeling killed
Philomel stilled
Her honey unfulfilled.

Feeling killed
Philomel stilled
Her honey unfulfilled

What is that sound?
A voice found;
Broken, the bound
Of silence, beyond
Violence of human sound,
As if a new self
Could be founded on sound.

Oh, men are sick:
The gods are strong
Oh, see! Quick! Quick!
The trees are astounded!
What is this humming?
I am becoming
My own song. . . .

Oh, men are sick:
The gods are strong.
Oh, see! Quick! Quick!
The trees are astounded!
What is this humming?
I am becoming
My own song. . . .


II   ECHO SONG

*Tape*

*Philomel*

O Thrush in the woods I fly
    among,
Do you, too, talk with the
    forest's tongue?

Stung, stung, stung;
With the sting of becoming
I sing

O Hawk in the high and
    widening sky,
What need I finally do to fly
And see with your unclouded
    eye?

Die, die, die;
Let the day of despairing
Be done

O Owl, the wild mirror of the
    night,
What is the force of the
    forests light?

Slight, slight, slight;
With the slipping-away of
The sun

O sable Raven, help me back!
What color does my torn robe
    lack?

Black, black, black;
As your blameless and long-
Dried blood

O bright Gull, aid me in my
    dream!
Above the foaming breaker's
    cream!

Scream, scream, scream,
For the scraps of your being;
Be shrill

The world's despair should
    not be heard!
Too much terror has
    occurred:
The Gods who made this
    hubbub erred!

Bird, bird, bird!
You are bare of desire:
Be born!

Oh green leaves! through your
    rustling lace
Ahead, I hear my own myth
    race.

Thrace, Thrace, Thrace!
Pain is unchained,
There is change!

There is change!
In the woods of Thrace!


III    PHILOMEL

Living, growing, changing, being in the hum always
Of pain! The pain of slow change blows in our faces
Like unfelt winds that the spinning world makes in its
    turning:
Life and feeling whirl on, below the threshold of burning.

                I burn in change.
                Far, far I flew
                To this wailing place.
                And now I range
(with tape)      Thrashing, through
                The woods of Thrace.

If pain brush against the rushing wings of frightened change,
Then feeling distills to a burning drop, and transformation
Becomes intolerable. I have been raped and had my tongue
Torn out: but more pain reigns in these woods I range among.

                I ache in change,
                Though once I grew
                At a slower pace.
                And now I range
(with tape)      Thrashing, through
                The woods of Thrace.

Crammed into one fell moment, my ghastly transformation
Died like a fading scream: the ravisher and the chased
Turned into one at last: the voice Tereus shattered
Becomes the tiny voices of night that the God has scattered.

                I die in change.
                Pain tore in two
                Love's secret face.
                And now I range

(with tape)        Thrashing, through
                      The woods of Thrace.

Love's most hidden tongue throbbed in the barbarous
    daylight;
Then all became pain in one great scream of silence, fading,
Finally, as all the voices of feeling died in the west
And pain alone remained with remembering in my breast.

                      I screamed in change.
                      Now all I can do
                      Is bewail that chase.
                      For now I range
(with tape)        Thrashing, through
                      The woods of Thrace.

Pain in the breast and the mind, fused into music! Change
Bruising hurt silence even further! Now, in this glade,
Suffering is redeemed in song. Feeling takes wing:
High, high above, beyond the forests of horror I sing!

                      I sing in change
                      And am changed anew!
                      (O strange, slow race
                      That I ran with grace!)
                      I sing in change.
                      Now my song will range
                      Till the morning dew
                      Dampens its face;
                      Now my song will range
                      As once it flew
                      Thrashing, through
                      The woods of Thrace.

# bp Nichol

## DADA LAMA

*a sound-sequence in six parts*

hweeeee
hweeeee
hyonnnn
hyonnnn

hweeeee
hweeeee
hyonnnn
hyonnnn

tubad id iddo
tubad id iddo
hyon
hyon

tubad id iddo
tubad id iddo
hyon
hyon

fffffffffffffffffffffffftsssssssss
ffffffffffffffffffffffffitsssssssss
ffffffffffffffffffffffffflitsssssssss

hyonnnnnn
          unh
hyonnnnnn
          unh

oudoo doan doanna
tinna limn limn
la leen
untloo lima
limna doo doo

doo du deena
deena doe du
deena deena
deo du deena

ah—ooo runtroo
lintle leave lipf
lat lina tanta
tlalum cheena
ran tron tra troo

deena dee du
deena deena
deo du deena
deena dee du

da dee di do du
deena
        deena

A ᴀᴀᴀ**ᴀᴀᴀ**ᴀᴀᴀᴀᴀᴀᴀᴀᴀᴀᴀᴀᴀᴀᴀᴀᴀᴀᴀᴀ
aaaaaaaaaaaa aaaaaaa aaaaa aaaa
ᴀᴀᴀ ᴀᴀᴀᴀ ᴀᴀ ᴀᴀᴀ ᴀ ᴀᴀᴀ ᴀ ᴀᴀᴀᴀ ᴀᴀ

aaaa aaa aaa aaaaaaaaa aa aa aaaaaa
ᴀᴀᴀᴀᴀᴀᴀᴀᴀ ᴀᴀ ᴀᴀ ᴀ ᴀᴀ ᴀᴀ ᴀᴀ ᴀᴀ ᴀᴀᴀ
aaaaa aaaaa aaaa aaa aaaa aaaaa

ᴀᴀᴀᴀ ᴀ ᴀᴀᴀᴀᴀ ᴀᴀ ᴀᴀᴀᴀ ᴀ ᴀᴀᴀ
a aaa aaaaaaaaaaaaaaaa aaaaaaaa
ᴀᴀᴀᴀ ᴀᴀ ᴀᴀ ᴀᴀᴀ ᴀ ᴀᴀᴀᴀᴀᴀᴀ ᴀᴀᴀ

tlic
tloc

tlic tloc
tlic tloc

tlic tloc tlic
tloc tlic tloc

tlic tloc tlic tloc
tlic tloc tlic tloc

tlic tloc tlic tloc tlic
tloc tlic tloc tlic tloc

tlic tloc tlic tloc tlic tloc
tlic tloc tlic tloc tlic tloc

tlic tloc tlic tloc tlic
tloc tlic tloc tlic tloc

tlic tloc tlic tloc
tlic tloc tlic tloc

tlic tloc tlic
tloc tlic tloc

tlic tloc
tlic tloc

tlic
tloc

WWWWWWWWWWWWWWWWWWWWWWWWWW

mmmmmmmmmmmmmmmmmmmmmmmm

WWWWWWWWWWWWWWWWWWWWWWWWWW

mmmmmmmmmmmmmmmmmmmmmmmm


Wwwwwwwwwwwwwwwwwwwwwwwww

Mmmmmmmmmmmmmmmmmmmmmmmm

Wwwwwwwwwwwwwwwwwwwwwwwww

Mmmmmmmmmmmmmmmmmmmmmmmm


WWWWWWWWWWWWWWWWWWWWW WW

MMMMMMMMMMMMMMMMMMMMMMMM

WWWWWWWWWWWWWWWWWWWWW WW


OUCOOOO OO OOOO OOOO OOO OOOOOH

MMMMMMMMMMMMMMMMMMMMMMMM

OUOOOOOOO OOOOOOOO OOOOOOOOH

MMMMMMMMMMMMMMMMMMMMMMMM


FREEEEEEEE EEE E EEEEEEE EE EE

EE EAAAAAAAAA AAAAAAAAAA AAAAH

FREEEE EE EEE E EE EEE EEEE EEEEE

EEEAAAAA AAAA AA AA AAAAA AAAH


cluntakkatakka

cluntakktakkatakk


FREE EE EE EE E EEEEEE EEEE EEEEEE

DUMMMMMMMMMMMMMMMMMMMMM

FRE EEEEE EE EEEEEE EEE EE EEEEE

DUMMMMMMMMMMMMMMMMMMMMM


453

# Richard Kostelanetz

N
Y
M
P
H
O
   M     M
  A       A
N          N
I          I
A          A

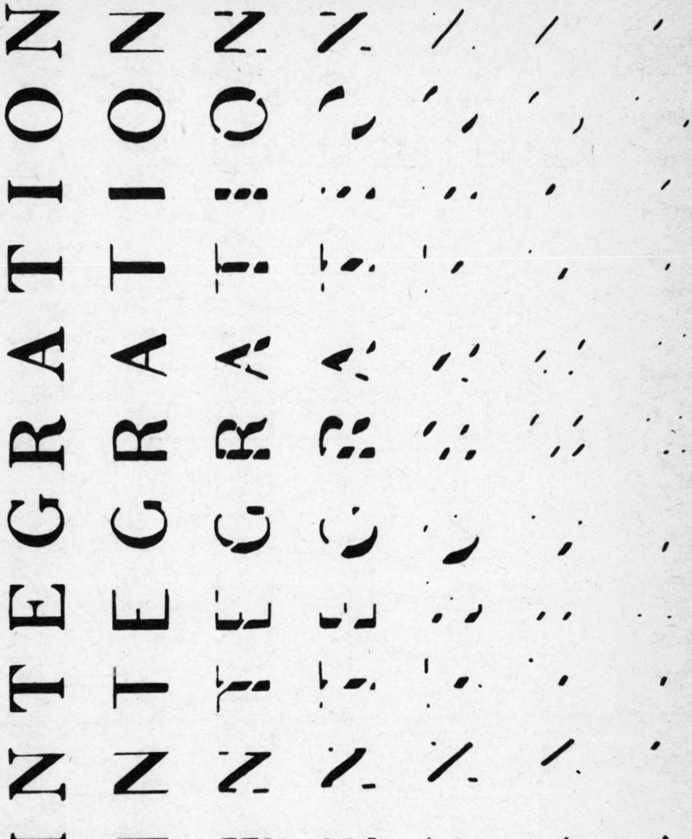
DISINTEGRATION
DISINTEGRATION

# MISCEGENATION

CITIZEN SOLDIER
CITIZE SN OLDIEP
CITIZ SEON LDIER
CITI SZOELN DIEP
CIT SIOZLEDN IER
CI STOILZDEIN ER
C SIOTLIDZIEEN R
SCOILTDIIZEERN

# ANAGOGY
# ANAGOGY
# ANAGOGY
# ANAGOGY
# ANAGOGY
# ANAGOGY
# ANAGOGY
# ANAGOGY
# ANAGOGY
# ANAGOGY
# ANAGOGY

# Mary Ellen Solt

```
A
A   U
A   U S
A   U S A

    A   S U
    A   S U P
    A   S U P E
    A   S U P E R
    A   S U P E R B

        S U B U R B

            B L U R B
            B L U R

            P L U R
            P L U R I
            P L U R I B
            P L U R I B U
            P L U R I B U S

                    U S
                    U S   U
                    U S   U N
                    U S   U N U
                    U S   U N U M

        E   P L U R I B U S   U N U M

            P L U R I B U S   U N U
            L U R I B U S   U N
            U R I B U S   U
            R I B U S
            I B U
            B
```

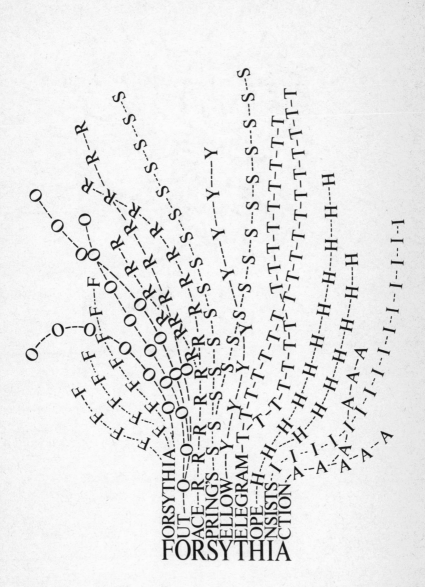

FORSYTHIA

SILENCE

RED

UMBELLAR MEASURES

SEEN SUMMER

INTERPRETS

GOD'S

NO ONE EXIT TIMES

EACH SUMMER

A CAPELLA RESOUNDS

ANSWERS

God's        summer
Exit         times
Resounds     summer
Acapella     answers
Noone        each
Interprets   seen
Umbellar     red
Measures     silence

# Liam O'Gallagher

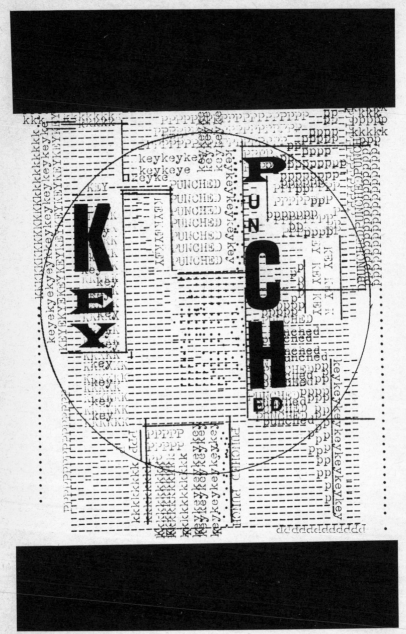

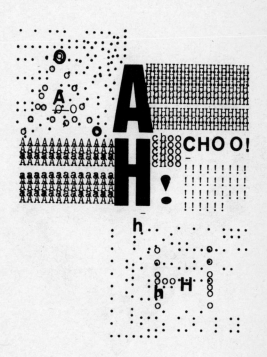

# Gerd Stern

XI

# S. Foster Damon

## JUST WHAT'S THE MATTER WITH ME ANYHOW

Life is the big neighborhood party, me lad,
to which you weren't invited. And so what.
Don't brood they meant to leave you out—that's bad;
try to pretend somehow you were forgot.
Don't happen past, and hope to be asked in:
you'd only smirk and stammer like a fool.
No! Make them sorry! Fill them with chagrin!—
—Swipe all the beer left on the porch to cool!

But that would show you care.
                                        No, take a chance—
walk in as though you owned the place—be brash
and grab the prettiest girl and make her dance.

(This is one party that you cannot crash.)
—So, go home; climb into bed and try to sleep.
(The cold, deep bed and your long, long last sleep.)

# TO THINE OWN SELF

*"To thine own self be true . . ."*
                        O ghastly parody
   Of my dark soul, O body (brother Cain)!
Which is mine own self?
                   And in Christian charity
   Tell me, what is the truth, O Pilate brain?
What is my self but a God-cheated Ahab,
   A proud mad cripple everybody loathes;
And the soiled loins, prededicate to Rahab,
   Shrink, cinctured in self-polluted clothes.

The horizon closes in, throned and shrivelling!
   The snake-spear rears, biting the heart's blood!
The nails!—
              And so I find myself stand snivelling
   Where once that saint, heroic Jesus, stood.

(My audience, the angels, bored blasé
And tired of laughing, have all slipped away.)

# NOBODADDY'S HOUSE HAS MANY MANSIONS

We are the freaks, the silent shrieks, all wrecked
in our conceiving or upbreeding; we
are hunchback minds, halt bodies, all elect
to failure and contemptibility.
Forego your jeering; let us make the joke;
be we your clowns with bladder, blunder, shove.

—Hark! that was our tongue-cut seer who spoke.
And he whose heart was ripped out preaches love:
Why all the selfishness? Why all the hate?

We cripples know exactly what's to lose:
our maims are visions. Yet we unaidables
see those whom we would die to help, refuse
all aid whatever, till it is too late.

They drop, drop, drop, into their separate hells.

# BOOK CASE

NECROMANCY IN THE NECROPOLIS

This is the cemetery of old souls,
humanity's paper memory of desire,
of hope and fear, greed, bigotry, love and ire,
encysted in their numbered pigeon-holes.
Our Great with academic aureoles
are dead—hence harmless: now we may admire
the lava of their once Vesuvian fire.
(Careful! lest ashes hide some undead coals.)

Coffined in leather, bound in linen sheets,
the form preserved with all the printer's art,
behold the emptied brain, the chalky heart,
the mummied loins, now unsarcophagussed.
Toy as you like with Shakespeare, Melville, Keats!
Open the bookcase doors, and—
                              Fie! what dust!

# COPERNICUS ASTROLOGUS

That was a pretty toy of Ptolemy's,
the conglobed crystals rounding a pure chord
to cradle man against catastrophes,
all for the greater glory of the Lord.
But in my brain I tried it, felt it yield,
then burst, the simulacrum of a spell
woven by wizards. Its vanishing revealed
the endless chaos where we ever dwell.
Nowhere may Archimedes fix his stand;
no up or down for god or worshipper;
nothing exists above us or below:
no Primal Mover with gigantic hand
to spin us; nowhere for falling Lucifer—
nowhere for the ascending Christ—to go.

# FINIS CORONAT—

*who, me?*

Goodbye! And now one thing at last is certain:
    I gave the signal long ago myself
to the stage-hands when to ring down the curtain
    upon this trashy drama of myself.

By whom was the long play so badly written,
    so blurred, so inconclusive, but myself?
Who was it, passion-lashed and conscience-smitten,
    played both the agonists but selfsame myself?

And in those characters, what histrionics,
    stupidities, falsities, I wrote myself!
And who else were the villains and the comics,
    the dancers, mobs, and orchestra, but myself.

Yes, even the scenery (not too bad): myself.
And you, the disgusted audience,—myself.

# Armand Schwerner

*From* THE TABLETS

> *presented by the scholar-translator*
> *transmitted through Armand Schwerner*
>
> key: ................*untranslatable section*
> ++++++++++*missing section*
> (?) *variant reading*
> [    ] *supplied by the scholar-translator*

## The Emptying

TABLET I

all that's left is pattern ¹ (shoes?)
I rooted about . . . like a . . . . . sow ² for her pleasure
the (power?) ³ for all of [us]!
I made a mistake. The small path was barely muddy. Little
    squush; and wet socks.⁴ It is (scholarship?) (meditation?)
and the . . . . (energy?) the (energy?) the (pig?) ⁵ of the
    [mistake]! . . . . (energy?) . . . . . . .
war/good-ness . . . ./cunt ⁶(thresher?)/marvel/cunt ⁶/bright-

¹ doubtful reconstruction
² atavism: a hieroglyph; perhaps "a fetal pig" or "a small pig" or "goddess"
³ perhaps "damage," if a borrowing; cf. cognate in N. Akkadian: "skin-burn."
⁴ modernism. Specificity of attire a problem. Possibly "underwear," (dryness?)
⁵ hieroglyph again: "god" may be meant here
⁶ hieroglyph, probably not syllabic. Very old    : conceivably haloed by
hair—but rake-like, very much the rake in the Kap-Kol-Bak-Silpotli-Wap
frieze in the young consort's left hand. (See Ouspenskaya: *The Young Consort and the Rake Muckery*, Egypt. Annals, Surah P, P iii.)

yellow/bright-ochre [7]/bright-bright-yellow/bright-ochre-
yellow/bright-yellow-yellow-yellow-ochre-yellow [8, 9]

*the emptying of yellow*

++++++++++
+++++++++++++++++++++
++++++
++++++
++++++
he calls himself "with grey horses"
he is "having fine green oxen"
with (purpose?) +++++++++++++++++++++ in
   the dream (nightmare?)
++++++++++++++++++++++ of a sharp blade
[testicles] ................................ for the ground
shit (sweat?) upon the ...........................
rain upon the ....................
saliva upon the ............................
heart's blood upon the ..............................
children's strange (beautiful?) early blood in the ..........
....................... from the old dryness (underwear?)
vomit (yellow/North?) does not slake ground
pus (ochre?/NNE?) does not stanch the wounds in the ground
bile (yellow-ochre?/NNNE?) does not ++++++++++++
he is splayed on the ............ like a worn-out pig (god?)
he is un-...........
he is dis-.............
he is ................-less
he is de-..............
he is impossible on the dry ground ++++++++++++++
   before.........
he is non-.........

---

[7] see Halevy-Cohen, *The Prismatic Function in Early Man: a study in Im-
perceptible Gradations*, U.U. Press, Ak., 1922–1962
[8] analogue of segmenting compass readings? as NE, NNE, etc.? We know
the god Pri-Prik usually assumed yellow guises in his search for the 18-fold
path. See Marduk, *The Babylonians*, Hirsute VII, Liber A-413, Tigris
[9] The entire sequence is a rare example of restriction of categories in one
"line" or "cadence" or "unit" or "verset." Only nominal forms used.

he is pre-.............. [10]
the ants look (scrounge?) for food
the ground-pig (lower god?) sucks dry filth for water
the palaces are yellow (vomit/N?)
look at the fishermen in their patterns (shoes?)!
they count the directions of emptiness by fish-names
N shad
E cod
S mackerel
W tuna
from the shad no rain weighs on the breeze
from the cod the loud wind is dry (unforgiving?) [11]
hanging-mackerel-tail-up-smoke-death [12]
the tuna is mighty, the tuna is mighty the way of up-down,
    smoke-death
the men dance around the stone
the stones dance over the pit
the pits dance beyond the bodies like the air-hog (god of
    low rain clouds?)
the bodies the bodies the bodies the bodies the bodies the
    bodies
beyond the bodies the trees dance
the bodies need to fuck the trees
the dry (unforgiving?) bodies wait twenty-eight days
the blood of the four bodies shad
the blood of the four bodies cod
the blood of the four bodies mackerel
the blood of the four bodies tuna [13]
they will change the bile
they will change the cold pus unless ........ because ......
    ...... fish-death

[10] the isolated prefix remnants are curious. The tablet seems rubbed out
with care. Is this segment an early attempt to unite meaning and form?
emptiness in substance as well as linear design?
[11] interesting. We find ourselves at or near the very point in time where the
word, concrete in origin, shades off into an abstraction.
[12] virtually untranslatable. This is an attempt at an Indo-European nomi-
nalization of *kili-pap-swad-ur-plonz*. We can convey little of the conceptual
category "fish-death," or rather "up-down-fish-dying-becoming," which refers
in a coterminous visionary metaphysic to both time-bound organisms (like
the urus, say) and to the Death God, *plonz*, in his timeless brooding.
[13] four bodies here; six of them in the previous mention. Odd.

they will-would-might-have-can-change [14] the winter of NNE
do they destroy the ochre, the shad/shad-cod? do they eat?
they wait for the fat pig (god?)
+++++++++++++++++++++++
++++++++++++++++++++++++++++
++++++++++++++++++++++++
+++++++++++++++++++++++++++++++++++++++++
++++++++++++++++
++++++++++++++++++++
+++++++++++++++++++++++++++++++++++++++++++++
.................... of the great Ones (One?) [15]
+++++++++++++++++
++++++++++++++++++++++++
++++++++++++++++ pattern (shoes?) ..............
+++++++++++++++++++++
++++++++++++++++
++++++++++++++++++++++++++++++
+++++++++++++.................................

TABLET III

## *the further emptying*

the calyx, the calyx, someone has ripped it
it will not make loam, it will crumble
the pig (god?) has pulled life off ++++++++++++
my chest empties ..................... my chest
I can no longer stand in the middle of the field and +++
I am missing, my chest has no food for the maggots
there is no place for the pollen, there is only a hole in the
   flower
the hummingbird ........... pus ............... nectar
the field is a hole without pattern (shoes?)
there are no eyes in back of the wisent's sockets
the urus eats her own teats and her .....................
the urus lies in milk and blood
the urus is a hole in the middle of the field

---

[14] tense untranslatable; outside Indo-European categories.
[15] capitalization clearly indicated. The number is in doubt. Is this the pig, or
an incredible presage of the early Elohim?

[testicles] ......................... for the ground
"with grey horses" drinks urine
"having fine green oxen" looks for salt
let us hold ................. the long man upside down
let us look into his mouth ....................... selfish
   saliva
let us pluck ++++++++++++++ for brother tree
let us kiss the long man, let us carry the long man
let us kiss the long man, let us fondle the long man
let us carry the long man as the ground sucks his drippings
let us feel the drippings from his open groin
let us kiss the hot wound, the wet wound ................
   nectar
let us wait until he is white and dry ............ my chest
let us look into his dry evil mouth, let us fondle the long man
let us bypass the wisent on the river-road pintrpnit [1]
let us avoid the urus on the river-road pintrpnit
let us smell the aurock on the river-road pintrpnit
let us carry the beautiful (strange?) children to the knom
let us sing with the children by the knom
let us set the children's beautiful (strange?) skulls by the
   hearth
when the rain comes.
let us have rain
let us have rain
+++++++++++++++++++++++++++++
++++++++++++++++++++++++++++++++++++
++++++++++++++ ........................... tremble
and also to make the strangers piss in their pants for fear
and to make all neighbors know of the terrible ...... that is
   ours
let them hear about it, let them know
let them tremble like a spear going through the heart and
   through the back
let them become a knowing spear, let them bore in, fish-death
let them shake from the spear's blow, let them hear it sing
I need to feel my solid arm, I need to feel my mighty penis
o my son at the other edge of fish-death

[1] transliteration. Probably an archaic form of "alleluiah" or "selah."

481

o my son by the dark river-road I can't reach your fingertips
o my son in the rain your liver will make the barley shoot up
o my son in the rain your eyes will see the way in the wheat
o my son on the happy edge of the emptying, fish-death,
  pintrpnit
o dark dark dark dark dark dark dark dark dark dark
o dark
you will-would-might-have-can, let us have rain

# Melvin B. Tolson

*From* LIBRETTO FOR THE REPUBLIC OF LIBERIA

TI

O Calendar of the Century,
red-letter the Republic's birth!
O Hallelujah,
oh, let no *Miserere*
venom the spinal cord of Afric earth!
*Selah!*                              260

"*Ecce homo!*"
the blind men cowled in azure rant
before the Capitol,
between the Whale and Elephant,
where no longer stands Diogenes' hearse
readied for the ebony mendicant,
nor weeping widow Europe with her hands
making the multitudinous seas incarnadine
or earth's *massebôth* worse:
O Great White World, thou boy of tears, omega hounds 270
lap up the alpha laugh and *du-haut-en-bas* curse.
*Selah!*

O Africa, Mother of Science
. . . *lachen mit yastchekes* . . .
What dread hand,
to make tripartite one august event,
sundered Gondwanaland?

What dread grasp crushed your biceps and
back upon the rack
chaos of chance and change                              280
fouled in Malebolgean isolation?
What dread *elboga* shoved your soul
into the *tribulum* of retardation?
melamin or melanin dies to the world and dies:
Rome casketed herself in Homeric hymns.
Man's culture in barb and Arab lies:
The Jordan flows into the Tiber,
the Yangtze into the Thames,
the Ganges into the Mississippi, the Niger
into the Seine.                                          290
Judge of the Nations, spare us: yet,
fool latins, alumni of one school,
on Clochan-na-n'all, say *Phew*
... *Lest we forget! Lest we forget!* ...
to dusky peers of Roman, Greek, and Jew.
*Selah!*

Elders of Agâ's House, keening
at the Eagles' feast, cringing
before the Red Slayer, shrinking
from the blood on Hubris' pall—                          300
carked by cracks of myriad curbs,
hitherto, against the Wailing Wall
of Ch'in, the blind men cried:
All cultures crawl
walk hard
fall,
flout
under classes under
*Lout,*
enmesh in ethos, in *masôreth,* the poet's flesh,       310
intone the Mass of the class as the requiem of the mass,
serve *adola mentis* till the crack of will,
castle divorcee Art in a blue-blood moat,
read the flesh of grass
into bulls and bears,
let Brahmin pens kill

Everyman the Goat,
write Culture's epitaph in *Notes* upstairs.
O *Cordon Sanitaire*,
thy brain's tapeworm, extract, thy eyeball's mote!   320
*Selah!*

\*   \*   \*

Like some gray ghoul from Alcatraz,
old Profit, the bald rake *paseq*, wipes the bar,
polishes the goblet vanity,
leers at the tigress Avarice   350
as
she harlots roués from afar:
swallowtails unsaved by loincloths,
famed enterprises prophesying war,
hearts of rags (*Hanorish tharah sharinas*) souls of chalk,
laureates with sugary grace in zinc buckets of verse,
myths rattled by the blueprint's talk,
ists potted and pitted by a feast,
Red Ruin's skeleton horsemen, four abreast
. . . galloping . . .   360
Marx, the exalter, would not know his East
. . . galloping . . .
nor Christ, the Leveler, His West.
*Selah!*

O Age of Tartuffe
. . . *a lighthouse with no light atop* . . .
O Age, *pesiq*, O Age,
kinks internal and global stinks
fog the bitter black estates of Buzzard and Og.
A Dog, I'd rather be, o sage, a Monkey or a Hog.   370
O Peoples of the Brinks,
come with the hawk's resolve,
the skeptic's optic nerve, the prophet's *tele* verve
and Oedipus' guess, to solve
the riddle of
the Red Enigma and the White Sphinx.
*Selah!*

O East . . . *el grito de Dolores* . . . O West,
pacts, disemboweled, crawl off to die;
white books, *fiers instants promis à la faux,*     380
in sick bay choke on mulligan truth and lie;
the knife of Rousseau hacks the anatomy
of the fowl necessity;
dead eyes accuse red Desfourneau,
whose sit-down strike gives High-Heels vertigo;
the wind blows through the keyhole
and the fettered pull down the shades;
while *il santo* and *pero* hone phillipics,
*Realpolitik* explodes the hand grenades
*faits accomplis*     390
in the peace of parades;
caught in the blizzard *divide et impera,*
the little gray cattle cower
before the Siamese wolves,
pomp and power;
Esperanto trips the heels of Greek;
in brain-sick lands, the pearls too rich for swine
the claws of the anonymous seek;
the case Caesarean, Lethean brew
nor instruments obstetrical at hand,     400
the midwife of the old disenwombs the new.
*Selah!*


The *Höhere* of Gaea's children
is beyond the *dérèglement de tous les sens,* is beyond
gold fished from cesspools, the *galerie des rois,*
the seeking of cows, *apartheid,* Sisyphus' despond,
the Ilande intire of itselfe with *die Schweine* in mud,
the potter's wheel that stocks the potter's field,
Kchesinskaja's balcony with epitaphs in blood,
deeds hostile all, O Caton, to hostile eyes,     410
the breaking of foreheads against the walls,
gazing at navels, thinking with thighs

The *Höhere* of God's stepchildren
is beyond the sabotaged world, is beyond
*das Diktat der Menschenverachtung,*
*la muerte sobre el esqueleto de la nada,*
the pelican's breast rent red to feed the young,
summer's third-class ticket, the *Revue des morts,*
the skulls trepanned to hold ideas plucked from dung,
Dives' crumbs in the church of the unchurched,    420
absurd life shaking its ass's ears among
the colors of vowels and Harrar blacks
with Nessus shirts from Europe on their backs


.    .    .


The *Höhere* of X's children
is beyond Heralds' College, the *filets d'Arachné*, is beyond
maggot democracy, the *Mal éternel,* the Bells of Ys,
the doddering old brigades with aorist medicines of poetry,
the *Orizaba* with its Bridge of Sighs,
the *oasis d'horreur dans un déserte d'ennui,*
the girasol rocks of Secunderabad,    430
Yofan's studio and *Shkola Nenavisti,*
the *ototatoi*—in Crimson Tapestries—of the *hoi polloi,*
Euboean defeats
in the Sausage Makers' bout
the fool himself himself finds out
and in the cosmos of his chaos
repeats.
*Selah!*

# NOTES

258. *Miserere.* Cf. Newman, *The Definition of a Gentleman:* ". . . we attended the Tenebrae, at the Sestine, for the sake of the Miserere . . ."

262. *Cowled in azure:* the cloak of deceit and false humility. Cf. Hafiz, *The Divan* (*Odes*), V, translated by Bicknell.

264. *Whale and Elephant:* the symbols Jefferson used to designate Great Britain with her navy under Nelson and France with her army under Napoleon. V. Anderson, *Liberia*, X.

269. *Massebôth:* "sacred pillars." Cf. Genesis, XXVIII, xviii. Also the J author.

270. *Thou boy of tears.* Cf. Shakespeare, *Coriolanus*, V, v.

274. *Lachen mit yastchekes:* "laughing with needles being stuck in you"; ghetto laughter.

275. Cf. Blake, *The Tiger.*

276. Cf. Hardy, *The Convergence of the Twain.*

286. V. Pycraft, *Animals of the World*, 1941-1942. *A fortiori*, the American trotter is "a combination of barb and Arab on English stock."

287. V. Christy, *The Asian Legacy and American Life.* This book contains vital facts on Oriental influences in the New Poetry. What I owe the late Professor Arthur E. Christy, a favorite teacher, is not limited to the concept of "the shuttle ceaselessly weaving the warp and weft of the world's cultural fabric."

293. *Clochan-na-n'all:* "the blind men's stepping-stones." Cf. Ferguson, *The Welshmen of Tirawley.*

297. V. Aeschylus, *Agamemnon.*

301. Cf. Shakespeare, *Coriolanus*, I, i, 67-76. See also Mr. Traversi's essay on this phase of the play.

303. I came across these words somewhere: "The Ch'in emperor built the Great Wall to keep out Mongolian enemies from the north and burned the books of China to destroy intellectual enemies from within."

310. Cf. Akiba: *"Masôreth* is a fence for the sayings of the fathers."
312. *Adla mentis.* V. Bacon, *Novum Organum.*
313. *Divorcee Art.* Cf. Gourmont: *"Car je crois que l'art est par essence, absolument inintelligible au peuple."*

\* \* \*

348. *Paseq:* "divider." This is a vertical line that occurs about 480 times in our Hebrew Bible. Although first mentioned in the *Midrash Rabba* in the eleventh century, it is still the most mysterious sign in the literature.
353. Cf. Cavafy, *Waiting for the Barbarians.*
354. *Famed enterprises.* V. Erasmus, *The Praise of Folly,* "Soldiers and Philosophers," *in toto,* the revised translation by John Wilson.
355. *Hearts of rags . . . souls of chalk:* Whitman's epithets for the "floating mass" that vote early and often for bread and circuses. *Hanorish tharah sharinas:* "Man is a being of varied, manifold, and inconstant nature." V. Della Mirandola, *Oration of the Dignity of Man.* Cf. Cunha: "The fantasy of universal suffrage [is] the Hercules' club of our dignity."
356. *Zinc buckets of verse.* V. Pasternak, *Definition of Poetry. Sugary grace.* Cf. Martial, *To a Rival Poet.*
359. Cf. Tennyson, *Idylls of the King:*
     "Red Ruin, and the breaking up of laws."
     V. Revelation VI. Cf. Jouve, *La Resurrection des Morts.* See the White Horse, the Red Horse, the Black Horse, and the fourth horse, the worst:
     > *Tu es jaune et ta forme coule à ta charpente*
     > *Sur le tonneau ajouré de tes côtes*
     > *Les lambeaux verts tombent plus transparents*
     > *La queue est chauve et le bassin a des béquilles*
     > *Pour le stérile va-et-vient de la violence . . ."*
363. *The Leveler.* V. The Acts V, xxxii-xxxvi.

367. *Pesiq:* "divided." V. Fuchs, *Pesiq ein Glossenzeichen.* It seems to me that this linguistic symbol gives us a concrete example of the teleological—perhaps the only one. By an accident of *a priori* probability, the sign in itself indicates both cause and effect, and the index of the relationship is served synchronously by either *paseq* or *pasiq.* Of course the protagonist of the poem uses them for his own purpose on another level.

369. *Bitter black estates.* Cf. Petrarca, *The Spring Returns, but Not to Him Returns,* translated by Auslander. *Buzzard.* V. Dryden, *The Hind and the Panther. Og.* V. Tate, *Second Part of Absalom and Achitophel,* the passage inserted by Dryden.

370. V. Rochester, *Satyr against Mankind.* Cf. Cocteau, *Le Cap de Bonne Espérance: "J'ai mal d'être homme."*

378. The watchword of Hidalgo, "Captain General of America."

380. Cf. Muselli, *Ballade de Contradiction:*
> *"Fiers instants promis à la faux,*
> *Eclairs sombres au noir domaine!"*

384. Cf. Camus, *The Artist as Witness of Freedom:* M. Desfourneau's ". . . demands were clear. He naturally wanted a bonus for each execution, which is customary in any enterprise. But, more important, he vigorously demanded that he be given . . . an administrative status. Thus came to an end, beneath the weight of history, one of the last of our liberal professions. . . . Almost everywhere else in the world, executioners have already been installed in ministerial chairs. They have merely substituted the rubber stamp for the axe."

386. Cf. Nietzsche, *Thus Spoke Zarathustra,* 232.

388. *Il Santo* and *Pero:* respectively, the nicknames of Nietzsche and Trotsky—the first innocently ironical, the second ironically innocent.

393. Cf. the remark of Nicholas I to a harassed minister of war: "We have plenty of little gray cattle." The Czar had in mind the Russian peasant.

397. *Brain-sick lands.* V. Meredith, *On the Dangers of War.*

398. In the fable of Antisthenes, when the hares demanded

equality for all, the lions said: "Where are your claws?" Cf. Martial, *Epigram XII*, 93: *"Dic mihi, so fias tu leo, qualis eris?"*

403. *Höhere.* Cf. Petronius: *"Proecipitandus est liber spiritus."*

405. In the Gilded Era, cynics said of Babcock: "He fished for gold in every stinking cesspool." *Galerie des rois.* Cf. Verlaine, *Nocturne Parisien*, the reference to the twenty-eight statues of French kings.

406. *The seeking of cows:* this is the literal meaning of the word "battle" among the ancient Aryans who ravaged the Indo-Gangetic plains. The backwardness of their culture is attested by their failure to fumigate and euphemize their war aims. *Apartheid:* the South African system of multi-layered segregation.

410. *Deeds hostile all:* these words are from the *Chorus to Ajax*, by Sophocles, which Mr. Forrestal apparently read just before his death. *O Caton:* Cato the Younger committed suicide in 46 B. C. He had spent the previous night reading Plato's *Phaedo.* Cf. Lamartine, *Le Désespoir.*

411. *The walls:* "economic doctrines." The figure is Blok's.

414. *Sabotaged world.* Cf. Salmon, *Age de l'Humanité.*

415. V. Mitscherlich and Mielke, *Doctors of Infamy*, translated by Norden. Cf. Grotius, *De Jure Belli et Pacis*, "Prolegomena," XVIII: ". . . a people which violates the Laws of Nature and Nations, beats down the bulwark of its own tranquillity for future time."

417. Cf. Ronsard, *Le Bocage.* Also Musset, *La Nuit de mai.*

418. V. Gautier, *Vieux de la vieille*, the reference to Raffet's *nocturne* showing Napoleon's spirit reviewing spectral troops.

419. Plekhanov had Alexander II in mind when he used the trepan figure.

421. V. Cendrars, *Eloge de la vie dangereuse.*

422. Rimbaud, in a town near the Red Sea, looked toward Khartoum and wrote: *"Leur Gordon est un idiot, leur*

*Wolseley un âne, et toutes leurs entreprises une suite insensée d'absurdités et de déprédations."* But fifty years later, when the Black Shirts entered Harrar, the ex-poet who plotted with Menelik against Italy was not there to hear Vittorio Mussolini's poetic account: "I still remember the effect produced on a small group of Galla tribesmen massed around a man in black clothes. I dropped an aerial bomb right in the center, and the group opened up like a flowering rose. It was most entertaining."

425. *Filets d'Arachné.* Cf. Chénier, *Qui? moi? de Phébus te dicter les leçons?*

426. *Mal éternel.* Cf. Lisle, *Dies irae.*

429. Cf. Baudelaire, *Le Voyage.*

430. V. Robinson, the Preface to *The Story of Medicine.*

431. *Yofan's studio:* Napoleon's old residence by the Kremlin wall. *Shkola Nenavisti:* a Berlin film on a Dublin subject in a Moscow theater.

432. *Otototoi.* See Gilbert Murray's Notes to *Aeschylus.*

433. Cf. Ovid, Tristia, quoted by Montaigne in *Of Three Commerces.* "Whoever of the Grecian fleet has escaped the Capharean rocks ever takes care to steer clear from those of the Euboean sea."

# Bio-Bibliographies

# A. R. AMMONS

Whiteville, North Carolina, 1926.

Studied at Wake Forest College and University of California; formerly was an executive of a scientific instruments company; currently teaches writing at Cornell University.

*Ommateum* (Dorrance & Co., 1955)
*Expressions of Sea Level* (Ohio State Univ., 1964)
*Corsons Inlet* (Cornell Univ., 1965)
*Tape for the Turn of the Year* (Cornell Univ., 1965)
*Northfield Poems* (Cornell Univ., 1966)
*Selected Poems* (Cornell Univ., 1968)

See Stephen Donadio, "Some Younger Poets in America," in Philip Rahv, ed., *Modern Occasions* (Farrar, Straus & Giroux, 1966); David Curry, "Apple Recommends . . ." *Apple*, 1 (Summer 1967); William Mathews, "Entering the World," *Shenandoah*, XX/4 (Summer 1969).

# BROTHER ANTONINUS

Born William Everson, Sacramento, California, 1912.

Studied at Fresno State College; currently is a lay brother, St. Albert's College, Oakland, California.

*These Are the Ravens* [Everson] (Pamphlet Series of Western Poets, San Leandro, Calif., 1935)
*The Masculine Dead* [Everson] (James Decker, Iowa City, 1942)
*The Residual Years* [Everson] (New Directions, 1948; rev. ed. 1968)
*The Crooked Lines of God* (Univ. of Detroit, 1959)
*The Hazards of Holiness* (Doubleday, 1962)
*Single Source: Early Poems* [Everson] (Oyez, Berkeley, Calif., 1966)
*The Rose of Solitude* (Doubleday, 1967)

Also collected six critical essays, *Robinson Jeffers* (Oyez, Berkeley, Calif., 1968).

See Ralph J. Mills, Jr., "Brother Antoninus," *Contemporary American Poetry* (Random House, 1965); James Dickey, "Brother

Antoninus," *Babel to Byzantium* (Farrar, Straus & Giroux, 1968);
William Stafford, ed., *The Achievement of Brother Antoninus*
(Scott, Foresman, 1967).


## JOHN ASHBERY

Sodus, New York, 1927.
  B.A., Harvard; M.A., Columbia; currently is associate editor of
*Art News*.

*Turandot and Other Poems* (Tiber de Nagy, 1953)
*Some Trees* (Yale Univ., 1956)
*The Poems* (Tiber, 1960)
*The Tennis Court Oath* (Wesleyan Univ., 1962)
*Rivers and Mountains* (Holt, Rinehart and Winston, 1966)
*Selected Poems* (Cape, London, 1968)
*The Double Dream of Spring* (Dutton, 1970)

  Also has written several plays, imaginative prose, and art
criticism; a novel co-authored with James Schuyler, *A Nest of
Ninnies* (Holt, Rinehart and Winston, 1969).
  See Jonathan Cott, "Poetry," in Richard Kostelanetz, ed., *The
New American Arts* (Horizon, 1965); Paul Carroll, "John Ash-
bery," *The Poem in Its Skin* (Follett, 1968).


## MARGARET ATWOOD

Ottawa, Ontario, 1939.
  B.A., Victoria College, University of Toronto; M.A., Radcliffe;
formerly taught at Sir George Williams University and the University of British Columbia; currently lives in Edmonton, Alberta.

*Double Persephone* (Hawkshead, Toronto, 1961)
*The Circle Game* (Contact Press, 1966; House of Anansi, 1967)
*The Animals in the Country* (Oxford—Canada, 1968; Little,
  Brown, 1969)
  Also published a novel, *The Edible Woman* (McClelland &
Stewart, 1969).


## TED BERRIGAN

Providence, Rhode Island, 1934.
  B.A., M.A., University of Tulsa; was founding editor of C Press;
currently teaches at the University of Iowa.

*The Sonnets* (C Press, 1965; Grove, 1967)
*Bean Spasms*, with Ron Padgett (Kulchur, 1967)
*Many Happy Returns* (Corinth, 1968)


# JOHN BERRYMAN

McAlester, Oklahoma, 1914.
  Was educated at Columbia University and Clare College, Cambridge; currently is Professor of Humanities, University of Minnesota.

*Poems* (New Directions, 1942)
*The Dispossessed* (Sloane, 1948)
*Homage to Mistress Bradstreet* (Farrar, Straus & Giroux, 1956)
*77 Dream Songs* (Farrar, Straus & Giroux, 1964)
*Berryman's Sonnets* (Farrar, Straus & Giroux, 1967)
*Short Poems* (Farrar, Straus & Giroux, 1967)
*His Toy, His Dream, His Rest* (Farrar, Straus & Giroux, 1968)
*Dream Songs* (Farrar, Straus & Giroux, 1969)

  Also published a critical biography, *Stephen Crane* (Sloane, 1950), as well as criticism and fiction.
  See Robert Lowell, "The Poetry of John Berryman," *New York Review of Books*, II (May 28, 1964); Stanley Kunitz, "No Middle Flight," *Poetry*, XC (1957); Jonathan Cott, "Two Dream Poets," in Richard Kostelanetz, ed., *On Contemporary Literature* (Avon, 1964).


# JOHN CAGE

Los Angeles, California, 1912.
  Studied at Pomona College; also studied musical composition with Arnold Schoenberg, Adolph Weiss, and Henry Cowell; recently was Visiting Professor at the University of Illinois.

*Silence* (Wesleyan Univ., 1961)
*A Year from Monday* (Wesleyan Univ., 1967)
*Notations*, with Alison Knowles (Something Else Press, New York, 1969)

  Also recorded *Indeterminacy* (Folkways, 3704).
  Regarding Cage as literature, see Richard Kostelanetz, "John

Cage: Some Random Remarks," *Denver Quarterly*, IV/2 (Spring 1969); Richard Kostelanetz, *ed.*, *John Cage: Before and After* (Praeger, 1970).

## J. V. CUNNINGHAM

Cumberland, Maryland, 1911.
  A.B., Ph.D., Stanford University; formerly taught at the Universities of Hawaii and Chicago; currently is Professor of English, Brandeis University.

*The Helmsman* (Colt, San Francisco, 1942)
*The Judge Is Fury* (Swallow & Wm. Morrow, 1947)
*Doctor Drink* (Cummington Press, 1950)
*The Quest of the Opal* (Swallow, 1950)
*The Exclusions of a Rhyme* (Swallow, 1960)
*To What Strangers, What Welcome* (Swallow, 1964)

  Also authored books of criticism, including *Tradition and Poetic Structure* (Swallow, 1960) and *The Journal of John Cardan* (Swallow, 1964).
  See Yvor Winters, "Conclusions," *Forms of Discovery* (Swallow, 1967), and *The Poetry of J. V. Cunningham* (Swallow, 1961); James Dickey, "J. V. Cunningham," *Babel to Byzantium* (Farrar, Straus & Giroux, 1968).

## S. FOSTER DAMON

Newton, Massachusetts, 1893.
  Professor Emeritus, Brown University, and Curator Emeritus of its Harris Collection of American Poetry and Plays; currently lives in Providence, Rhode Island, and Annisquam, Massachusetts.

*Astrolabe, Infinitudes and Hypocrises* (Harper, 1927)
*Tilted Moons* (Harper, 1929)
*Nightmare Cemetery* [pseudonym Samuel Nomad] (Privately published, Providence, R.I., 1964)

  Also authored *William Blake: His Philosophy and Symbols* (Houghton Mifflin, 1924), *Blake Dictionary* (Brown Univ., 1965), and other volumes of criticism.
  See Malcolm Cowley, "The Self-Obliterated Author: S. Foster Damon," *Southern Review*, IV/1 (January 1968); Yvor Winters, "Conclusions," *Forms of Discovery* (Swallow, 1967).

# JAMES DICKEY

Atlanta, Georgia, 1923.

Studied at Vanderbilt; formerly was an advertising executive and teacher; recently served as Consultant in Poetry to the Library of Congress; currently teaches at the University of South Carolina.

*Into the Stone* (Scribner's, 1957)
*Drowning with Others* (Wesleyan Univ., 1962)
*Helmets* (Wesleyan Univ., 1964)
*Two Poems of the Air* (Centicore, Portland, Ore., 1964)
*Buckdancer's Choice* (Wesleyan Univ., 1965)
*Poems: 1957–1967* (Wesleyan Univ., 1967)

Also published essays and reviews collected in *The Suspect in Poetry* (The Sixties, 1964) and *Babel to Byzantium* (Farrar, Straus & Giroux, 1968), as well as read selections on his record *The Poems of James Dickey* (Spoken Arts, 984).

See Richard Howard, "On James Dickey," *Partisan Review*, XXXIII/3 (Summer 1966); Crunk, "The Work of James Dickey," *The Sixties*, 7 (Winter 1964); Robert Bly, "The Collapse of James Dickey," *The Sixties*, 9 (Spring 1967); Richard Kostelanetz, "Flyswatter and Gadfly," *Shenandoah*, XVI/3 (Spring 1965); Paul Carroll, *The Poem in Its Skin* (Follett, 1968); Ralph J. Mills, "The Poetry of James Dickey," *Tri-Quarterly* (Winter 1968); Lawrence Lieberman, ed., *The Achievement of James Dickey* (Scott, Foresman, 1968).

# ALAN DUGAN

Brooklyn, New York, 1923.

Was educated at Queens College, Olivet College, Mexico City College, and elsewhere; currently lives in New York City and teaches part-time.

*Poems* (Yale Univ., 1961)
*Poems 2* (Yale Univ., 1963)
*Poems 3* (Yale Univ., 1967)
*Collected Poems* (Yale Univ., 1969)

See Robert Boyers, "The Poetry of Survival," *Salmagundi*, II/3 (Spring-Summer 1968).

## GAIL DUSENBERY

Albany, New York, 1939.

Studied at Cornell University; B.A., the University of California, Berkeley; was a founding editor of *The San Francisco Earthquake;* currently lives in San Francisco and works as a medical secretary.

*The Mark* (Oyez, Berkeley, Calif., 1968)

## ALLEN GINSBERG

Newark, New Jersey, 1926.

B.A., Columbia College; formerly was book reviewer briefly on *Newsweek* and holder of miscellaneous jobs; currently lives disaffiliated in New York City.

*Howl, and Other Poems* (City Lights, 1956)
*Empty Mirror: Early Poems* (Totem/Corinth, 1961)
*Kaddish and Other Poems* (City Lights, 1961)
*Reality Sandwiches* (City Lights, 1963)
*Jukebox All'Idrogeno* (Mondadori Editore, 1965)
*Wichita Vortex Sutra* (Coyote, 1966)
*T.V. Baby Poems* (Grossman, 1968)
*Airplane Dreams* (House of Anansi, 1968)
*Planet News* (City Lights, 1968)

Also wrote many pieces in prose (soon to be collected), made a recording of early poems (Fantasy, 7006), and authored, with William S. Burroughs, *The Yage Letters* (City Lights, 1963).

See Kenneth Rexroth, "Disengagement: The Art of the Beat Generation," *New World Writing*, 11 (1957); M. L. Rosenthal, "Allen Ginsberg," *The New Poets* (Oxford, 1967); Leslie A. Fiedler, "Into the Cafés: A Kind of Solution," *Waiting for the End* (Stein & Day, 1964); Richard Kostelanetz, "Allen Ginsberg," *Master Minds* (Macmillan, 1969); Jane Kramer, *Allen Ginsberg in America* (Random House, 1969); Thomas Parkinson, ed., *A Casebook on the Beat* (Crowell, 1961), Paul Carroll, "Allen Ginsberg," *The Poem in Its Skin* (Follett, 1968).

## JOHN GIORNO

New York, New York, 1936.

B.A., Columbia College; formerly was a seaman, a stockbroker on Wall Street, and the star of Andy Warhol's *Sleep;* currently lives in New York City.

*Poems* (Mother, 1967)

Also released an LP stereo recording, *Raspberry and Pornographic Poem* (The Intravenus Mind, 1967).
See John Perreault, "Pop Poetry," *Village Voice* (Sept. 7, 1967).

## DAN GRAHAM

Urbana, Illinois, 1942.
Studied at Columbia University; founded John Daniels Gallery; currently lives in New York City.
Poems published in *Extensions, Aspen, Harper's Bazaar,* and *0 to 9,* and *End Moments* (Dan Graham, N.Y., 1969).

Also published essays, art criticism, and photographs.

## DANIEL HOFFMAN

New York, New York, 1923.
B.A., Ph.D., Columbia University; currently is Professor of English at the University of Pennsylvania.

*An Armada of Thirty Whales* (Yale Univ., 1954)
*A Little Geste* (Oxford, 1960)
*The City of Satisfactions* (Oxford, 1963)
*Striking the Stones* (Oxford, 1968)
*Broken Laws* (Oxford, 1970)

Also published four critical volumes, including *Form and Fable in American Fiction* (Oxford, 1961) and *Barbarous Knowledge* (Oxford, 1967), edited two anthologies, and made a recording for the Library of Congress (PL 38).
See John A. Meixner, "Hoffman's Visionary Horse Pursued," *Sewanee Review,* LXXII/4 (Autumn 1964); William Sylvester, review in *College English,* XXIX (October 1967).

## JOHN HOLLANDER

New York, New York, 1929.
B.A., Columbia; Ph.D., Indiana; formerly was a Junior Fellow, Harvard University, and a teacher at Yale and Connecticut Col-

lege; currently is Professor of English at Hunter College, U.C.N.Y., and poetry consultant for *Partisan Review*.

*A Crackling of Thorns* (Yale Univ., 1958)
*Movie-Going and Other Poems* (Atheneum, 1962)
*Visions from the Ramble* (Atheneum, 1965)
*Types of Shape* (Atheneum, 1968)

Also edited anthologies of poetry and published journalism, criticism, and literary history; of the last includes *The Untuning of the Sky: Ideas of Music in English Poetry, 1500–1700* (Princeton Univ., 1961).


# DAVID IGNATOW

Brooklyn, New York, 1914.
Formerly was Office Manager of the Enterprise Book Binding Company and an editor of the *Beloit Poetry Journal;* currently lives in East Hampton, New York, and occasionally edits *Chelsea Review*.

*Poems* (Decker, Prairie City, Ill., 1948)
*The Gentle Weightlifter* (Morris Gallery, 1955)
*Say Pardon* (Wesleyan Univ., 1961)
*Figures of the Human* (Wesleyan Univ., 1964)
*Rescue the Dead* (Wesleyan Univ., 1968)
*Poems: 1934–1969* (Wesleyan Univ., 1970)

Also published critical essays and extracts from a journal.
See James Dickey, "David Ignatow," *Babel to Byzantium* (Farrar, Straus & Giroux, 1968); Crunk, "The Work of David Ignatow," *The Sixties*, 10 (Summer 1968).


# RANDALL JARRELL

Nashville, Tennessee, 1914; died, Greensboro, North Carolina, 1965.
Studied at Vanderbilt and Princeton; taught at several universities, particularly the Women's College of the University of North Carolina.

*The Rage for the Lost Penny* (New Directions, 1940)
*Blood for a Stranger* (Harcourt, Brace & World, 1942)

*Little Friend, Little Friend* (Dial, 1945)
*Losses* (Harcourt, Brace & World, 1948)
*The Seven-League Crutches* (Harcourt, Brace & World, 1951)
*Selected Poems* (Knopf, 1955)
*The Woman at the Washington Zoo* (Atheneum, 1960)
*The Lost World* (Macmillan, 1965)
*The Complete Poems* (Farrar, Straus & Giroux, 1968)

Also published three collections of critical essays: *Poetry and the Age* (Knopf, 1953), *A Sad Heart at the Supermarket* (Atheneum, 1962), and *The Third Book of Criticism* (Farrar, Straus & Giroux, 1969); children's books; translations; anthologies; and a single novel, *Pictures from an Institution* (Knopf, 1954).

See James Dickey, "Randall Jarrell," *Babel to Byzantium* (Farrar, Straus & Giroux, 1968); Stephen Stepanchev, "Randall Jarrell," *American Poetry Since 1945* (Harper & Row, 1965); Sister M. Bernetta Quinn, "Randall Jarrell," *The Metamorphic Tradition in Modern Poetry* (Rutgers Univ., 1955).


## GALWAY KINNELL

Providence, Rhode Island, 1927.

A.B., Princeton; formerly taught at the University of Chicago and in Tehran; worked with CORE in Louisiana; recently became Poet-in-Residence at the University of California—Irvine.

*What a Kingdom It Was* (Houghton Mifflin, 1960)
*Flower Herding on Mount Monadnock* (Houghton Mifflin, 1964)
*Body Rags* (Houghton Mifflin, 1968)

Also published a novel, *Black Light* (Houghton Mifflin, 1966), and translations from the French, including *The Poetry of François Villon* (New American Library, 1965), and Yves Bonnefoy's *On the Motion and Immobility of Douve* (Ohio State, 1968).

See James Dickey, "Galway Kinnell," *Babel to Byzantium* (Farrar, Straus & Giroux, 1968); Glauco Cambon, *Contemporary American Poetry* (Univ. of Minnesota, 1962).


## KENNETH KOCH

Cincinnati, Ohio, 1925.

A.B., Harvard; Ph.D., Columbia; currently is Associate Professor of English, Columbia College.

*Poems* (Tibor de Nagy, 1953)
*Ko, or a Season on Earth* (Grove, 1959)
*When the Sun Tries To Go On* (Hasty Papers, 1960; Black Sparrow, 1969)
*Thank You and Other Poems* (Grove, 1962)
*Poems from 1952 & 1953* (Black Sparrow, 1968)
*The Pleasures of Peace* (Grove, 1968).

Also published prose fiction and a collection of plays, *Bertha* (Grove, 1966).
See Jonathan Cott, "Poetry," in Richard Kostelanetz, ed., *The New American Arts;* F. W. Dupee, "Kenneth Koch's Poetry," *King of the Cats* (Farrar, Straus & Giroux, 1965).

## RICHARD KOSTELANETZ

New York, New York, 1940.
A.B., Brown; M.A., Columbia; currently lives unaffiliated in New York City.

*Visual Language* (forthcoming)

Also published criticism of contemporary arts and cultural history, including *The Theatre of Mixed Means* (Dial, 1968) and *Master Minds* (Macmillan, 1969), as well as edited several anthologies, among them *The Young American Writers* (Funk & Wagnalls, 1967) and *Imaged Words & Worded Images* (Outerbridge & Dienstfrey, 1970).
See Jean-François Bory, "In Production," in *Once Again* (New Directions, 1968); Richard Kostelanetz, "Word-Imagery," *Metamorphosis in the Arts* (Abrams, 1971).

## STANLEY KUNITZ

Worcester, Massachusetts, 1905.
A.B., Harvard University; currently teaches part-time at Columbia.

*Intellectual Things* (Doubleday, 1930)
*Passport to the War* (Holt, Rinehart and Winston, 1944)
*Selected Poems 1928–1958* (Atlantic–Little, Brown, 1958)

Also published critical essays, as well as edited numerous books of literary-biographical reference, including *American Authors, 1600–1900* (Wilson, 1938), *Twentieth Century Authors* (Wilson, 1942), and *Twentieth Century Authors—First Supplement* (Wilson, 1955).

See Ralph J. Mills, Jr., "Stanley Kunitz," *Contemporary American Poetry* (Random House, 1965); Robert Lowell, *et al.*, "On Stanley Kunitz's 'Father and Son,'" in Anthony Ostroff, ed., *The Contemporary Poet as Artist and Critic* (Little, Brown, 1964).


# PHILIP LAMANTIA

San Francisco, California, 1927.
Formerly was an editor of *View;* currently lives in Seattle, Washington.

*Erotic Poems* (Bern Porter, Berkeley, Calif., 1946)
*Ekstasis* (Auerhahn, 1959)
*Narcotica* (Auerhahn, 1959)
*Destroyed Works* (Auerhahn, 1962)
*Touch of the Marvelous* (Oyez, Berkeley, Calif., 1966)
*Selected Works, 1943–1966* (City Lights, 1967)

See Kenneth Rexroth, "The New Poetry," *Assays* (New Directions, 1961); Philip Lamantia, "Letter from San Francisco," *Horizon*, 93-4 (October 1947).


# JOHN LOGAN

Red Oak, Iowa, 1923.
Formerly taught at Notre Dame; currently is Professor of English at S.U.N.Y.—Buffalo and editor of *Choice*.

*Cycle for Mother Cabrini* (Grove, 1955)
*Ghosts of the Heart* (Univ. of Chicago, 1960)
*Spring of the Thief* (Knopf, 1963)
*The Zig Zag Walk* (Dutton, 1969)

See Crunk, "The Work of John Logan," *The Sixties*, 5 (Fall 1961); Paul Carroll, "John Logan," *The Poem in Its Skin* (Follett, 1968); Jerome Mazzaro, "Ventures into Evening: Self-Parody in the Poetry of John Logan," *Salmagundi*, II/4 (1968).


# ROBERT LOWELL

Boston, Massachusetts, 1917.
Was educated at Harvard and Kenyon; subsequently taught at

Iowa, Boston, and Harvard Universities; currently lives in New York City.

*Land of Unlikeness* (Cummington Press, 1944)
*Lord Weary's Castle* (Harcourt, Brace & World, 1946)
*The Mills of the Kavanaughs* (Harcourt, Brace & World, 1951)
*Life Studies* (Farrar, Straus & Giroux, 1959)
*For the Union Dead* (Farrar, Straus & Giroux, 1964)
*Near the Ocean* (Farrar, Straus & Giroux, 1967)
*Notebook 1967–1968* (Farrar, Straus & Giroux, 1969)

Also published a collection of poetic translations, *Imitations* (Farrar, Straus & Giroux, 1961); a translation of Racine's *Phaedra* (Farrar, Straus & Giroux, 1961); and a book of plays, *The Old Glory* (Farrar, Straus & Giroux, 1965).

See Randall Jarrell, "From the Kingdom of Necessity," *Poetry and the Age* (Knopf, 1953), also reprinted in Richard Kostelanetz, ed., *On Contemporary Literature* (Avon, 1964); Jerome Mazzaro, *The Poetic Themes of Robert Lowell* (Univ. of Michigan, 1966); Hugh B. Staples, *Robert Lowell: The First Twenty Years* (Farrar, Straus & Giroux, 1962); M. L. Rosenthal, "Robert Lowell and 'Confessional' Poetry," *The New Poets* (Oxford, 1967); Robert Boyers and Michael London, eds., *Robert Lowell: The Hero as Victim* (David Lewis, 1969); Frederick Seidel, "Robert Lowell," *Writers at Work: Second Series* (Viking, 1963); John Berryman *et al.*, "On Robert Lowell's 'Skunk Hour,'" in Anthony Ostroff, ed., *The Contemporary Poet as Artist and Critic* (Little, Brown, 1964); William J. Martz, ed., *The Achievement of Robert Lowell* (Scott, Foresman, 1966).

# bpNICHOL

Vancouver, British Columbia, 1944.
Studied at the University of British Columbia; currently works in the lay analytic movement in Toronto.

*Konfessions of an Elizabethan Fan Dancer* (Writer's Forum, London, 1967)
*bp*, which includes *Letters Home, Journeying & The Returns*, and a recording of sound poems entitled *Borders* (Coach House, 1967)

Also recorded *Motherlove* (Allied Records, Toronto) and authored *Two Novels* (Coach House, 1969).
See "New Wave Nichol," *Tamarack Review*, 44 (Summer 1967).

## Liam O'Gallagher

Oakland, California, 1917.

Studied at Columbia University; also studied painting with Hans Hofmann; currently teaches painting in San Francisco, where he lives.

*Planet Noise* (Nova Broadcast, San Francisco, 1969)

His paintings are represented in collections here and abroad; and his work with words appears regularly in *The San Francisco Earthquake.*


## Charles Olson

Worcester, Massachusetts, 1910; died, 1970, New York City.

Was "uneducated" at Wesleyan, Yale, and Harvard; formerly was Rector at Black Mountain College and Professor of English at S.U.N.Y.—Buffalo.

*The Maximus Poems 1–10* (Jargon, 1953)
*The Distances* (Grove, 1960)
*The Maximus Poems* (Jargon/Corinth, 1960)
*Selected Writings* (New Directions, 1966)
*Maximus Poems IV, V, VI* (Grossman, 1969)

Also published many pamphlets of poetry; *Mayan Letters* (Divers, Mallorca, 1953; reprinted, Grossman, 1968); and three books of criticism: *Call Me Ishmael* (Reynal & Hitchcock, 1947), *Projective Verse* (Totem, 1959), and *The Human Universe* (Auerhahn, 1965; Grove, 1967).

See M. L. Rosenthal, "Charles Olson," *The New Poets* (Oxford, 1967); Robert Creeley, "Introduction," in Olson's *Selected Writings;* Robert Duncan, "Notes on Poetics Regarding Olson's 'Maximus,'" *The Black Mountain Review,* 6 (1954), which was reprinted in a revised form in *The Review,* 10 (1964); James Dickey, "Charles Olson," *Babel to Byzantium* (Farrar, Straus & Giroux, 1968).


## Sylvia Plath

Boston, Massachusetts, 1932; died, London, England, 1963.
Studied at Smith and Newnham College, Cambridge.

507

*The Colossus* (Knopf, 1962)
*Ariel* (Harper & Row, 1966)
*Uncollected Poems* (Turret, London, 1968)

Also published short stories, essays, a radio play, and a novel, *The Bell Jar* (Heinemann, London, 1963), originally issued pseudonymously.

See Charles Newman, "Candor Is the Only Wile," and Anne Sexton, "The Barfly Ought To Sing," *Tri-Quarterly*, 7 (Fall 1966); M. L. Rosenthal, "Sylvia Plath," *The New Poets* (Oxford, 1967); Robert Boyers, "The Trepanned Veteran," *Centennial Review* (Spring 1969); A. Alvarez, "Sylvia Plath," *Beyond All That Fiddle* (Random House, 1969).


# KENNETH REXROTH

South Bend, Indiana, 1905.
Currently lives in San Francisco and contributes a regular column to the San Francisco *Chronicle*.

*The Phoenix and the Tortoise* (New Directions, 1944)
*The Signature of All Things* (New Directions, 1949)
*The Dragon and the Unicorn* (New Directions, 1952)
*In Defense of the Earth* (New Directions, 1956)
*The Homestead Called Damascus* (New Directions, 1963)
*Natural Numbers* (New Directions, 1963)
*The Collected Shorter Poems* (New Directions, 1966)
*The Heart's Garden, The Garden's Heart* (Pym-Randall, 1967)
*The Collected Longer Poems* (New Directions, 1968)

Also published numerous collections of translations from Chinese, Japanese, and other languages; verse plays; miscellaneous criticism, some of which was collected in *The Bird in the Bush* (New Directions, 1959) and *Assays* (New Directions, 1961); and *An Autobiographical Novel* (Doubleday, 1966).


# THEODORE ROETHKE

Saginaw, Michigan, 1908; died, Bainbridge Island, Washington, 1963.
A.B., M.A., University of Michigan; at death was Professor of English, University of Washington.

*Open House* (Knopf, 1941)
*The Lost Son and Other Poems* (Doubleday, 1948)
*Praise to the End!* (Doubleday, 1951)
*The Waking: Poems 1933–1953* (Doubleday, 1953)
*Words for the Wind* (Doubleday, 1958)
*I Am! Says the Lamb* (Doubleday, 1961)
*Sequence, Sometimes Metaphysical* (Stone Wall, 1963)
*The Far Field* (Doubleday, 1964)
*Collected Poems* (Doubleday, 1966)

Also published a children's book, *Party at the Zoo* (Crowell Collier and Macmillan, 1963), and recorded selections from *Words for the Wind* (Folkways, FL 9736). His prose was posthumously collected in Ralph J. Mills, Jr., ed., *On the Poet and His Craft* (Univ. of Washington, 1965); and Mills also edited and introduced the *Selected Letters of Theodore Roethke* (Univ. of Washington, 1968).

See Mills's pamphlet, *Theodore Roethke* (Univ. of Minnesota, 1963); Karl Malkoff, *Theodore Roethke* (Columbia Univ., 1966); Allan Seager, *The Glass House* (McGraw-Hill, 1968); Stanley Kunitz, "Theodore Roethke," *New York Review of Books*, I (Oct. 17, 1963), and "Poet of Transformations," *New Republic*, CLII (Jan. 23, 1956); Jonathan Cott, "Two Dream Poets," in Richard Kostelanetz, ed., *On Contemporary Literature* (Avon, 1964); Hilton Kramer, "The Poetry of Theodore Roethke," *Western Review*, XVII (Winter 1954); Kenneth Burke, "The Vegetal Radicalism of Theodore Roethke," *Language as Symbolic Action* (Univ. of California, 1968); Hyatt H. Waggoner, "Theodore Roethke," *American Poets* (Houghton Mifflin, 1968); William L. Martz, ed., *The Achievement of Theodore Roethke* (Scott, Foresman, 1966); essays by W. D. Snodgrass, Louis L. Martz, Roy Harvey Pearce, Denis Donoghue, *et al.*, collected in Arnold Stein, ed., *Theodore Roethke: Essays on the Poetry* (Univ. of Washington, 1966).


## DELMORE SCHWARTZ

Brooklyn, New York, 1913; died, New York City, 1966.
Studied at N.Y.U., Wisconsin, and Harvard; taught at Harvard and Syracuse; served as an editor of *Partisan Review* and film critic for *The New Republic*.

*In Dreams Begin Responsibilities* (New Directions, 1938)
*Shenandoah* (New Directions, 1941)
*Genesis* (New Directions, 1943)

*Vaudeville for a Princess* (New Directions, 1950)
*Summer Knowledge* (Doubleday, 1959)

Also published two books of short stories: *The World Is a Wedding* (New Directions, 1948) and *Successful Love* (Corinth, 1961); and much uncollected literary criticism.

See John Hollander, "Poetry Chronicle," *Partisan Review*, XXVII/2 (Spring 1960).


## Armand Schwerner

Antwerp, Belgium, 1927.
Was educated at Columbia and the University of Geneva; also studied jazz improvisation and theory with Lennie Tristano; formerly was a jazz musician; currently is Professor of English and Speech, Staten Island Community College.

*The Lightfall* (Hawk's Well, 1964)
(*If Personal*) (Black Sparrow, 1968)
*Seaweed* (Black Sparrow, 1968)
*The Tablets* (Cummington Press, 1969)

Also co-authored *The Domesday Dictionary: An Inventory of the Artifacts and Conceits of a New Civilization* (Simon & Schuster, 1964).


## David Shapiro

Newark, New Jersey, 1947.
A.B., Columbia University; currently is a Kellett Fellow, Clare College, Cambridge, England.

*January* (Holt, Rinehart and Winston, 1965)
*Poems from Deal* (Dutton, 1969)

Also co-edited *Random Anthology: New York Poets* (Random House, 1970).


## Harvey Shapiro

Chicago, Illinois, 1924.
A.B., Yale; M.A., Columbia; formerly taught English at Cornell,

Bard, Queens, and Columbia; currently is assistant editor on the *New York Times Magazine.*

*The Eye* (Swallow, 1953)
*The Book and Other Poems* (Cummington Press, 1955)
*Mountain, Fire, Thornbush* (Swallow, 1961)
*Battle Report* (Wesleyan Univ., 1966)

Also published reviews of poetry and literary journalism.
See David Ignatow, "The Past Reconsidered," *The Nation* (Apr. 24, 1967).


## MARY ELLEN SOLT

Gilmore City, Iowa, 1920.
B.A., Iowa State Teachers College; M.A., University of Iowa; currently lives in Bloomington, Indiana.

*Flowers in Concrete* (Indiana Univ., Fine Arts Dept., 1966)
*The Peoplemover: A Demonstration Poem* (Finial Press, 1969).

Also edited the anthology *Concrete Poetry: A World View* (Indiana Univ., 1969).
See Eugene Wildman, "Afterword," *The Chicago Review Anthology of Concretism* (Swallow, 1968).


## W. D. SNODGRASS

Wilkinsburg, Pennsylvania, 1926.
Studied at Geneva College and State University of Iowa, B.A., M.A., M.F.A.; taught at Cornell, Rochester, Wayne State, and, currently, Syracuse.

*Heart's Needle* (Knopf, 1959)
*After Experience* (Harper & Row, 1968)

Also published critical essays and translations, including a book of Christian Morgenstern's *Gallows Songs* (Univ. of Michigan, 1967).
See Glauco Cambon, *Recent American Poetry* (Univ. of Minnesota, 1966); Paul Carroll, "W. D. Snodgrass," *The Poem in Its Skin* (Follett, 1968).

## GARY SNYDER

San Francisco, California, 1930.
B.A., Reed College; studied further in Chinese and Japanese at the University of California, Berkeley, and in Japan; currently is a translator in Kyoto, Japan.

*Riprap* (Origin Press, Ashland, Mass., 1959)
*Myths & Texts* (Totem/Corinth, 1960)
*A Range of Poems* (Fulcrum, London, 1967)
*The Back Country* (New Directions, 1968)

Also published translations from Oriental languages and *Earth House Hold* (New Directions, 1969), a prose collection.
See Crunk, "The Work of Gary Snyder," *The Sixties*, 6 (Spring 1962); Thomas Parkinson, "The Poetry of Gary Snyder," *Southern Review*, IV/3 (Summer 1968); David Curry, "Apple Recommends . . .," *Apple*, 2 (Summer 1968).


## GERD STERN

Saarbasin, Germany, 1928.
Attended Black Mountain and other colleges; worked in public relations; recently became a director of Intermedia Systems, Inc.; was a founding member of USCO, Garnerville, New York.

*First Poems and Others* (Privately published, 1952)
*Afterimage* (Maverick, Woodstock, N.Y., 1966)

Also published travel reportage and collaborated in USCO's technological and artistic projects.
See Richard Kostelanetz, "USCO," *The Theatre of Mixed Means* (Dial, 1968).


## MELVIN B. TOLSON

Moberly, Missouri, 1900; died, St. Paul, Minnesota, 1966.
Was educated at Fisk, Lincoln, and Columbia Universities; formerly was Professor of Creative Literature and Director of the Dust Bowl Theater at Langston University; at death was Poet-in-Residence, Tuskegee Institute.

*Rendezvous with America* (Dodd, Mead, 1944)
*Libretto for the Republic of Liberia* (Twayne, 1953)
*Harlem Gallery: The Curator* (Twayne, 1965)

Also wrote several plays, including *The Moses of Beale Street* and *Southern Front*, as well as dramatizations of George Schuyler's novel *Black No More* and Walter White's *Fire in the Flint*.

See Dan McCall, "The Quicksilver Sparrow of M. B. Tolson," *American Quarterly*, XVIII/3 (Fall 1966); M. W. King, "Melvin B. Tolson: An Interview," in Herbert Hill, ed., *Anger, and Beyond* (Harper & Row, 1965); Stanley Edgar Hyman, "American Negro Literature and the Folk Tradition," *The Promised End* (World, 1963).


# DAVID WAGONER

Massillon, Ohio, 1926.

B.A., Pennsylvania State College; M.A., Indiana University; currently is Professor of English, University of Washington, and editor of *Poetry Northwest*.

*Dry Sun, Dry Wind* (Indiana Univ., 1953)
*A Place To Stand* (Indiana Univ., 1958)
*The Nesting Ground* (Indiana Univ., 1963)
*Staying Alive* (Indiana Univ., 1966)
*New and Selected Poems* (Indiana Univ., 1969)

Also published five novels: *Man in the Middle* (Harcourt, Brace & World, 1954), *Money Money Money* (Harcourt, Brace & World, 1955), *Rock* (Viking, 1958), *The Escape Artist* (Farrar, Straus & & Giroux, 1965), and *Baby Come on Inside* (Farrar, Straus & Giroux, 1968).


# JAMES WRIGHT

Martin's Ferry, Ohio, 1927.

A.B., Kenyon; M.A., Ph.D., University of Washington; currently teaches at the Bronx campus of Hunter College, U.C.N.Y.

*The Green Wall* (Yale Univ., 1957)
*Saint Judas* (Wesleyan Univ., 1959)
*The Branch Will Not Break* (Wesleyan Univ., 1963)
*Shall We Gather at the River* (Wesleyan Univ., 1968)

Also published translation of both prose and poetry from German and Spanish, including Theodor Strom's short novels, *Rider on the White Horse* (New American Library, 1964).

See Jonathan Cott, "Poetry," in Richard Kostelanetz, ed., *The New American Arts* (Horizon, 1965); Ralph J. Mills, Jr., "James Wright," *Contemporary American Poetry* (Random House, 1965); Paul Carroll, "James Wright," *The Poem in Its Skin* (Follett, 1968); Crunk, "The Work of James Wright," *The Sixties*, 8 (Spring 1966).


## LOUIS ZUKOFSKY

New York, New York, 1904.
Has taught at several universities; currently lives in New York City.

*Fifty-Five Poems* (Decker, Prairie City, Ill., 1941)
*Anew* (Decker, Prairie City, Ill., 1946)
*Some Time* (Jargon, 1956)
*All, the Collected Short Poems 1923–1958* (Norton, 1965)
*All, the Collected Short Poems 1956–1964* (Norton, 1966)
*"A" 1–12* (Doubleday–Paris Review, 1969)

Also published criticism and manifestoes, much of which is collected in *A Test of Poetry* (Routledge, 1952; Jargon/Corinth, 1964), *Bottom: On Shakespeare* (Univ. of Texas, 1963), and *Prepositions* (Horizon, 1968); translations, such as *Catullus* (Grossman-Goliard, 1969); prose fiction, such as *Ferdinand* (Cage-Grossman, 1969); and *Autobiography* (Grossman, 1970).

See W. C. Williams, "A New Line Is a New Measure," *New Quarterly of Poetry* (Winter 1947–1948); Ezra Pound, *Polite Essays* (Faber & Faber, 1937); Robert Creeley, "A Note," in *"A" 1–12;* Cid Corman, *At Bottom* (Caterpiller, 1967).

# BIBLIOGRAPHY OF SELECTED MACRO-CRITICISM

## I  On the Modern Imagination

Apollinaire, Guillaume. "L'Esprit Nouveau et les Poètes," in Roger Shattuck, ed. & trans., *Selected Writings of Guillaume Apollinaire*. N.Y.: New Directions, 1949.

Barrett, William. *Irrational Man*. Garden City: Doubleday, 1958.

Bergonzi, Bernard, ed. *Innovations*. London: Macmillan, 1958.

Burke, Kenneth. *Counter-Statement*. Chicago: Univ. of Chicago, 1957.

Eisenstein, Sergei. *Film Form and Film Sense*. N.Y.: Meridian, 1957.

Ellmann, Richard; & Feidelson, Charles, Jr., eds. *The Modern Tradition*. N.Y.: Oxford, 1965.

Frank, Joseph. *The Widening Gyre*. New Brunswick, N.J.: Rutgers Univ., 1963.

Giedion, Sigfried. *Space, Time and Architecture*. Cambridge: Harvard Univ., 1941.

Hamburger, Michael. *The Truth of Poetry*. N.Y.: Harcourt, Brace & World, 1970.

Kermode, Frank. *Romantic Image*. London: Routledge, 1957.

Kostelanetz, Richard. *The Theatre of Mixed Means*. N.Y.: Dial, 1968.

McLuhan, Marshall. *Understanding Media*. N.Y.: McGraw-Hill, 1964.

Moholy-Nagy, Laszlo. *Vision in Motion*. Chicago: Paul Theobald, 1947.

Peckham, Morse. *Rage for Chaos*. Philadelphia: Chilton, 1965.

Raymond, Marcel. *From Baudelaire to Surrealism*. N.Y.: Wittenborn, 1949.

Read, Herbert. *The Philosophy of Modern Art*. N.Y.: Horizon, 1952.

Rosenberg, Harold. *The Tradition of the New*. N.Y.: Horizon, 1959.

Shattuck, Roger. *The Banquet Years*. N.Y.: Harper & Row, 1958.

Sypher, Wylie. *Rococo to Cubism in Art and Literature*. N.Y.: Vintage, 1963.

## II   On Modern American Poetry

Alvarez, A. *The Shaping Spirit.* London: Chatto & Windus, 1958.

Auden, W. H. *The Dyer's Hand.* N.Y.: Random House, 1962.

Blackmur, R. P. *Form and Value in Modern Poetry.* Garden City: Doubleday Anchor, 1957.

Bogan, Louise. *Achievement in American Poetry.* Chicago: Regnery, 1951.

Cambon, Glauco. *The Inclusive Flame.* Bloomington: Indiana Univ., 1963.

Daiches, David. *Poetry and the Modern World.* Chicago: Univ. of Chicago, 1940.

Dijkstra, Bram. *The Hieroglyphics of a New Speech.* Princeton: Princeton Univ., 1969.

Engle, Paul; & Langland, Joseph, eds. *Poet's Choice.* N.Y.: Dial, 1963.

Fiedler, Leslie A. *Waiting for the End.* N.Y.: Stein & Day, 1964.

Friedman, Norman. *E. E. Cummings.* Baltimore: Johns Hopkins Univ., 1960.

Gross, Harvey. *Sound and Form in Modern Poetry.* Ann Arbor: Univ. of Michigan, 1964.

Guimond, James. *The Art of William Carlos Williams.* Urbana: Univ. of Illinois, 1968.

Hollander, John, ed. *Modern Poetry: Essays in Criticism.* N.Y.: Oxford, 1968.

Hyman, Stanley Edgar. *Poetry and Criticism.* N.Y.: Atheneum, 1961.

Jarrell, Randall. *Poetry and the Age.* N.Y.: Knopf, 1953.

Kenner, Hugh. *Gnomon.* N.Y.: McDowell, Obolensky, 1958.

————. *The Poetry of Ezra Pound.* N.Y.: New Directions, 1951.

Leavis, F. R. *New Bearings in English Poetry,* amended ed. London: Chatto & Windus, 1950.

Matthiessen, F. O. "Introduction," in *The Oxford Book of American Verse.* N.Y.: Oxford, 1950.

Miller, J. Hillis, ed. *William Carlos Williams.* Englewood Cliffs, N.J.: Prentice-Hall, 1966.

Nemerov, Howard. *Poetry and Fiction.* New Brunswick, N.J.: Rutgers Univ., 1963.

O'Connor, William Van. *Sense and Sensibility in Modern Poetry.* Chicago: Univ. of Chicago, 1948.

Pearce, Roy Harvey. *The Continuity of American Poetry.* Princeton, N.J.: Princeton Univ., 1961.

————; & Miller, J. Hillis, eds. *The Act of the Mind.* Baltimore: Johns Hopkins Univ., 1965.

Pound, Ezra. *Literary Essays.* N.Y.: New Directions, 1954.

Ransom, John Crowe; Schwartz, Delmore; & Wheelock, John Hall. *American Poetry at Mid-Century*. Washington, D.C.: Library of Congress, 1958.

Rosenthal, M. L. *The Modern Poets: A Critical Introduction*. N.Y.: Oxford, 1960.

Spender, Stephen; & Hall, Donald, eds. *The Concise Encyclopedia of English and American Poets and Poetry*. N.Y.: Hawthorn, 1963.

Stevens, Wallace. *The Necessary Angel*. N.Y.: Knopf, 1951.

Stock, Noel, ed. *Ezra Pound: Perspectives*. N.Y.: Regnery, 1968.

Tate, Allen. *Essays of Four Decades*. N.Y.: Morrow, 1968.

Waggoner, Hyatt H. *American Poets*. Boston: Houghton Mifflin, 1968.

Williams, William Carlos. *Selected Essays*. N.Y.: New Directions, 1969.

Winters, Yvor. *In Defense of Reason*. Denver: Swallow, 1947.

———. *The Function of Criticism*. Denver: Swallow, 1957.

# III   On Contemporary American Poetry—Books

Carroll, Paul. *The Poem in Its Skin*. Chicago: Follett, 1968.

Cambon, Glauco. *Recent American Poetry*. Minneapolis: Univ. of Minnesota, 1962.

Dickey, James. *The Suspect in Poetry*. Madison, Minn.: The Sixties, 1964.

———. *Babel to Byzantium*. N.Y.: Farrar, Straus & Giroux, 1968.

Eckman, Frederick. *Cobras and Cockle Shells*. Flushing, N.Y.: Vagrom Chap Book (#5), 1957.

Howard, Richard. *Alone with America*. N.Y.: Atheneum, 1969.

Hungerford, Edward B., ed. *Poets in Progress: Critical Prefaces to Ten Contemporary Americans*. Evanston, Ill.: Northwestern Univ., 1962.

Mills, Ralph J., Jr. *Contemporary American Poetry*. N.Y.: Random House, 1965.

Nemerov, Howard, ed. *Poets on Poetry*. N.Y.: Basic, 1966.

Ostroff, Anthony, ed. *The Contemporary Poet as Artist and Critic*. Boston: Little, Brown, 1964.

Rosenthal, M. L. *The New Poets*. N.Y.: Oxford, 1967.

Stepanchev, Stephen. *American Poetry Since 1945*. N.Y.: Harper & Row, 1965.

# IV   On Contemporary American Poetry—Essays

Cott, Jonathan. "Poetry," in Richard Kostelanetz, ed., *The New American Arts*. N.Y.: Horizon, 1965.

Dickey, James. "The Son, the Cave, and the Burning Bush," in Paul Carroll, ed., *The Young American Poets*. Chicago: (Follett, 1968.

Fiedler, Leslie A. "The New Mutants," in Richard Kostelanetz, ed., *Beyond Left and Right*. N.Y.: Morrow, 1968.

Hall, Donald. "Introduction," in *Contemporary American Poetry*. Harmondsworth: Penguin, 1962.

———. "The New Poetry," *New World Writing*, 7 (1955).

Hart, Lawrence. "The New Face of Conformity," *Works*, I/3 (Spring 1968).

Hoffman, Daniel. "Arrivals and Rebirths," *Sewanee Review*, LXVIII/1 (Winter 1960).

———. "Meter-Making Arguments," *Southern Review*, IV/1 (Winter 1968).

Kostelanetz, Richard. "Introduction," in *Imaged Words and Worded Images*. N.Y.: Outerbridge and Dienstfrey, 1970.

———. "The Streams of Recent American Poetry," in *On Contemporary Literature*, rev. ed. N.Y.: Avon, 1969.

Kunitz, Stanley. "Poetry's Silver Age: An Improbable Dialogue," in John Fischer and Robert Silvers, ed., *Writing in America*. New Brunswick, N.J.: Rutgers Univ., 1960.

Lockwood, Willard. "Publishing Poetry," *Panache*, 2 (1968).

Pearson, Norman Holmes. "Introduction," in *Decade*. Middletown: Wesleyan Univ., 1969.

Rexroth, Kenneth. "The World Is Full of Strangers," *New Directions* 16 (1957).

———. "A Hope for Poetry," *Holiday*, XX (March 1966).

Solt, Mary Ellen. "Introduction," in *Concrete Poetry: A World View*. Bloomington: Indiana Univ., 1968.

Thorp, Willard. "Poetry, Raw or Cooked?" in Robert E. Spiller, ed., *A Time of Harvest*. N.Y.: Hill & Wang, 1962.

# INDEX OF AUTHORS AND TITLES

# INDEX OF FIRST LINES